SCHOOL ATLAS

Editorial Adviser
Dr Patrick Wiegand

OXFORD
UNIVERSITY PRESS

Great Clarendon Street, Oxford OX2 6DP

Oxford University Press is a department of the University of Oxford.
It furthers the University's objective of excellence in research, scholarship,
and education by publishing worldwide in

Oxford   New York

Auckland Cape Town Dar es Salaam Hong Kong Karachi
Kuala Lumpur Madrid Melbourne Mexico City Nairobi
New Delhi Shanghai Taipei Toronto

With offices in

Argentina Austria Brazil Chile Czech Republic France Greece
Guatemala Hungary Italy Japan Poland Portugal Singapore
South Korea Switzerland Thailand Turkey Ukraine Vietnam

Oxford is a registered trade mark of Oxford University Press
in the UK and in certain other countries

© Oxford University Press 2006

First published 2006

Reprinted with corrections 2007

© Maps copyright Oxford University Press

ISBN 978 0 19 832700 4 (hardback)

ISBN 978 0 19 832699 1 (paperback)

1 3 5 7 9 10 8 6 4 2

Printed in Singapore by KHL Printing Co. Pte Ltd

Paper used in the production of this book is a natural, recyclable product
made from wood grown in sustainable forests. The manufacturing process
conforms to the environmental regulations of the country of origin.

Acknowledgements

Illustrations by:
Mark Duffin pp 5 (satellite), 7 (compass), 72, 73; Tracey Learoyd pp 78, 79; Tracey Learoyd and Adrian Smith p 10 *and thereafter* (landscape pictograms); ODI pp 27, 86, 87 (population figures)

The publishers would also like to thank the following for permission to reproduce the following photographs:
Alamy pp 18t (Robert Harding World Imagery), 18tc (The Photolibrary Wales), 18c (Geogphotos), 18bc (Worldwide Picture Library), 24tc (Jon Arnold Images), 24bc (D.Rowland), 25bl (The Photolibrary Wales), 30br (Robert Harding World Imagery), 30tr (A.Jenny), 30tc (C.Pefley), 30blc (N.Cameron), 30bl (D.Young-Wolff), 30brc (allOver photography), 30bc (H.Salvadori), 31tl (Jon Arnold Images), 31bl (R.Naude), 37tcr (foodfolio), 47tr (B.Cruickshank), 47ct (R.Fried), 49cbl (C.Ehlers), 49ct (Robert Harding World Imagery), 53bl (J.Marshall/ Tribaleye Images), 53*inset* (Dinodia Images), 53tr (Images of Africa Photobank), 60cbl (Atmosphere Picture Library), 60bl (Buzz Pictures), 64cb (Sue Cunningham Photographic), 65ctl (Robert Harding World Imagery), 65ctc (M.Vautier), 65cbr (P.Fridman), 65cbl (Network Photographers), 69tl (Robert Harding World Imagery), 72bl (Worldwide Picture Library), 72br (K.Welsh), 76tc (Robert Harding World Imagery), 76bc (ashfordplatt), 78t (Worldwide Picture Library), 79tl (FLPA), 81bl (PCL), 81br (SUNNYphotography.com), 84t (A.Arbib), 85c (R.Cooke); Corbis pp 18b (C.Gryniewicz), 19b (R.Ergenbright), 24t (R.Antrobus), 24b (D.Croucher), 37tr (T.Gipstein), 37tcl (V.Rastelli), 37br (Spaceborne Imaging Radar-C/X-band), 53blc (G.Mendel), 53tcr (C.Osborne), 54tl (R.De La Harpe/Gallo Images), 55t (C.Gryniewicz/Ecoscene), 55ct (T.Mukoya/Reuters), 60ctl (R.Cummins), 60tr (E.Young), 60br (J.Sugar), 64ct (W.Kaehler), 65 (W.Kaehler), 68tl (G.Rowell), 73bl (J.Van Hasselt), 73br (WildCountry), 76tr (R.Watts), 77tr (R.A.Cooke), 77bl (W.Kaehler), 77bc (G.Rowell), 84c (F.Prouser/Reuters); Images courtesy Jesse Allen, based on data from the MODIS Rapid Response Team at NASA GSFC pp 42cr, 42br; Empics pp 25tr (M.Egerton), 25tl (A.Grant/AP),

25cr (G.Copley/PA), 25br (M.Egerton), 53tlc (G.Barker); Frank Lane Picture Agency p 76tl; Getty Images 31bc (C.Aslund), 31br (AFP), 37cb (G.Niu), 47bl (China Photos), 47bcr (L.Jin), 47cb (G.Niu), 49cbr (Y.Tsuno), 53br (C.Kober), 65tc (F.Bueno), 65cr (J.Jangoux), 77br (F.Lemmens), 82tl (J.Sartore), 82bl (G.Wiltsie), 83cb (D.Day), 85b (L.Fievet); Lonely Planet Images pp 37tl (D.Tomlinson), 47tl (K.Lieb), 49bl (O.Strewe), 53tl (J.Elk III), 53tcl (T.Wheeler), 54br (A.Blomqvist), 54tc (C.Fredriksson), 54tr (M.Reardon), 54bc (M.Fletcher), 55b (B.Bachmann), 60ctr (D.Peevers), 64t (R.Gomes), 79b (P.Horton); Image courtesy NASA/GSFC/MITI/ERSDAC/JAROS and U.S./Japan ASTER Science Team p 47br; Image Courtesy NASA/TRMM p 42cl; Image courtesy A. Piatanesi/Istituto Nazionale di Geofisica e Vulcanologia, Italy p 43cr; Pictures Colour Library p 53trc (W.Dentith); Punchstock pp 49cb (Photodisc), 65tr (Brand X Pictures), 83t (Photodisc); Rex Features pp 30tl (Sipa Press), 37ct (M.Frassineti/AGF), 49tr (Sipa Press); Guido Alberto Rossi pp 76br, 77tl; Images courtesy Ted Scambos, National Snow and Ice Data Center, University of Colorado, Boulder, based on data from MODIS pp 68bl, 68br; Science Photo Library pp 5bl (NRSC Ltd), 19t (S.Stammers), 19c (S.Stammers), 37bl (B.Edmaier), 43bl (Digital Globe/ Eurimage), 43br (Digital Globe/ Eurimage), 46bc (CNES/1989 Distribution Spot Image), 46tl (Planetary Visions Ltd), 60tl (E.Young/Agstock), 60bc (D.Parker), 61bl (Digital Globe/ Eurimage), 61br (Digital Globe/ Eurimage), 61t (NOAA), 65bl (NASA), 68tr (NASA), 69c (US Geological Survey), 79tr (D.Parker); Still Pictures pp 47tc (X.Zhen/UNEP), 49br (K.Yashiro/UNEP), 53bcl (J.Schytte), 53brc (R.Giling), 53bcr (J.Schytte), 54bl (Altitude), 55cb (D.Blell), 64b (A.Gunnartz), 82cr (R.Giling), 83ct (J.Schytte), 83b (S.Sprague), 84b (H.Tin)

The photographs and illustrations were sourced by Pictureresearch.co.uk

The page design is by Adrian Smith

The publishers are grateful to the following colleagues in geography education for their helpful comments and advice during the development stages of this atlas: Kirsty Cook, Karen Elliot, Donna Forrester, Mel Gibson, Geoff Gilbert, Robin Robson, John Ziltener.

2 Contents

- Atlas literacy ——————— 4–5
- Atlas numeracy ————— 6–7

British Isles

British Isles   Political ——————— 8–9

United Kingdom
Scotland ——————— 10–11

United Kingdom
Northern Ireland and
Southern Scotland ——— 12

United Kingdom
Northern England ——— 13

United Kingdom
Wales and
South West England ——— 14

United Kingdom
Southern England ——— 15

British Isles
Ireland ——————— 16–17

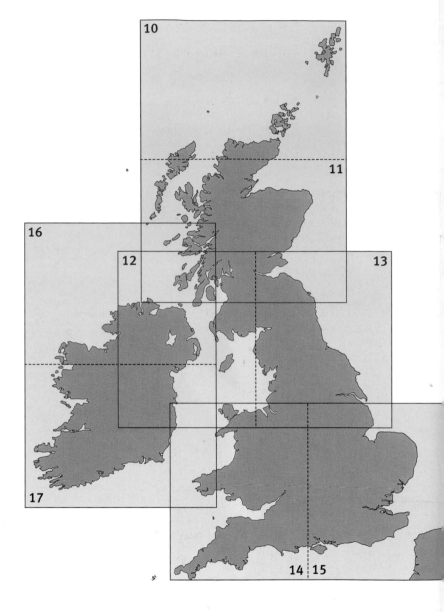

British Isles   Relief ——————— 18

British Isles   Geology ——————— 19

British Isles   Climate ——————— 20

British Isles   Water and flooding —— 21

British Isles   Population ——————— 22

United Kingdom   Fuel and industry ——— 23

United Kingdom   Tourism ——————— 24

British Isles   Sport ——————— 25

British Isles   Road and rail connections — 26

British Isles   Air and sea connections ——— 27

Contents 3

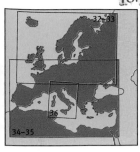

Europe

Europe | Relief — 28
Europe | Political
European Union — 29
Europe | Climate — 30
Europe | Tourism — 31
Northern Europe — 32–33
Southern Europe — 34–35
Italy — 36
Italy | *a closer look* — 37

Asia

Asia | Relief — 38
Asia | Political — 39
South West
and South Asia — 40–41
Bangladesh | Flooding — 42
Indian Ocean | Tsunami — 43
East and
South East Asia — 44–45
China | *a closer look* — 46–47
Japan — 48
Japan | *a closer look* — 49

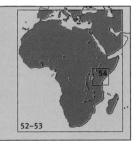

Africa

Africa | Relief — 50
Africa | Political — 51
Africa — 52–53
Kenya — 54
Kenya | *a closer look* — 55

North America

North America | Relief — 56
North America | Political — 57
United States of America — 58–59
California — 60
Hurricane Katrina — 61

South America

South America — 62
South America | Political — 63
Brazil | *a closer look* — 64–65

Oceania

Oceania — 66–67

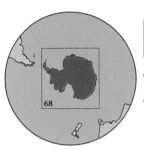

Antarctica

Antarctica — 68
Antarctica | Tourism
Natural resources — 69

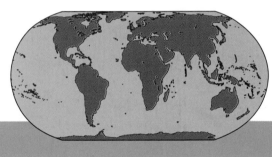

World

World | Political — 70–71
World | Relief — 72–73
World | Temperature and rainfall — 74
World | Climate regions — 75
World | Biomes — 76–77
World | Earthquakes and volcanoes — 78–79
World | Population — 80–81
World | Development — 82–83
World | Globalisation and aid — 84
World | Connections — 85

● Data files — 86–87
● Data sets — 88–91
● Index — 92–96

© Oxford University Press

4 Atlas literacy

Map language

Title
names the map area

Sub-title
describes what the map shows

Key (also called a legend)
explains the symbols
used on the map

Scale
shows how large
the map is.

Scale information
can be shown
- as a statement
- as a ratio (also called
  a representative
  fraction)
- as a scale line

Information panel
provides extra information,
often about extremes
or records

Map locator
shows where the map
area is on a smaller
scale map

Globe locator
shows where the map
area is on the globe

Comparitor
shows how large the
map area is compared
to the British Isles

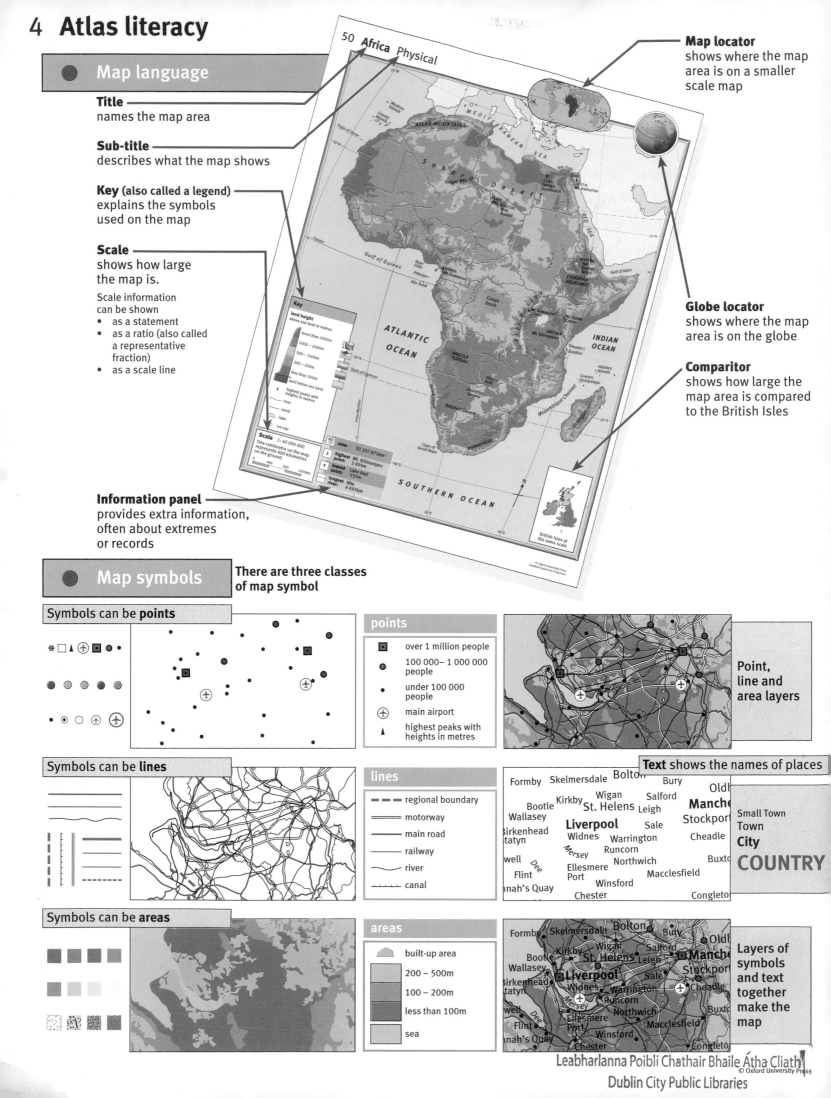

Africa Physical

Map symbols

There are three classes
of map symbol

Symbols can be **points**

points

- ▣ over 1 million people
- ● 100 000 – 1 000 000 people
- • under 100 000 people
- ⊕ main airport
- ▲ highest peaks with heights in metres

Point,
line and
area layers

Symbols can be **lines**

lines

- ▬ ▬ regional boundary
- ═══ motorway
- ─── main road
- ─── railway
- ─── river
- ┴┴┴ canal

Text shows the names of places

Formby Skelmersdale Bolton Bury Oldh
Kirkby Wigan Salford
Bootle St. Helens Leigh **Manche**
Wallasey Liverpool Sale Stockpor
Birkenhead Widnes Warrington Cheadle
Prestatyn Runcorn
Mersey Northwich Buxto
Ellesmere
Flint Port Winsford Macclesfield
annah's Quay Chester Congleto

Small Town
Town
City
COUNTRY

Symbols can be **areas**

areas

- built-up area
- 200 – 500m
- 100 – 200m
- less than 100m
- sea

Layers of
symbols
and text
together
make the
map

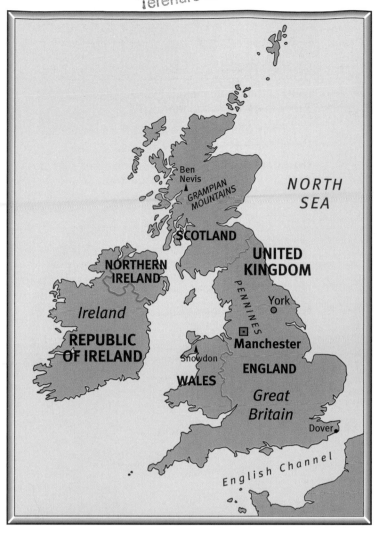

Type on maps

Type face gives clues to word meaning.

Great Britain *Ireland*	islands
UNITED KINGDOM **REPUBLIC OF IRELAND**	countries
ENGLAND SCOTLAND WALES **NORTHERN IRELAND**	parts of the United Kingdom
PENNINES *GRAMPIAN MOUNTAINS*	physical features
Ben Nevis Snowdon	mountain peaks
NORTH SEA *English Channel*	sea areas
Manchester York Dover	settlements

Abbreviations and brackets

Words are often shortened on maps.

UK	United Kingdom
USA	United States of America
UAE	United Arab Emirates

R.	River
Mt.	Mount
Is.	Island
Pen.	Peninsula

A country name in brackets shows that a place is part of that country.

Corsica is part of France.
Sardinia is part of Italy.

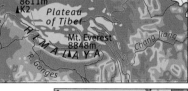

Satellite images and map styles

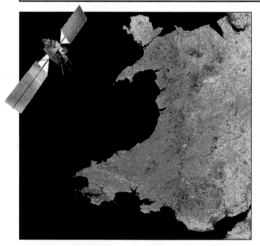

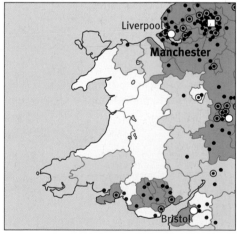

Satellite images show radiation from different types of land use on the Earth as colours.

These colours are often very different from those that would be seen on an aerial photograph.

Key	
orange	rough pasture
red	forest and woodland
dark blue	urban areas

Topographic maps show the main features of the physical landscape as well as settlements, communications and boundaries.

Key	
	land between 200m and 500m
	motorway
⊕	main airport

Thematic maps show information about themes such as geology, climate, tourism and sport.

This map shows population.

Key	
	areas with over 250 people per square kilometre
○	cities with between 400 000 and 1 000 000 people
•	towns with between 25 000 and 100 000 people

6 Atlas numeracy

The Earth is a sphere*.

Two sets of imaginary lines help us describe where places are on the Earth.

All the lines are numbered and some have special names.

* It is actually slightly flattened at the north and south poles.

Longitude

Lines of longitude measure distance east or west. These lines are called **meridians**.

The **Prime Meridian** (also called the Greenwich Meridian) is at longitude 0°.

The **International Date Line** (on the other side of the Earth) is based on longitude 180°.

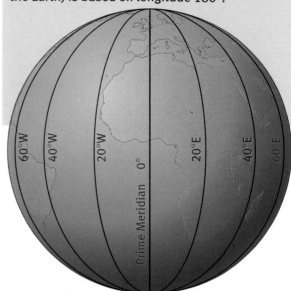

Latitude

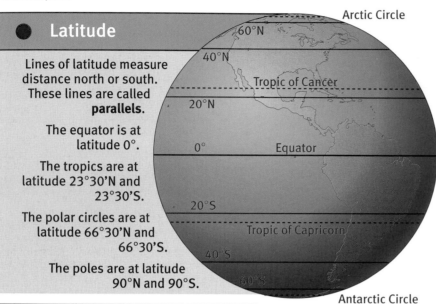

Lines of latitude measure distance north or south. These lines are called **parallels**.

The equator is at latitude 0°.

The tropics are at latitude 23°30'N and 23°30'S.

The polar circles are at latitude 66°30'N and 66°30'S.

The poles are at latitude 90°N and 90°S.

Map projections

There are many ways of showing the spherical surface of the Earth on a flat map.

Most world maps in this atlas use the Eckert IV projection.

This shows land masses at their correct size in relation to each other but there is some distortion in shape.

World map used in the United Kingdom.

World map used in Australia.

This world map (called an Oblique Aitoff) allows a good view of the northern hemisphere.

Grid codes

In this atlas, the lines of latitude and longitude are used to make a grid.

The columns of the grid have letters.

The rows of the grid have numbers.

Numbers and letters together make a grid code that can be used to describe where places are on the Earth.

Abuja is in B4   Durban is in C2

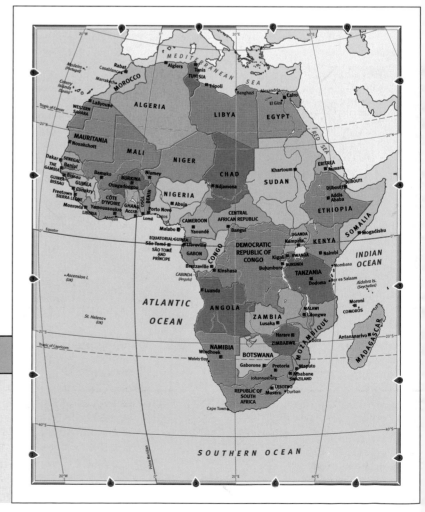

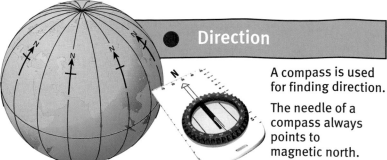

Direction

A compass is used for finding direction.

The needle of a compass always points to magnetic north.

North on atlas maps follows the lines of longitude.

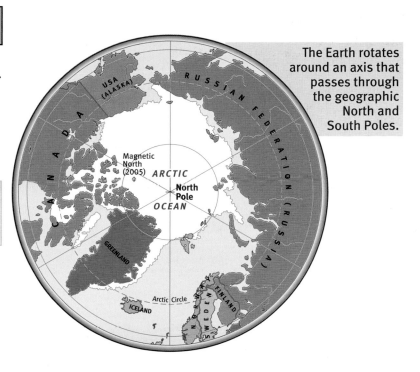

The Earth rotates around an axis that passes through the geographic North and South Poles.

Scale

Maps are much, much smaller than the areas they show. A few centimetres on the map stand for very many kilometres on the ground.

This map has a ratio (or representative fraction) of 1: 55 000 000. The map is 55 million times smaller than the area it shows.

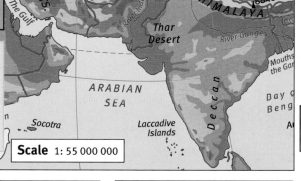

Scale 1: 55 000 000

Each division on the scale line is one centimetre.

The scale line shows how many kilometres are represented by one centimetre.

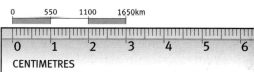

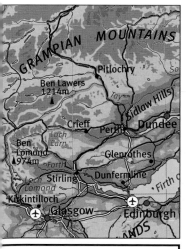

Scale One centimetre on the map represents **25** kilometres on the ground.

0   25   50   75km

The distance between Glenrothes and Dunfermline is about 25km

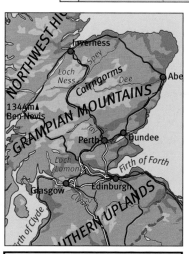

Scale One centimetre on the map represents **50** kilometres on the ground.

0   50   100   150km

The distance between Perth and Edinburgh is about 50km

Scale One centimetre on the map represents **100** kilometres on the ground.

0   100   200   300km

The distance between Glasgow and Dundee is about 100km

Larger scale
smaller area
more detail

Smaller scale
larger area
less detail

On world maps the scale is only true along the equator.

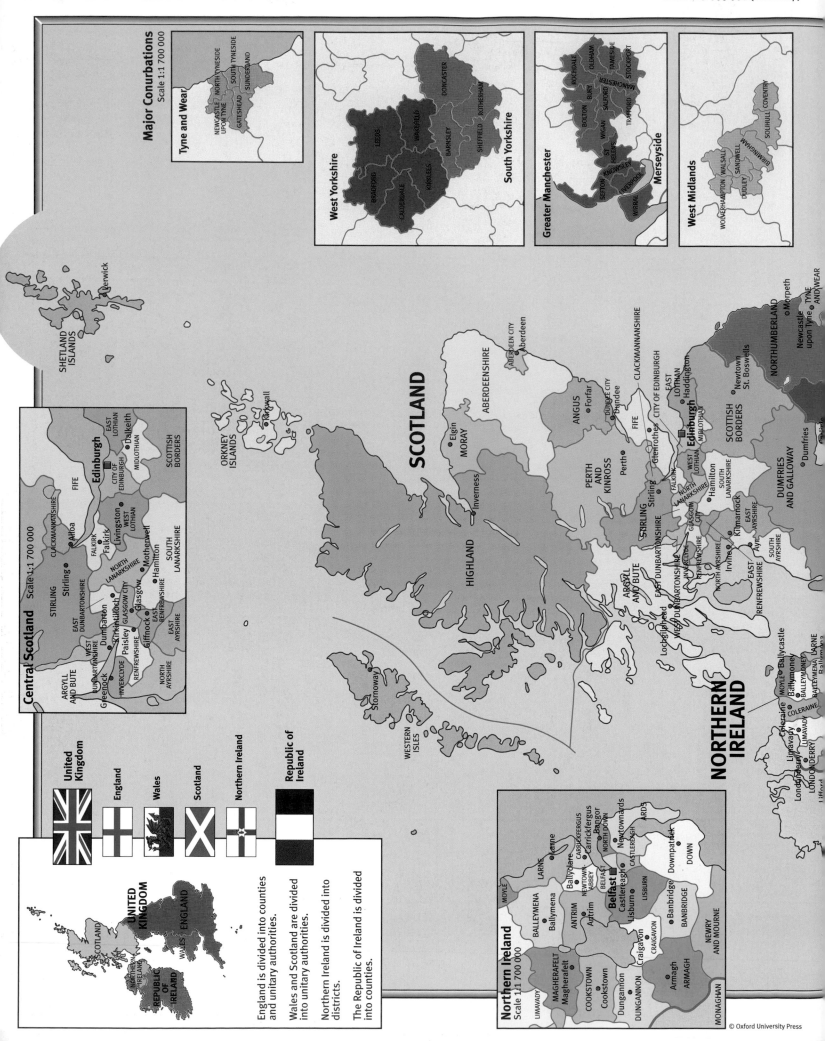

Major Conurbations
Scale 1:1 700 000

Tyne and Wear
NEWCASTLE UPON TYNE, NORTH TYNESIDE, SOUTH TYNESIDE, GATESHEAD, SUNDERLAND

West Yorkshire
LEEDS, BRADFORD, CALDERDALE, KIRKLEES, WAKEFIELD

South Yorkshire
BARNSLEY, DONCASTER, ROTHERHAM, SHEFFIELD

Greater Manchester
BOLTON, BURY, ROCHDALE, OLDHAM, WIGAN, SALFORD, MANCHESTER, TAMESIDE, TRAFFORD, STOCKPORT, ST HELENS, KNOWSLEY, SEFTON, LIVERPOOL, WIRRAL

Merseyside

West Midlands
WOLVERHAMPTON, WALSALL, SANDWELL, DUDLEY, BIRMINGHAM, SOLIHULL, COVENTRY

Central Scotland
Scale 1:1 700 000

EAST LOTHIAN, Edinburgh, Dalkeith, CITY OF EDINBURGH, MIDLOTHIAN, SCOTTISH BORDERS, FIFE, CLACKMANNANSHIRE, Alloa, Stirling, STIRLING, FALKIRK, Falkirk, Livingston, WEST LOTHIAN, Motherwell, Hamilton, NORTH LANARKSHIRE, SOUTH LANARKSHIRE, WEST DUNBARTONSHIRE, Dumbarton, Kirkintilloch, Glasgow, GLASGOW CITY, Paisley, EAST RENFREWSHIRE, Giffnock, EAST DUNBARTONSHIRE, INVERCLYDE, RENFREWSHIRE, Greenock, ARGYLL AND BUTE, NORTH AYRSHIRE, EAST AYRSHIRE

SHETLAND ISLANDS, Lerwick

ORKNEY ISLANDS, Kirkwall

SCOTLAND
ABERDEEN CITY, Aberdeen, ABERDEENSHIRE, Elgin, MORAY, ANGUS, Forfar, DUNDEE CITY, Dundee, FIFE, CITY OF EDINBURGH, Edinburgh, EAST LOTHIAN, Haddington, MIDLOTHIAN, SCOTTISH BORDERS, Newtown St. Boswells, NORTHUMBERLAND, Morpeth, Newcastle upon Tyne, TYNE AND WEAR, PERTH AND KINROSS, Perth, Glenrothes, Stirling, STIRLING, FALKIRK, Falkirk, WEST LOTHIAN, NORTH LANARKSHIRE, Hamilton, SOUTH LANARKSHIRE, GLASGOW CITY, Glasgow, Inverness, HIGHLAND, ARGYLL AND BUTE, Lochgilphead, WEST DUNBARTONSHIRE, EAST DUNBARTONSHIRE, INVERCLYDE, RENFREWSHIRE, NORTH AYRSHIRE, Irvine, Kilmarnock, EAST AYRSHIRE, SOUTH AYRSHIRE, Ayr, DUMFRIES AND GALLOWAY, Dumfries, SCOTTISH BORDERS

WESTERN ISLES, Stornoway

NORTHERN IRELAND
MOYLE, Ballycastle, Ballymoney, BALLYMONEY, LARNE, Larne, BALLYMENA, Ballymena, Coleraine, COLERAINE, Limavady, LIMAVADY, Londonderry, LONDONDERRY

Flags
United Kingdom
England
Wales
Scotland
Northern Ireland
Republic of Ireland

England is divided into counties and unitary authorities.

Wales and Scotland are divided into unitary authorities.

Northern Ireland is divided into districts.

The Republic of Ireland is divided into counties.

UNITED KINGDOM, SCOTLAND, WALES, ENGLAND, NORTHERN IRELAND, REPUBLIC OF IRELAND

Northern Ireland
Scale 1:1 700 000

MOYLE, LARNE, Larne, Ballyclare, Carrickfergus, CARRICKFERGUS, Bangor, NORTH DOWN, Newtownards, ARDS, NEWTOWN ABBEY, BELFAST, Belfast, Castlereagh, CASTLEREAGH, Lisburn, LISBURN, Downpatrick, DOWN, BALLYMENA, Ballymena, ANTRIM, Antrim, Banbridge, BANBRIDGE, Craigavon, CRAIGAVON, NEWRY AND MOURNE, MAGHERAFELT, Magherafelt, COOKSTOWN, Cookstown, Dungannon, DUNGANNON, Armagh, ARMAGH, LIMAVADY, MONAGHAN

© Oxford University Press

Teesside
Scale 1:1 700 000

Hartlepool
South Bank
REDCAR & CLEVELAND
Middlesbrough
MIDDLESBROUGH
Durham
HARTLEPOOL
Stockton-on-Tees
Darlington
DARLINGTON
STOCKTON-ON-TEES
DURHAM
NORTH YORKSHIRE

Thames Valley
Scale 1:1 700 000

BUCKINGHAMSHIRE
SLOUGH
Maidenhead
Slough
WINDSOR AND
MAIDENHEAD
Bracknell
BRACKNELL
FOREST
SURREY
Reading
READING
WEST
BERKSHIRE
Newbury
Wokingham
WOKINGHAM
HAMPSHIRE
WILTSHIRE

ENGLAND

Norwich
NORFOLK
SUFFOLK
Ipswich
ESSEX
Chelmsford
Southend-on-Sea
Southend
THURROCK
Rochester
MEDWAY
KENT
Maidstone
London
Kingston upon Thames
GREATER LONDON
EAST SUSSEX
Lewes
Brighton
BRIGHTON AND HOVE
Hove
WEST SUSSEX
Chichester
PORTSMOUTH
Portsmouth
ISLE OF WIGHT

CITY OF KINGSTON UPON HULL
Kingston upon Hull
NORTH EAST LINCOLNSHIRE
Grimsby
NORTH LINCOLNSHIRE
Scunthorpe
LINCOLNSHIRE
Lincoln
CAMBRIDGESHIRE
Peterborough
PETERBOROUGH
Cambridge
BEDFORDSHIRE
Bedford
Luton
LUTON
HERTFORDSHIRE
Hertford

EAST RIDING OF YORKSHIRE
Beverley
York
YORK
NORTH YORKSHIRE
Northallerton
Leeds
WEST YORKSHIRE
SOUTH YORKSHIRE
Sheffield
NOTTINGHAMSHIRE
Nottingham
NOTTINGHAM CITY
DERBYSHIRE
Matlock
DERBY CITY
Derby
RUTLAND
Oakham
LEICESTERSHIRE
LEICESTER CITY
Leicester
Glenfield
NORTHAMPTONSHIRE
Northampton
MILTON KEYNES
Milton Keynes
Aylesbury
BUCKINGHAMSHIRE
WINDSOR AND MAIDENHEAD
Reading
WOKINGHAM
Winchester
HAMPSHIRE
Southampton
SOUTHAMPTON
Bournemouth
BOURNEMOUTH

DURHAM
Durham
STOCKTON-ON-TEES
DARLINGTON
MIDDLESBROUGH
HARTLEPOOL
CUMBRIA
LANCASHIRE
Preston
BLACKPOOL
Blackpool
BLACKBURN WITH DARWEN
Blackburn
GREATER MANCHESTER
Manchester
Warrington
WARRINGTON
MERSEYSIDE
Liverpool
HALTON
Widnes
CHESHIRE
Chester
FLINTSHIRE
Mold
WREXHAM
Wrexham
DENBIGHSHIRE
Ruthin
CONWY
Conwy

York
NORTH YORKSHIRE
SOUTH YORKSHIRE
Sheffield
STAFFORDSHIRE
Stafford
STOKE-ON-TRENT
Stoke-on-Trent
TELFORD AND WREKIN
Telford
SHROPSHIRE
Shrewsbury
POWYS
WEST MIDLANDS
Birmingham
WARWICKSHIRE
Warwick
WORCESTERSHIRE
Worcester
HEREFORDSHIRE
Hereford
MONMOUTHSHIRE
GLOUCESTERSHIRE
Gloucester
OXFORDSHIRE
Oxford
SWINDON
Swindon
WILTSHIRE
Trowbridge
Thornbury
SOUTH GLOUCESTERSHIRE
BRISTOL
Bristol
BATH & NORTH EAST SOMERSET
Bath
NORTH SOMERSET
Weston-super-Mare
SOMERSET
Taunton
DORSET
Dorchester
Poole
POOLE
DEVON
Exeter
TORBAY
Torquay
Plymouth
PLYMOUTH
CORNWALL
Truro

NEWPORT
Newport
TORFAEN
CAERPHILLY
RHONDDA CYNON TAFF
MERTHYR TYDFIL
BLAENAU GWENT
THE VALE OF GLAMORGAN
BRIDGEND
Cardiff
CARDIFF
SWANSEA
Swansea
NEATH PORT TALBOT
CARMARTHENSHIRE
Carmarthen
Llandrindod Wells
CEREDIGION
Aberaeron
GWYNEDD
Caernarfon
ISLE OF ANGLESEY
Llangefni
PEMBROKESHIRE
Haverfordwest

WALES

UNITED KINGDOM

Douglas
ISLE OF MAN

CHANNEL ISLANDS

Isles of Scilly

Thames Valley / Greater London references
Isles of Scilly

REPUBLIC OF IRELAND

Belfast
ANTRIM
ARDS
NEWTOWNABBEY
CARRICKFERGUS
NORTH DOWN
CASTLEREAGH
LISBURN
DOWN
Newry
NEWRY AND MOURNE
BANBRIDGE
CRAIGAVON
ARMAGH
Armagh
MAGHERAFELT
COOKSTOWN
DUNGANNON
Dungannon
OMAGH
Omagh
STRABANE
FERMANAGH
Enniskillen

DONEGAL
Sligo
SLIGO
LEITRIM
Carrick-on-Shannon
Castlebar
MAYO
ROSCOMMON
Roscommon
Longford
LONGFORD
CAVAN
Cavan
Monaghan
MONAGHAN
MEATH
Trim
LOUTH
Dundalk
Dublin
DUBLIN
Mullingar
WEST MEATH
Naas
KILDARE
Wicklow
WICKLOW
GALWAY
Galway
OFFALY
Tullamore
Portlaoise
LAOIS
Carlow
CARLOW
Kilkenny
KILKENNY
WEXFORD
Wexford
CLARE
Ennis
LIMERICK
Limerick
TIPPERARY
Clonmel
WATERFORD
Waterford
KERRY
Tralee
CORK
Cork

South Wales
Scale 1:1 700 000

MONMOUTHSHIRE
Pontypool
TORFAEN
Cwmbran
Ebbw Vale
NEWPORT
Newport
NORTH SOMERSET
Merthyr Tydfil
R-HONDDA CYNON TAFF
Hengoed
CAERPHILLY
Cardiff
CARDIFF
Barry
THE VALE OF GLAMORGAN
BRIDGEND
Bridgend
NEATH PORT TALBOT
Tonypandy
Port Talbot
SWANSEA
Swansea

1 MERTHYR TYDFIL
2 BLAENAU GWENT

Greater London
Scale 1:850 000

ENFIELD
BARNET
HARROW
HILLINGDON
HOUNSLOW
EALING
BRENT
HARINGEY
WALTHAM FOREST
HAVERING
REDBRIDGE
BARKING
NEWHAM
HACKNEY
CAMDEN
ISLINGTON
CITY
TOWER HAMLETS
GREENWICH
BEXLEY
LEWISHAM
SOUTHWARK
LAMBETH
WANDSWORTH
RICHMOND UPON THAMES
KINGSTON UPON THAMES
MERTON
SUTTON
CROYDON
BROMLEY
HAMMERSMITH
KENSINGTON AND CHELSEA
CITY OF WESTMINSTER

1 KENSINGTON AND CHELSEA
2 CITY OF WESTMINSTER
3 HAMMERSMITH
4 TOWER HAMLETS

Transverse Mercator Projection © Oxford University Press

UK Government website www.direct.gov.uk
National Statistics Online www.statistics.gov.uk

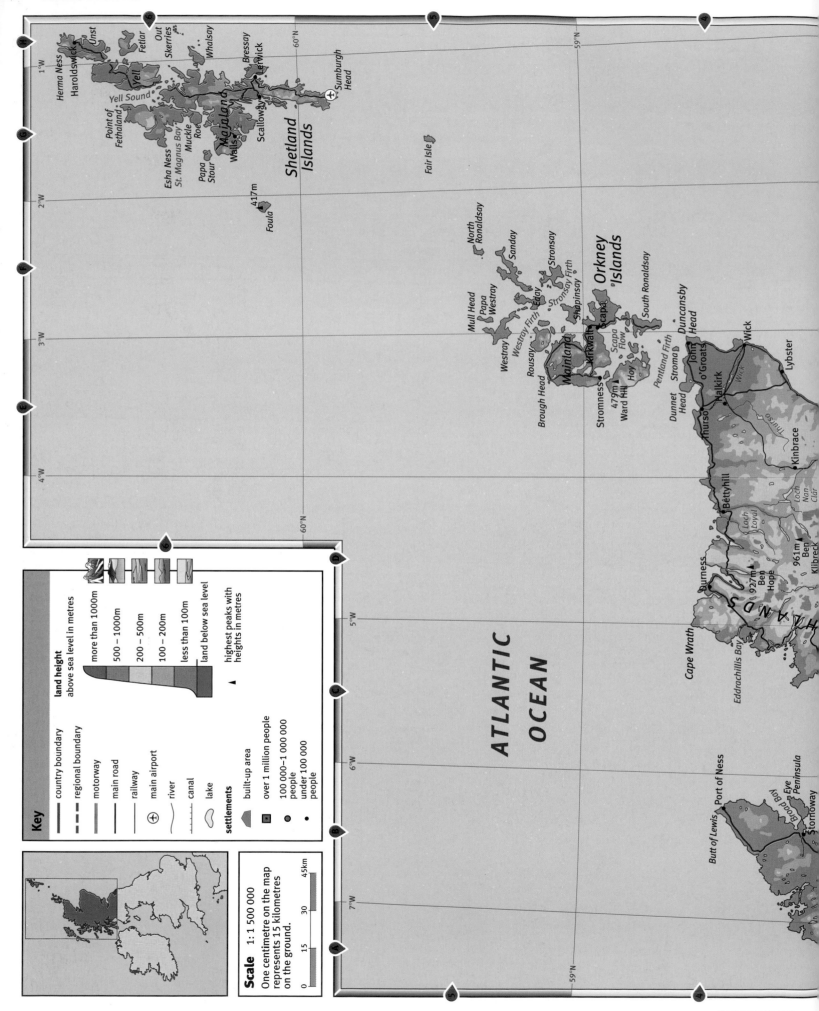

Shetland Islands

Herma Ness
Unst
Haroldswick
Fetlar
Out Skerries
Whalsay
Bressay
Lerwick
Yell
Yell Sound
Point of Fethaland
Mainland
Scalloway
Walls
Esha Ness
St. Magnus Bay
Muckle Roe
Papa Stour
417m
Foula
Sumburgh Head

Fair Isle

Orkney Islands

North Ronaldsay
Sanday
Stronsay
Stronsay Firth
Mull Head
Papa Westray
Eday
Rousay
Westray Firth
Shapinsay
Scapa
South Ronaldsay
Westray
Mainland
Kirkwall
Scapa Flow
Hoy
Duncansby Head
Brough Head
Stromness
479m
Ward Hill
Pentland Firth
Stroma
John o'Groats
Wick
Dunnet Head
Thurso
Halkirk
Wick
Lybster

ATLANTIC OCEAN

Kinbrace
Bettyhill
Loch Nan Clàr
Loch Loyal
Durness
927m
Ben Hope
961m
Ben Klibreck

Cape Wrath
Eddrachillis Bay
HIGHLANDS

Butt of Lewis
Port of Ness
Broad Bay
Eye Peninsula
Stornoway

Key

land height
above sea level in metres

| more than 1000m |
| 500 – 1000m |
| 200 – 500m |
| 100 – 200m |
| less than 100m |
| land below sea level |

▲ highest peaks with heights in metres

country boundary
regional boundary
motorway
main road
railway
⊕ **main airport**
river
canal
lake

settlements

■ built-up area
over 1 million people
■ 100 000–1 000 000 people
● under 100 000 people

Scale 1:1 500 000
One centimetre on the map represents 15 kilometres on the ground.

0   15   30   45km

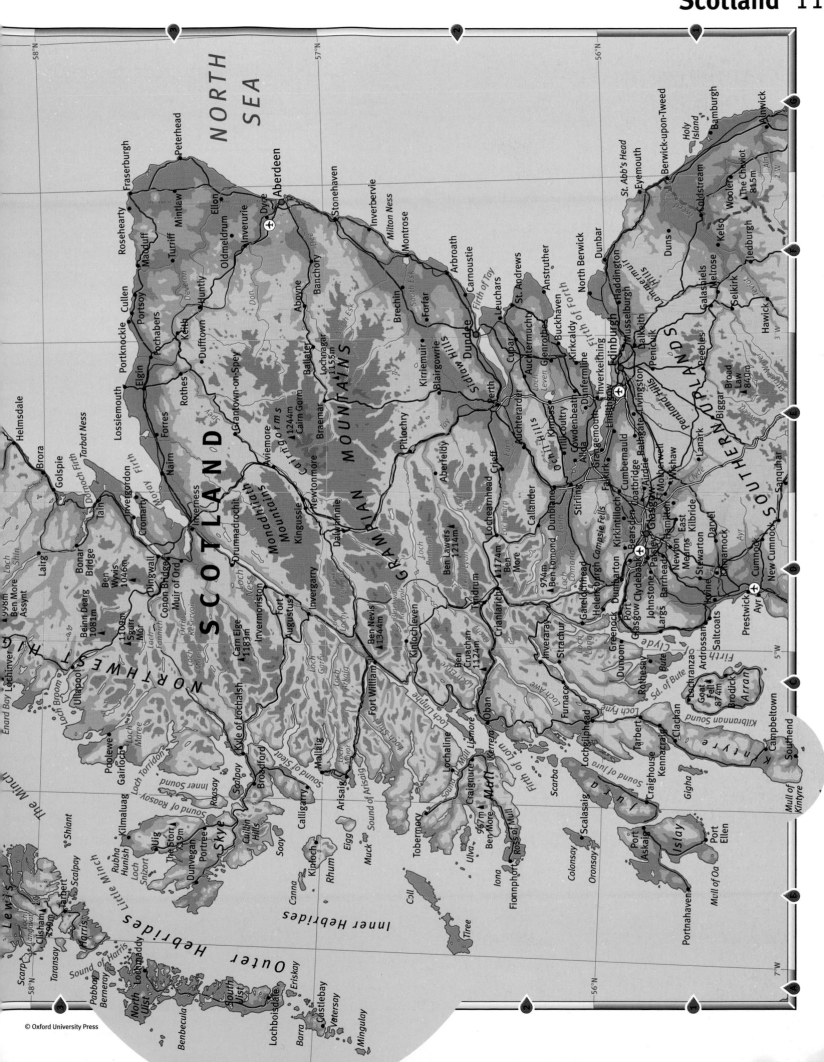

NORTH SEA

ENGLAND

country boundary
regional boundary
motorway
main road
railway
main airport
river
canal
lake

settlements

built-up area
over 1 million people
100 000–1 000 000 people
under 100 000 people

land height
above sea level in metres

more than 1000m
500 – 1000m
200 – 500m
100 – 200m
less than 100m
land below sea level
highest peaks with heights in metres

Scale 1: 1 500 000
One centimetre on the map
represents 15 kilometres
on the ground.

0   15   30   45km

Broad Law 840m
The Cheviot 815m
Peel Fell 602m
Cross Fell 893m
Skiddaw 931m
Scafell Pike 978m
Helvellyn 950m
Mickle Fell 790m
Whernside 737m
Ingleborough 723m
Pen-y-Ghent 693m
Great Whernside 704m
Ward's Stone 560m
The Peak 636m

© Oxford University Press

Key

———	country boundary
– – –	regional boundary
═══	motorway
———	main road
——	railway
✈	main airport
∿	river
┼┼┼┼	canal
⬭	lake

settlements

⬢	built-up area
▣	over 1 million people
⬤	100 000–1 000 000 people
•	under 100 000 people

land height
above sea level in metres

more than 1000m	
500 – 1000m	
200 – 500m	
100 – 200m	
less than 100m	
land below sea level	
▲	highest peaks with heights in metres

Scale 1: 1 500 000

One centimetre on the map represents 15 kilometres on the ground.

0   15   30   45km

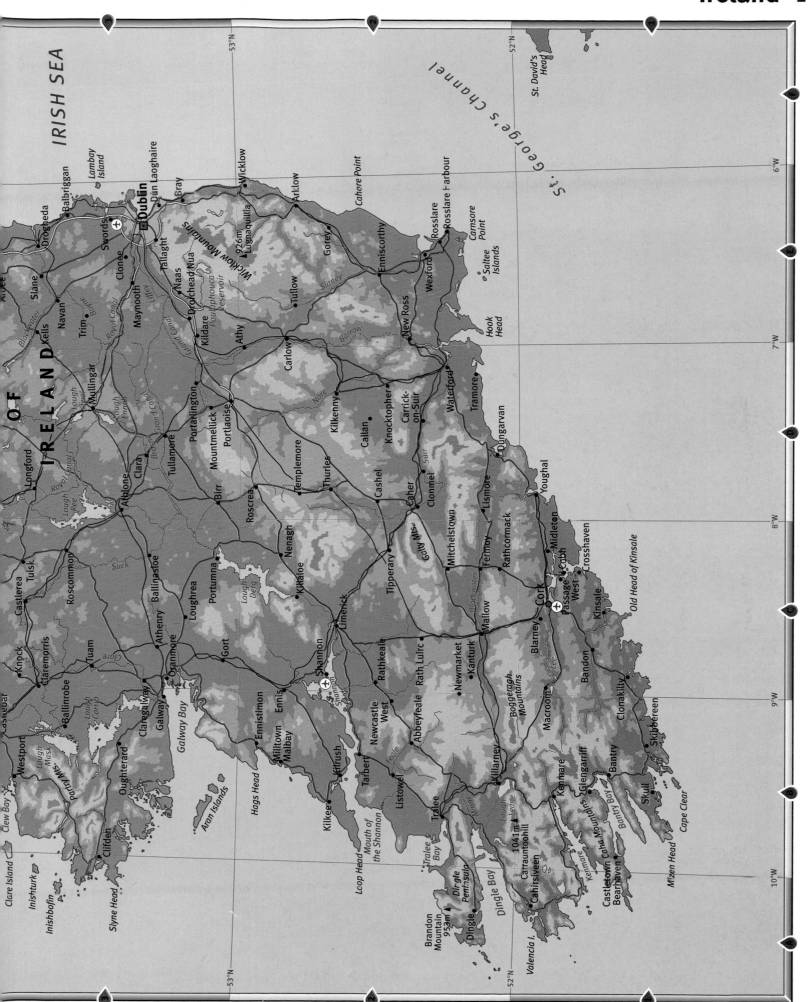

IRISH SEA

REPUBLIC OF IRELAND

St. George's Channel

St. David's Head

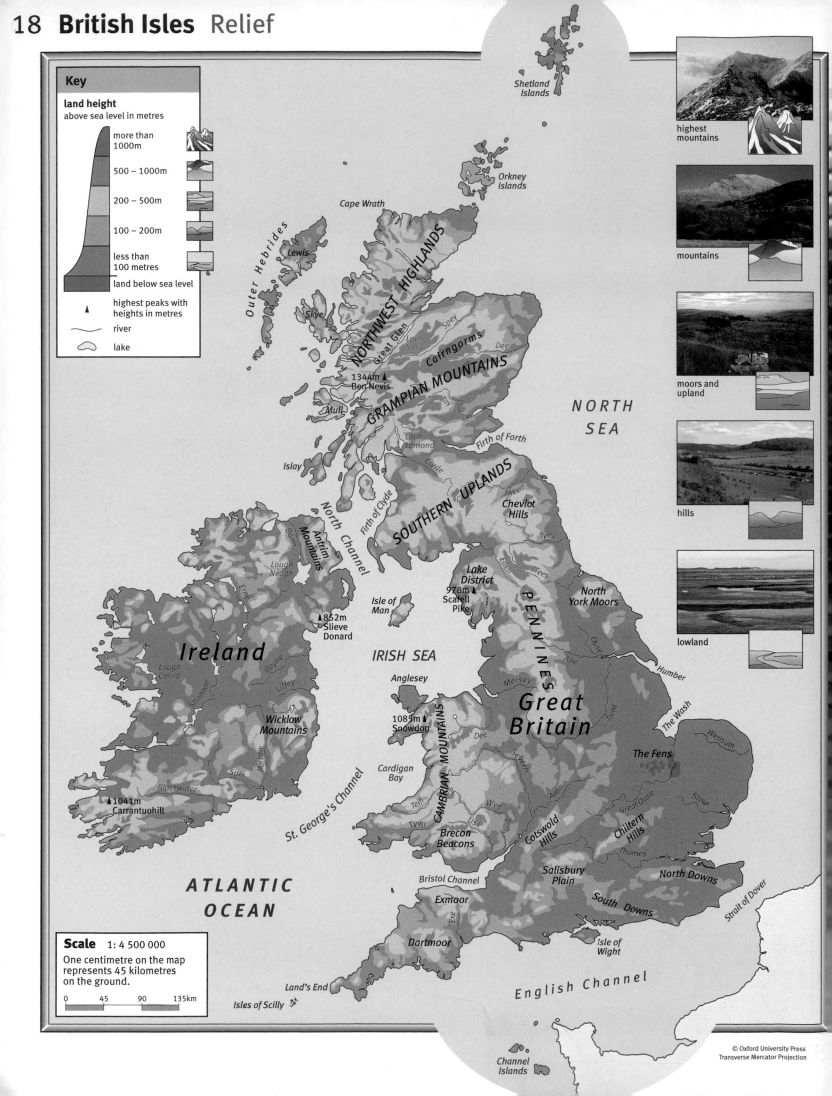

Key

land height
above sea level in metres

more than 1000m

500 – 1000m

200 – 500m

100 – 200m

less than 100 metres

land below sea level

▲ highest peaks with heights in metres

river

lake

highest mountains

mountains

moors and upland

hills

lowland

Shetland Islands

Orkney Islands

Cape Wrath

Outer Hebrides

Lewis

Skye

NORTHWEST HIGHLANDS

Great Glen

Loch Ness

Spey

Cairngorms

Dee

GRAMPIAN MOUNTAINS

1344m ▲ Ben Nevis

Mull

Tay

Loch Lomond

Firth of Forth

Clyde

NORTH SEA

Islay

Firth of Clyde

SOUTHERN UPLANDS

Tweed

Cheviot Hills

Tyne

North Channel

Bann

Antrim Mountains

Lough Neagh

Erne

Ireland

Lough Corrib

Shannon

Boyne

Liffey

Barrow

Suir

Blackwater

▲ 1041m Carrantuohill

Wicklow Mountains

▲ 852m Slieve Donard

Isle of Man

IRISH SEA

Lake District

978m ▲ Scafell Pike

Eden

Tees

PENNINES

North York Moors

Ouse

Aire

Mersey

Humber

The Wash

Wensum

Anglesey

1085m ▲ Snowdon

CAMBRIAN MOUNTAINS

Dee

Great Britain

Severn

Trent

Great Ouse

The Fens

Stour

Chiltern Hills

Cardigan Bay

Teifi

Tywi

Usk

Wye

Avon

Cotswold Hills

Thames

North Downs

St. George's Channel

Brecon Beacons

Salisbury Plain

South Downs

Strait of Dover

Bristol Channel

Exmoor

Exe

Isle of Wight

ATLANTIC OCEAN

Dartmoor

Land's End

English Channel

Isles of Scilly

Channel Islands

Scale 1: 4 500 000

One centimetre on the map represents 45 kilometres on the ground.

0   45   90   135km

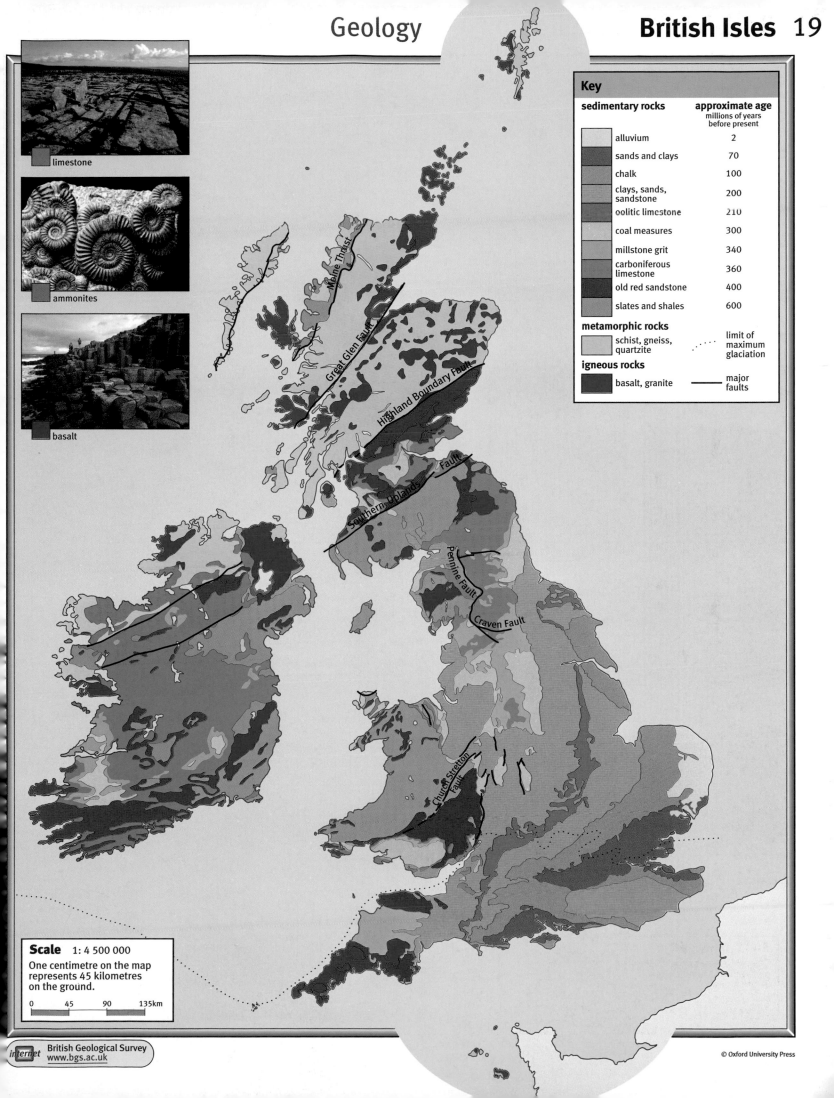

limestone

ammonites

basalt

Key

sedimentary rocks	approximate age millions of years before present
alluvium	2
sands and clays	70
chalk	100
clays, sands, sandstone	200
oolitic limestone	210
coal measures	300
millstone grit	340
carboniferous limestone	360
old red sandstone	400
slates and shales	600

metamorphic rocks

schist, gneiss,
quartzite

.... limit of
maximum
glaciation

igneous rocks

basalt, granite

——— major
faults

Moine Thrust

Great Glen Fault

Highland Boundary Fault

Southern Uplands Fault

Pennine Fault

Craven Fault

Church Stretton Fault

Scale 1: 4 500 000

One centimetre on the map
represents 45 kilometres
on the ground.

0   45   90   135km

British Geological Survey
www.bgs.ac.uk

© Oxford University Press

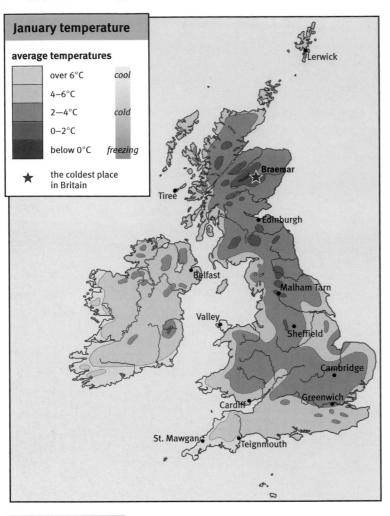

January temperature

average temperatures

over 6°C	*cool*
4–6°C	
2–4°C	*cold*
0–2°C	
below 0°C	*freezing*

★ the coldest place in Britain

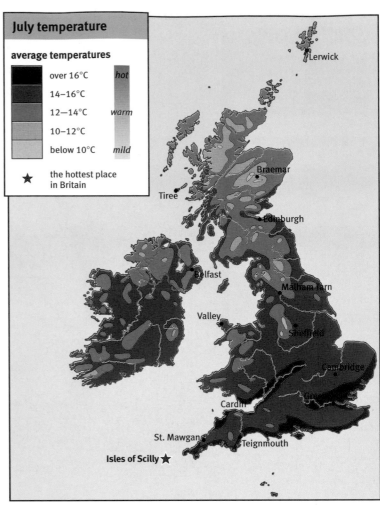

July temperature

average temperatures

over 16°C	*hot*
14–16°C	
12—14°C	*warm*
10–12°C	
below 10°C	*mild*

★ the hottest place in Britain

Isles of Scilly ★

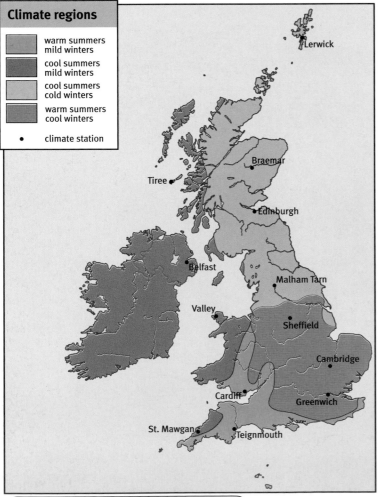

Climate regions

- warm summers mild winters
- cool summers mild winters
- cool summers cold winters
- warm summers cool winters
- • climate station

internet | Met Office www.metoffice.gov.uk | BBC Weather Centre www.bbc.co.uk/weather

Climate graphs

for selected British climate stations

▇ average monthly rainfall in milimetres

〜 average monthly temperature in °C

9m height above sea level

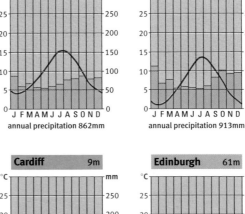

Belfast 63m
annual precipitation 862mm

Braemar 339m
annual precipitation 913mm

Cambridge 26m
annual precipitation 1112mm

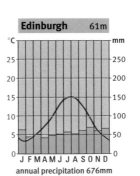

Cardiff 9m
annual precipitation 554mm

Edinburgh 61m
annual precipitation 676mm

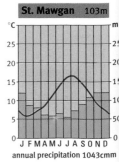

St. Mawgan 103m
annual precipitation 1043cmm

Transverse Mercator Projection © Oxford University Press

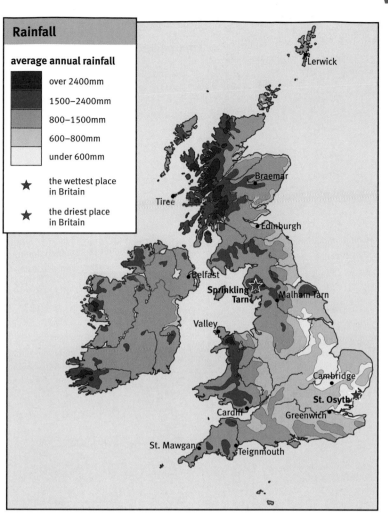

Rainfall

average annual rainfall

- over 2400mm
- 1500–2400mm
- 800–1500mm
- 600–800mm
- under 600mm

★ the wettest place in Britain

★ the driest place in Britain

Lerwick

Braemar

Tiree

Edinburgh

Belfast

Sprinkling Tarn

Malham Tarn

Valley

Cambridge

St. Osyth

Cardiff

Greenwich

St. Mawgan

Teignmouth

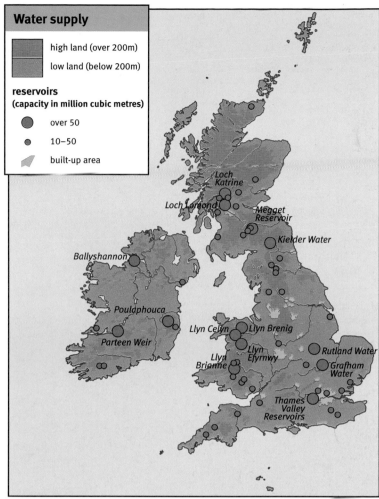

Water supply

- high land (over 200m)
- low land (below 200m)

reservoirs (capacity in million cubic metres)

- ⬤ over 50
- • 10–50
- built-up area

Loch Katrine

Loch Lomond

Megget Reservoir

Kielder Water

Ballyshannon

Pouldphouca

Llyn Celyn

Llyn Brenig

Parteen Weir

Llyn Efyrnwy

Rutland Water

Llyn Brianne

Grafham Water

Thames Valley Reservoirs

Climate data

averages are for 1971-2001

Valley 10m — climate station and its height above sea level

Greenwich	7m	Jan	Feb	Mar	Apr	May	Jun	Jul	Aug	Sep	Oct	Nov	Dec	YEAR
temperature (°C)		5.2	5.2	7.4	9.3	12.6	15.7	18.2	18.0	15.1	11.6	7.9	6.1	11.0
rainfall (mm)		52	34	42	45	47	53	38	47	57	62	52	54	583

Lerwick	82m	Jan	Feb	Mar	Apr	May	Jun	Jul	Aug	Sep	Oct	Nov	Dec	YEAR
temperature (°C)		3.6	3.4	4.1	5.3	7.7	9.8	11.7	12.0	10.3	8.2	5.6	4.1	7.2
rainfall (mm)		135	108	122	74	54	59	59	78	115	132	152	150	1238

Malham Tarn	381m	Jan	Feb	Mar	Apr	May	Jun	Jul	Aug	Sep	Oct	Nov	Dec	YEAR
temperature (°C)		1.8	1.8	3.4	5.5	8.7	11.2	13.4	13.1	10.9	7.8	4.4	2.7	7.1
rainfall (mm)		165	116	134	91	85	97	95	123	130	152	156	175	1519

Sheffield	131m	Jan	Feb	Mar	Apr	May	Jun	Jul	Aug	Sep	Oct	Nov	Dec	YEAR
temperature (°C)		4.0	4.2	6.2	8.1	11.4	14.2	16.6	16.4	13.7	10.3	6.7	4.9	9.8
rainfall (mm)		87	63	68	63	56	67	51	64	64	74	78	92	827

Teignmouth	3m	Jan	Feb	Mar	Apr	May	Jun	Jul	Aug	Sep	Oct	Nov	Dec	YEAR
temperature (°C)		6.4	6.4	7.6	9.0	12.0	14.7	17.1	16.9	14.8	11.9	8.9	7.4	11.1
rainfall (mm)		102	83	68	55	52	51	36	57	67	83	84	113	851

Tiree	9m	Jan	Feb	Mar	Apr	May	Jun	Jul	Aug	Sep	Oct	Nov	Dec	YEAR
temperature (°C)		5.4	5.2	6.1	7.4	9.8	11.8	13.6	13.8	12.2	10.2	7.5	6.2	9.1
rainfall (mm)		143	98	105	67	54	62	78	99	119	143	137	135	1240

Valley	10m	Jan	Feb	Mar	Apr	May	Jun	Jul	Aug	Sep	Oct	Nov	Dec	YEAR
temperature (°C)		5.8	5.6	6.9	8.5	11.3	13.6	15.7	15.8	14.0	11.4	8.4	6.7	10.3
rainfall (mm)		82	60	67	52	45	51	49	68	73	90	101	92	830

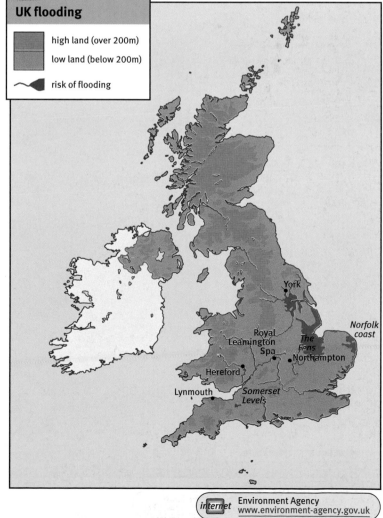

UK flooding

- high land (over 200m)
- low land (below 200m)
- risk of flooding

York

Royal Leamington Spa

The Fens

Norfolk coast

Northampton

Hereford

Lynmouth

Somerset Levels

internet Environment Agency
www.environment-agency.gov.uk

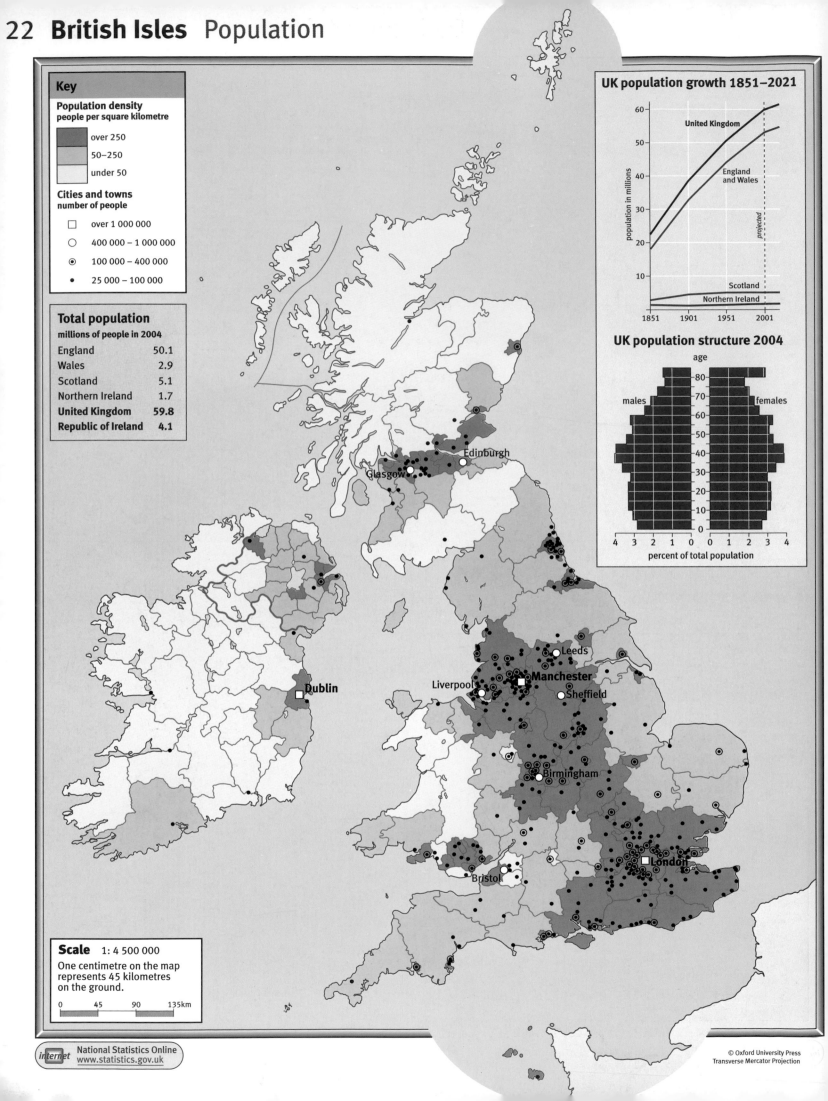

Key

Population density
people per square kilometre

- over 250
- 50–250
- under 50

Cities and towns
number of people

- □ over 1 000 000
- ○ 400 000 – 1 000 000
- ◉ 100 000 – 400 000
- • 25 000 – 100 000

Total population

millions of people in 2004

England	50.1
Wales	2.9
Scotland	5.1
Northern Ireland	1.7
United Kingdom	**59.8**
Republic of Ireland	**4.1**

UK population growth 1851–2021

- United Kingdom
- England and Wales
- Scotland
- Northern Ireland

population in millions: 10, 20, 30, 40, 50, 60
years: 1851, 1901, 1951, 2001
projected

UK population structure 2004

age
males — females
80, 70, 60, 50, 40, 30, 20, 10, 0
percent of total population: 4 3 2 1 0 0 1 2 3 4

Scale 1: 4 500 000

One centimetre on the map
represents 45 kilometres
on the ground.

0   45   90   135km

Edinburgh
Glasgow
Dublin
Liverpool Manchester Leeds
Sheffield
Birmingham
Bristol
London

National Statistics Online
www.statistics.gov.uk

© Oxford University Press
Transverse Mercator Projection

Key

Fossil fuel

- coalfield
- coal mine
- oil field
- oil pipeline
- gas field
- gas pipeline

Largest power stations

- burning coal, oil or gas
- using water power
- using nuclear power
- using wind power

Manufacturing industry
main centres of selected industries

- oil refining
- steel
- motor vehicles
- electronics and computers
- clothing and footwear
- built-up area

Scale 1: 5 000 000

One centimetre on the map
represents 50 kilometres
on the ground.

0   50   100   150km

UK employment 1984–2004

millions of people

25

20 — Tertiary activity

15

10

5 — Secondary activity

— Primary activity

0

1984   1994   2004

Department of Trade and Industry
www.dti.gov.uk

© Oxford University Press

Magnus
Penguin E.
Tern
Statfjord
Comorants
Brent
Ninian
North Alwyn
Dunbar
Nuggets
Schiehallion
Foinaven
Frigg
Bruce
Beryl
Harding
Claymore
Macculloch
Captain
Scott
Britannia
Blake
Alloa
Forties
Nelson
Causeymire
Mungo
Madoes
Pierce
Shearwater
Elgin
Jade
Bittern
Franklin
Judy
Luichart
Deanie
Peterhead
Fasnakyle
Glenmoriston
Fort William
Errochty
Kinlocheven
Clunie
Rannock
Tummel
Lochay
Clachan
Sloy
Kinross
Markinch
Cruach
Mhor
Longannet
Torness
Glasgow
Grangemouth
Broxburn
Cockenzie
Hunterston
Edinburgh
Beinn
an Tuirc
Motherwell
Bowbeat
Hawick
Tongland
Newcastle
upon Tyne
Prudhoe
Hartlepool
North Tees
Teesside
Teesside
Murdoch
Belfast
Kendal
North
Morecambe
Eggborough
Ferrybridge
Scunthorpe
West
Sole
Heysham
Hull
Saltend
Carrack
South
Morecambe
Lennox
Leeds
Galleon
Viking
Hamilton
Manchester
Killingholme
Liverpool
Sheffield
South
Indefatigable
Stanlow
Cottam
Killingholme
North Hoyle
Ince
Leman
Dinorwig
Connah's
Quay
Fiddler's Ferry
Sandbach
West Burton
Wrexham
Crewe
Burnaston
Ratcliffe-on-Soar
Scroby
Sands
Rugeley
Nottingham
Carno
Wolverhampton
Leicester
Norwich
Rheidol
Birmingham
Solihull
Kettering
Penrhyddlan
Coventry
Rushden
Cambridge
Llidiart-y-waun
Northampton
Wellingborough
Sizewell
Longbridge
Milton
Keynes
Hitchin
Cowley
Watford
Borehamwood
Milford Haven
Cwmbran
Didcot
Reading
Coryton
Pembroke
Llanwern
London
Kingsnorth
Cardiff
Swindon
Barking
Port Talbot
Bristol
Tilbury
Bridgend
Newbury
Bracknell
Guildford
Dungeness
Aberthaw
Street
Hinkley
Point
Fawley
Wytch
Farm

Key

- National Parks
- Areas of outstanding natural beauty
- Protected coast
- ✳ World Heritage site

Major tourist attractions (more than 1 million visitors per year)

- historic buildings
- museums and galleries
- zoos, parks and gardens
- theme parks and piers
- built-up area

Scale   1: 4 500 000

One centimetre on the map represents 45 kilometres on the ground.

| 0 | 45 | 90 | 135km |

Holidays in the UK and abroad

Numbers of holidays taken by UK residents
millions

- holidays in the UK
- holidays abroad

(bar chart, y-axis 0 to 40)
1981, 1991, 2001

Central London

0   3 km

- British Museum
- National Portrait Gallery
- Madame Tussauds
- Somerset House
- National Gallery
- Tower of London
- Science Museum
- Tate Modern
- National History Museum
- London Eye
- Westminster Abbey
- Victoria and Albert Museum

internet British Tourist Authority www.visitbritain.org   UNESCO world heritage sites http://whc.unesco.org

© Oxford University Press
Transverse Mercator Projection

Shetland

Hoy and West Mainland   ✳ The Heart of Neolithic Orkney

Kyle of Tongue

South Lewis, Harris, and North Uist

Assynt Coigach

✳ St. Kilda

Wester Ross

The Cuillin Hills

Knoydart   Cairngorms   Aberdeen

Ben Nevis and Glen Coe

Loch Rannoch and Glen Lyon

Knapdale   Loch Lomond and the Trossachs

Jura   Old and New Towns of Edinburgh   ✳ Edinburgh Castle

North Arran   Glasgow   Strathclyde Country Park

New Lanark

Giant's Causeway

Antrim Coast and Glens

Sperrin   Belfast   Northumberland

Strangford Lough   Hadrian's ✳ Wall   Newcastle upon Tyne

Mourne   North Pennines   Durham Cathedral & Castle

Lake District   Windermere Lake Cruises   Yorkshire Dales   North York Moors

Fountain's Abbey & Studley Royal Park ✳   Nidderdale   Flamingoland

Forest of Bowland   York Minster

Blackpool Pleasure Beach   Saltaire ✳   Leeds

Pleasureland   Lincolnshire Wolds

Liverpool- Maritime Mercantile City   Manchester   Sheffield

Anglesey   Albert Dock   Peak District   Norfolk Coast

Castles & Town Walls of King Edward ✳   Chester Zoo   Alton Towers

Stoke-on-Trent   Derwent Valley Mills   Nottingham   Pleasure Beach, Great Yarmouth

Snowdonia   Ironbridge Gorge   Drayton Manor   Thetford Forest Park   The Broads

Lleyn   Coventry   Suffolk Coast and Heaths

Shropshire Hills   Birmingham   Willen Lake and Park

Pembrokeshire Coast   Fairlands Valley Park

Brecon Beacons   Wye Valley   Cotswolds   Blenheim ✳ Palace   Chilterns

Blaenavon ✳   Oxford   Tower of London ✳✳   Kew Gardens   Maritime Greenwich

Gower   Cardiff   Bristol   North Wessex Downs   Legoland   Westminster Palace/Abbey ✳   Canterbury Cathedral

Ashton Court Estate   ✳ Bath   Stonehenge/ Avebury ✳   Kent Downs

Exmoor   Cranborne Chase   South Downs   High Weald

Blackdown Hills   Eastbourne Pier

Dartmoor   Dorset   Isle of Wight

Eden Project   Cornwall   Dorset and East Devon Coast   New Forest

Isles of Scilly

Loch Einich, Cairngorms

The Cotswolds

The Needles, Isle of Wight

Edinburgh Castle

Sports venues 2005

major clubs or grounds

- Association Football
- Rugby Union
- Rugby League
- Cricket
- major sports stadium or centre
- built-up area

Scale 1: 4 500 000
One centimetre on the map represents 45 kilometres on the ground.

0   45   90   135km

Goodison Park
6 November 2005

Millenium Stadium, Cardiff
19 March 2005

Old Trafford
15 October 2005

The Oval
22 September 2005

Millenium Stadium, Cardiff

UK sport
www.uksport.gov.uk

BBC sport
www.bbc.co.uk/sport

© Oxford University Press

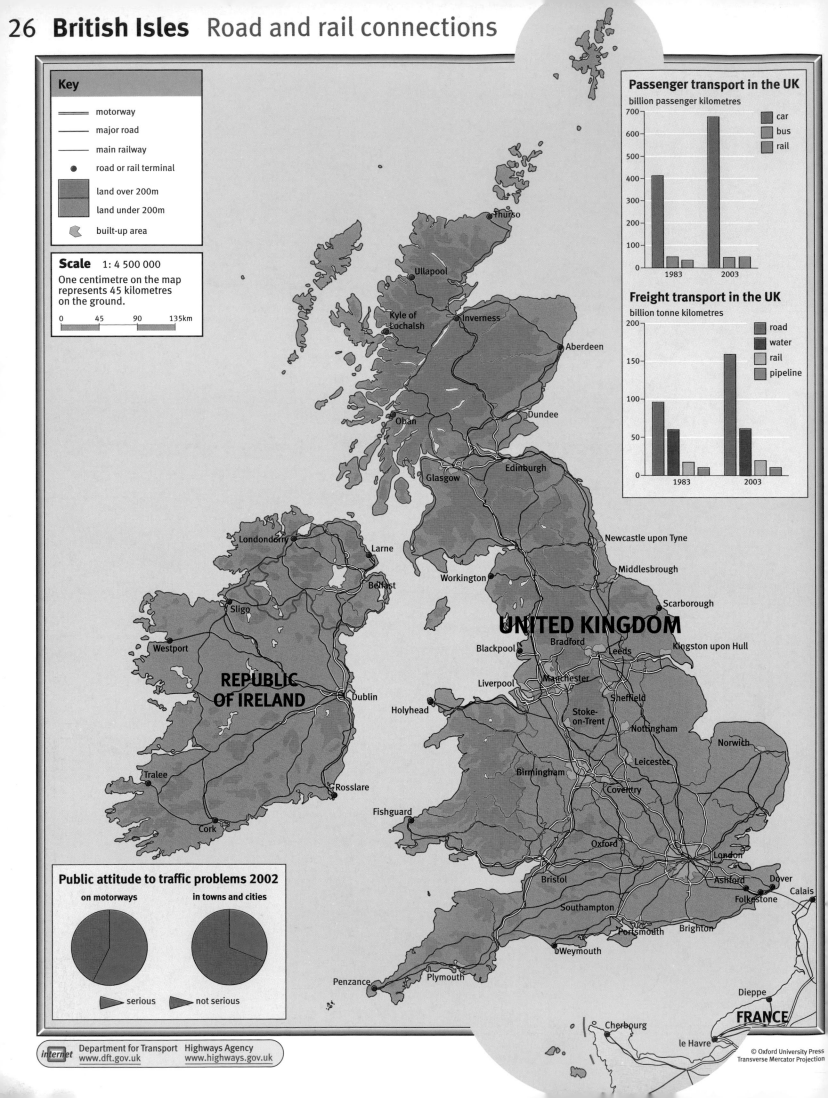

Key

- motorway
- major road
- main railway
- ● road or rail terminal
- land over 200m
- land under 200m
- built-up area

Scale 1: 4 500 000

One centimetre on the map represents 45 kilometres on the ground.

0   45   90   135km

Passenger transport in the UK

billion passenger kilometres

- car
- bus
- rail

700
600
500
400
300
200
100

1983   2003

Freight transport in the UK

billion tonne kilometres

- road
- water
- rail
- pipeline

200

150

100

50

0

1983   2003

Thurso
Ullapool
Kyle of Lochalsh
Inverness
Aberdeen
Oban
Dundee
Glasgow
Edinburgh
Newcastle upon Tyne
Middlesbrough
Workington
Scarborough

Londonderry
Larne
Belfast
Sligo
Westport

REPUBLIC OF IRELAND

Dublin
Holyhead

UNITED KINGDOM

Bradford
Blackpool
Leeds
Kingston upon Hull
Liverpool   Manchester
Sheffield
Stoke-on-Trent
Nottingham
Norwich
Leicester
Birmingham
Coventry

Tralee
Rosslare
Fishguard
Cork

Oxford
London
Bristol
Ashford   Dover
Calais
Folkestone
Southampton
Brighton
Portsmouth
Weymouth
Penzance   Plymouth

Dieppe

FRANCE

Cherbourg
le Havre

Public attitude to traffic problems 2002

on motorways   in towns and cities

▶ serious   ▶ not serious

internet Department for Transport
www.dft.gov.uk   Highways Agency
www.highways.gov.uk

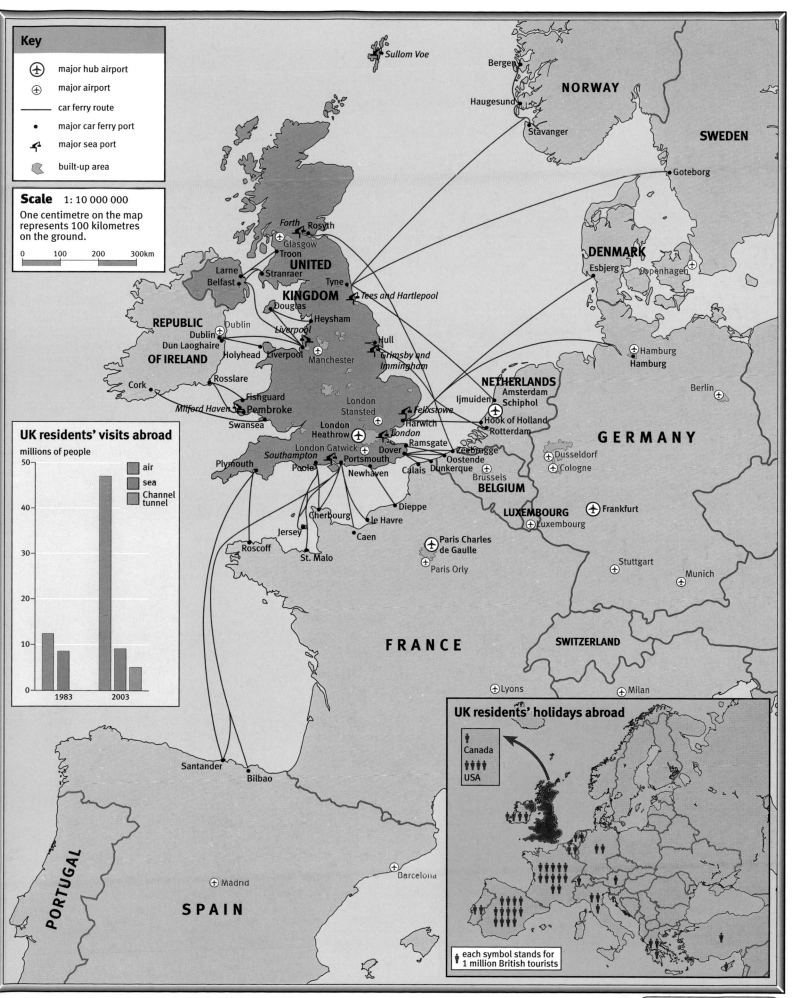

Key

- ✈ major hub airport
- ⊕ major airport
- — car ferry route
- • major car ferry port
- ⊁ major sea port
- ⬟ built-up area

Scale 1: 10 000 000

One centimetre on the map represents 100 kilometres on the ground.

0   100   200   300km

UK residents' visits abroad

millions of people

50

40

30

20

10

0
      1983   2003

- air
- sea
- Channel tunnel

UK residents' holidays abroad

- 👤 Canada
- 👤👤👤 USA

each symbol stands for 1 million British tourists

Sullom Voe

Bergen
Haugesund
Stavanger

NORWAY

SWEDEN

Goteborg

Forth · Rosyth
Glasgow
Troon

UNITED

Larne
Belfast
Stranraer
Tyne

KINGDOM

Douglas
Heysham

DENMARK
Esbjerg
Copenhagen

REPUBLIC

Dublin
Dun Laoghaire
Liverpool
Liverpool
Manchester

Hull
Grimsby and Immingham

Hamburg
Hamburg

Holyhead
OF IRELAND

Berlin

Cork
Rosslare

NETHERLANDS
Amsterdam
Schiphol

Fishguard
Pembroke
Milford Haven
Swansea

London
Stansted

Felixstowe
Harwich

Ijmuiden
Hook of Holland
Rotterdam

GERMANY

London
Heathrow
London

Ramsgate

Zeebrugge

Dusseldorf
Cologne

Plymouth
Southampton
Poole
Portsmouth
Newhaven

London Gatwick
Dover
Calais
Dunkerque

Oostende
Brussels
BELGIUM

LUXEMBOURG
Luxembourg

Frankfurt

Cherbourg
Dieppe
le Havre

Jersey
Caen

Roscoff
St. Malo

Paris Charles
de Gaulle
Paris Orly

Stuttgart

Munich

FRANCE

SWITZERLAND

Santander
Bilbao

Madrid

Barcelona

PORTUGAL

SPAIN

Lyons
Milan

internet National Statistics Online www.statistics.gov.uk

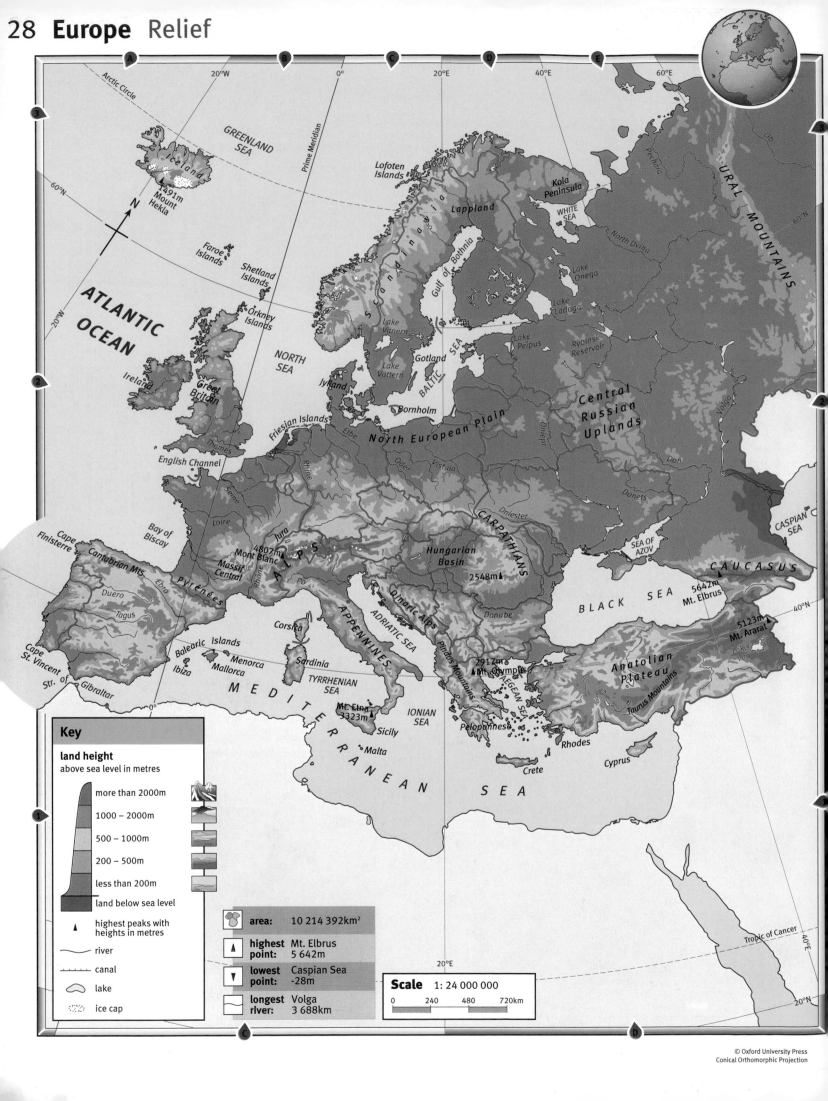

Key

land height
above sea level in metres

- more than 2000m
- 1000 – 2000m
- 500 – 1000m
- 200 – 500m
- less than 200m
- land below sea level

▲ highest peaks with heights in metres

river

canal

lake

ice cap

area:	10 214 392km²	
highest point:	Mt. Elbrus	5 642m
lowest point:	Caspian Sea	-28m
longest river:	Volga	3 688km

Scale 1: 24 000 000

0   240   480   720km

© Oxford University Press
Conical Orthomorphic Projection

ATLANTIC OCEAN

MEDITERRANEAN SEA

NORTH SEA

BALTIC SEA

BLACK SEA

ICELAND — Reykjavik

REPUBLIC OF IRELAND — Dublin, Belfast

UNITED KINGDOM — London, Edinburgh, Manchester, Birmingham

NORWAY — Oslo

SWEDEN — Stockholm, Göteborg

FINLAND — Helsinki

DENMARK — Copenhagen, Hamburg

ESTONIA — Tallinn

LATVIA — Riga

LITHUANIA — Vilnius

RUSSIAN FEDERATION (RUSSIA) — Moscow, St. Petersburg, Nizhniy-Novgorod

KALININGRAD (Russia)

BELARUS — Minsk

POLAND — Warsaw, Krakow

NETHERLANDS — Amsterdam, Rotterdam

GERMANY — Berlin, Düsseldorf

BELGIUM — Brussels

LUXEMBOURG — Luxembourg

FRANCE — Paris, Bordeaux, Lyons, Marseilles

CZECH REP. — Prague

SLOVAKIA — Bratislava

AUSTRIA — Vienna

SWITZERLAND — Bern

LIECHTENSTEIN

SLOVENIA — Ljubljana

HUNGARY — Budapest

UKRAINE — Kiev, Kharkov, Donets'k, Odessa

Volgograd, Rostov-on-Don

MOLDOVA — Chisinau

ROMANIA — Bucharest

CROATIA — Zagreb

BOSNIA–HERZEGOVINA — Sarajevo

SERBIA — Belgrade

MONTENEGRO — Podgorica

ITALY — Rome, Milan, Naples

Munich

SAN MARINO

MONACO

ANDORRA

SPAIN — Madrid, Barcelona, Valencia, Seville

PORTUGAL — Lisbon, Oporto

Gibraltar (UK)

Ceuta (Sp), Melilla (Sp)

BULGARIA — Sofia

FYRO MACEDONIA — Skopje

ALBANIA — Tiranë

GREECE — Athens

TURKEY — Ankara, Istanbul, Izmir, Adana

GEORGIA — Tbilisi

CYPRUS — Nicosia

MALTA — Valletta

Arctic Circle

Prime Meridian

0° 20°E 40°E 60°E

60°N 60°N

40°N

20°W

Tropic of Cancer

European Union

REPUBLIC OF IRELAND, UNITED KINGDOM, SWEDEN, FINLAND, DENMARK, ESTONIA, LATVIA, LITHUANIA, NETHERLANDS, BELGIUM, GERMANY, LUXEMBOURG, CZECH REP., POLAND, FRANCE, AUSTRIA, SLOVAKIA, SLOVENIA, HUNGARY, ROMANIA, ITALY, PORTUGAL, SPAIN, BULGARIA, GREECE, MALTA, CYPRUS

Key

colours show countries

SPAIN — country names are shown like this

■ capital city

• other major city

	population: 655 884 785 *
largest country:	Ukraine 603 698km²
country with most people:	Germany 82 689 000
largest city:	Istanbul, Turkey 9 946 000

* does not include Russian Federation

Scale 1: 24 000 000

0 240 480 720km

European Union Gateway
http://europa.eu.int/index_en.htm

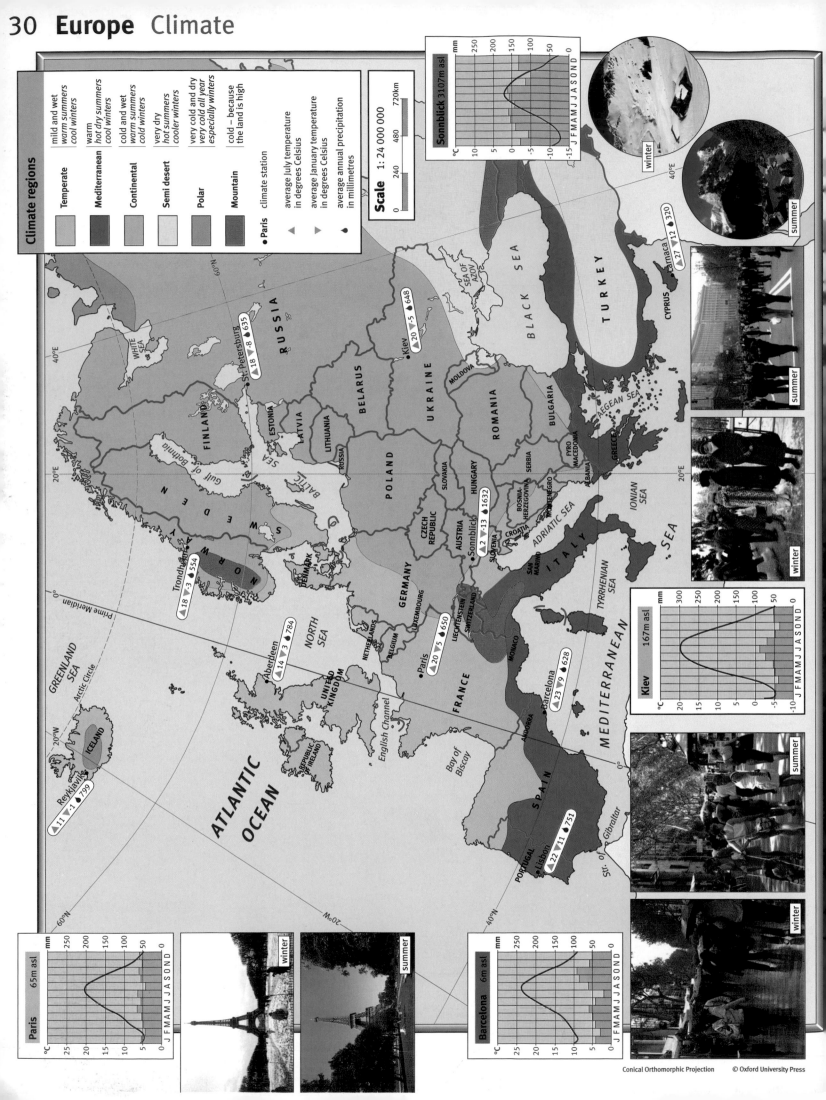

Climate regions

Temperate	mild and wet / *warm summers* / *cool winters*
Mediterranean	warm / *hot dry summers* / *cool winters*
Continental	cold and wet / *warm summers* / *cold winters*
Semi desert	very dry / *hot summers* / *cooler winters*
Polar	very cold and dry / *very cold all year* / *especially winters*
Mountain	cold – because / *the land is high*

• Paris   climate station

◀ average July temperature in degrees Celsius
▶ average January temperature in degrees Celsius
● average annual precipitation in millimetres

Scale 1: 24 000 000

0   240   480   720km

Conical Orthomorphic Projection   © Oxford University Press

Climate stations (◀ July °C ▶ January °C ● precipitation mm):

- Reykjavik ◀11 ▶-1 ●799
- Trondheim ◀18 ▶3 ●554
- St. Petersburg ◀18 ▶-8 ●635
- Kiev ◀20 ▶-5 ●648
- Aberdeen ◀14 ▶3 ●784
- Paris ◀20 ▶5 ●650
- Sonnblick ◀2 ▶-13 ●1632
- Barcelona ◀23 ▶9 ●628
- Lisbon ◀22 ▶11 ●751
- Larnaca ◀27 ▶12 ●320

Climate graphs:
- Sonnblick 3107m asl
- Kiev 167m asl
- Paris 65m asl
- Barcelona 6m asl

Region labels: GREENLAND SEA, Arctic Circle, ICELAND, ATLANTIC OCEAN, NORTH SEA, WHITE SEA, BALTIC SEA, Gulf of Bothnia, NORWAY, SWEDEN, FINLAND, RUSSIA, ESTONIA, LATVIA, LITHUANIA, BELARUS, DENMARK, REPUBLIC OF IRELAND, UNITED KINGDOM, English Channel, NETHERLANDS, BELGIUM, LUXEMBOURG, GERMANY, POLAND, UKRAINE, MOLDOVA, CZECH REPUBLIC, SLOVAKIA, AUSTRIA, LIECHTENSTEIN, SWITZERLAND, HUNGARY, FRANCE, Bay of Biscay, ANDORRA, MONACO, SPAIN, PORTUGAL, Str. of Gibraltar, ITALY, SAN MARINO, SLOVENIA, CROATIA, BOSNIA-HERZEGOVINA, MONTENEGRO, SERBIA, ALBANIA, FYRO MACEDONIA, ROMANIA, BULGARIA, GREECE, TURKEY, CYPRUS, BLACK SEA, SEA OF AZOV, ADRIATIC SEA, TYRRHENIAN SEA, IONIAN SEA, AEGEAN SEA, MEDITERRANEAN SEA, Prime Meridian

summer / winter

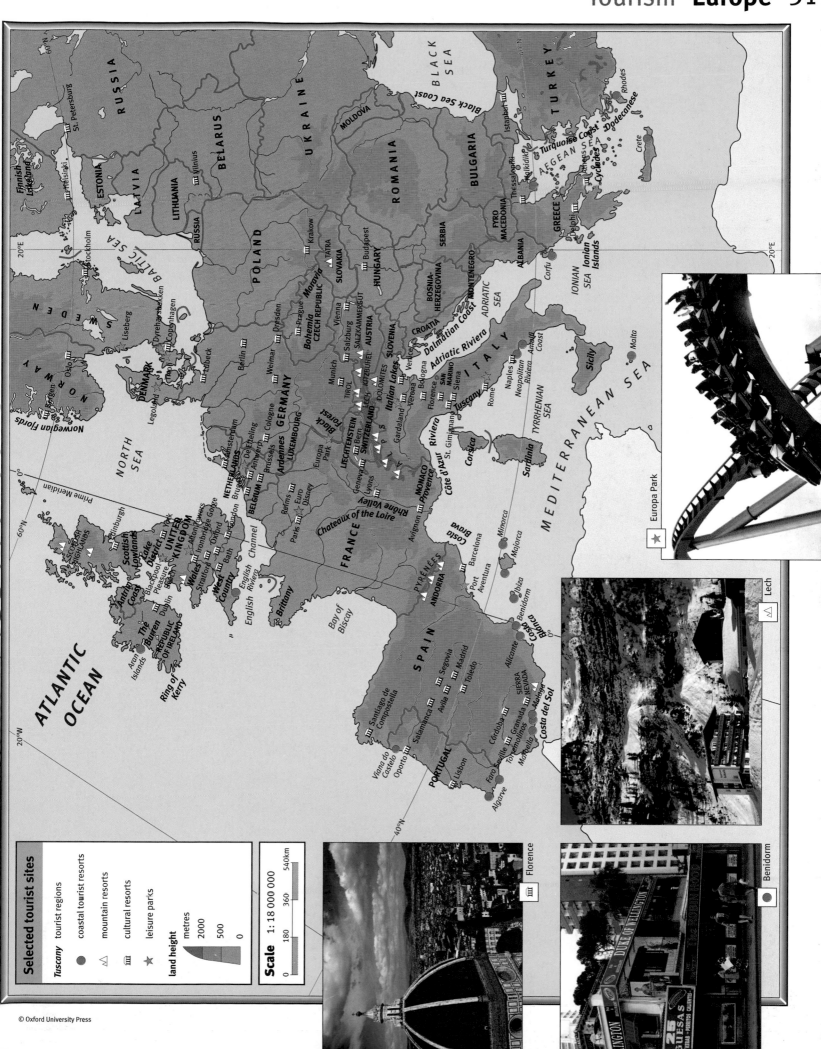

ATLANTIC
OCEAN

ICELAND

Reykjavík
Akureyri
Mount Hekla
1491
Höfn
Ísafjörður
Arctic Circle

NORWEGIAN
SEA

Vesterålen Is.
Lofoten Is.
Bodø

N O R W A Y
S W E D E N
Scandinavia

Trondheim
Galdhøpiggen
2470m
Glåma
Bergen
Stavanger
Oslo
Uppsala
Lake Vänern
Stockholm
Lake Vättern
Jönköping
Göteborg
Skagerrak
Kattegat
Ålborg
DENMARK
Århus
Copenhagen
Malmö
Odense
Bornholm
Kiel
Indalsä

NORTH
SEA

Faroe
Islands
(Den.)

Shetland
Islands

Outer
Hebrides
Orkney
Islands

1344m
Ben Nevis
Inverness
Aberdeen
Dundee
Glasgow
Edinburgh
Newcastle
upon Tyne
Belfast
Galway
REPUBLIC
OF IRELAND
Dublin
Manchester
Liverpool
Leeds
UNITED
KINGDOM
Cork
Birmingham
Cardiff
London
Bristol
Plymouth
Thames
Southampton
Strait of Dover
Land's End
Isles of
Scilly
English Channel
Channel
Islands
Brest
le Havre
Rouen
Rennes
le Mans
Paris
Orléans
Nantes
Tours
FRANCE
Nancy
Reims
Lille
Calais
Norwich
The Hague
Rotterdam
Amsterdam
NETHERLANDS
Antwerp
Essen
BELGIUM
Brussels
Bonn
Frisian Is.
Bremen
Elbe
Hamburg
Rostock
Szczecin
Hannover
Berlin
Poznań
Leipzig
Wrocław
Dresden
GERMANY
Düsseldorf
Cologne
LUXEMBOURG
Luxembourg
Frankfurt-
am-Main
Prague
CZECH REP.
Brno
Nuremberg
Strasbourg
Rhine
Stuttgart
Saône
Dijon
Basel
Zürich
Bern
SWITZERLAND
LIECHTENSTEIN
Innsbruck
Munich
Salzburg
Linz
Bratislava
Vienna
AUSTRIA
Danube
Loire
Seine

Bay of Biscay

60°N

50°N

10°W

20°W

30°W

70°N

10°W

0°
Prime Meridian

10°E

A   B   C   D   E
3
2
1

BARENTS SEA

North Cape

Tromsø

Lappland

Inarijärvi

Murmansk

Kandalaksha

Kola Peninsula

White Sea

Ukhta

Pechora

Arctic Circle

Luleå

Kemi

Oulu

Severodvinsk
Arkhangel'sk

Syktyvkar

Kellefte

Umeå

Vaasa

FINLAND

Petrozavodsk

Lake Onega

North Dvina

Kotlas

Gulf of Bothnia

Tampere

Lake Ladoga

Kirov

Åland

Turku

Helsinki

St. Petersburg

Vologda

Gulf of Finland

Tallinn

Lake Peipus

Novgorod

Rybinsk Reservoir

Rybinsk

Yaroslavl'

Volga

Nizhniy-Novgorod

Kazan'

ESTONIA

Pskov

Tver'

Vladimir

G. of Riga

Gotland

LATVIA

Riga

Moscow

Ryazan

Baltic Sea

Daugavpils

Daugava

Vitsyebsk

Smolensk

Tula

RUSSIAN FEDERATION
(RUSSIA)

Penza

Klaipéda

LITHUANIA

Kaunas

Mahilyow

Bryansk

Orel

Lipetsk

Tambov

Kaliningrad RUSSIA

Vilnius

Minsk

Dnieper

Homyel'

Kursk

Voronezh

Gdansk

North European Plain

Białystok

BELARUS

Pripet

Don

Bydgoszcz

POLAND

Brest

Vistula

Warsaw

Łodz

Lublin

Kiev

Kharkiv

Katowice

Zhytomyr

UKRAINE

Krakow

L'viv

Shakhty

strava

Vinnytsya

Dnipropetrovsk

Donets'k

Rostov-on-Don

SLOVAKIA

Dniester

Chernivtsi

Kryvyy Rih

Zaporizhzhya

Mariupol

CARPATHIANS

Miskolc

MOLDOVA

Odessa

Kherson

SEA OF AZOV

Krasnodar

Budapest

Debrecen

ROMANIA

Chişinău

Kerch'

Crimea

© Oxford University Press

50°N

Cork
Birmingham
Cardiff
UNITED KINGDOM
Norwich
Plymouth
Bristol
London
The Hague
Southampton
Amsterdam
Rotterdam
Land's End
Isles of Scilly
English Channel
Strait of Dover
Calais
Antwerp
Essen
Frisian Is.
Kiel
Rostock
Hamburg
Bremen
Szczecin
Berlin
Poznań
NETHERLANDS
BELGIUM
Lille
Brussels
Düsseldorf
Cologne
Hannover
Leipzig
Dresden
Wrocław
Channel Islands
Brest
le Havre
Rouen
Reims
LUXEMBOURG
Luxembourg
Bonn
GERMANY
Frankfurt-am-Main
Prague
CZECH REP
Rennes
le Mans
Paris
Orléans
Nancy
Strasbourg
Stuttgart
Nuremberg
Linz
Brno
Bratislav
Nantes
Tours
Dijon
Basel
Zürich
Bern
Munich
Salzburg
Vienna
AUSTRIA
Bay of Biscay
FRANCE
Limoges
Clermont-Ferrand
Geneva
Lake Geneva
SWITZERLAND
LIECHTENSTEIN
Innsbruck
Graz
A Coruña
Cape Finisterre
Gijón
Santander
Oviedo
León
Bilbao
Bordeaux
Lyons
4807m Mont Blanc
Ljubljana
SLOVENIA
Zagre
Vigo
Cantabrian Mts.
Bordogne
St-Étienne
MASSIF CENTRAL
Grenoble
Milan
Venice
Trieste
CROATIA
Oporto
Douro
Valladolid
Duero
San Sebastián
Garonne
Toulouse
Nîmes
Avignon
Turin
Módena
Verona
Po
Bologna
SAN MARINO
Split
PORTUGAL
Coimbra
SPAIN
Madrid
Tagus
Zaragoza
ANDORRA
PYRÉNÉES
Rhône
Marseilles
Nice
MONACO
Genoa
Florence
ITALY
APPENNINES
ADRIATIC SEA
Dinar
Lisbon
Guadiana
Ebro
Valencia
Barcelona
Corsica (France)
Elba
Rome
Faro
Sierra Morena
Guadalquivir
Murcia
Alicante
Balearic Islands
Menorca
Ajaccio
Sardinia (Italy)
Sássari
Naples
Vesuvius 1277m
Bari
Cape St. Vincent
Jerez de la Frontera
Cádiz
Sierra Nevada
Cartagena
Palma
Mallorca
Ibiza
TYRRHENIAN SEA
Cágliari
Salerno
Tarant
Tangier
Málaga
Gibraltar (UK)
MEDITER
Palermo
Messina
Réggio Calabria
Ceuta (Sp.)
Tétouan
Melilla (Sp.)
Oran
Algiers
Blida
Bejaïa
Skikda
Annaba
Bizerte
Tunis
Mt Etna 3323m
Sicily
Catánia
Fès
Meknès
Oudja
Sidi-Bel-Abbès
Ech Cheliff
Constantine
Sétif
Sousse
Valletta
MALTA
MOROCCO
ATLAS MOUNTAINS
Bouârfa
Aïn Sefra
El Bayadh
Bou Saâda
Djelfa
Biskra
Tébessa
TUNISIA
Gafsa
Sfax
Gabès
Béchar
Tozeur
30°N
Beni-Abbès
ALGERIA
Touggourt
Tripoli
Misratah
Timimoun
Prime Meridian
El Golea
Hassi Messaoud
10 E
Sirt
LIBYA

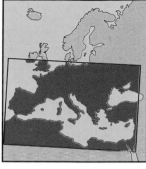
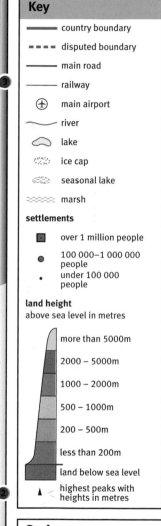
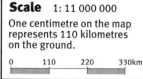

Key

	country boundary
	regional boundary
	main road
	railway
✈	main airport
	river
	lake
	ice cap

settlements

▪	over 1 million people
●	100 000–1 000 000 people
•	under 100 000 people

land height
above sea level in metres

more than 5000m

2000 – 5000m

1000 – 2000m

500 – 1000m

200 – 500m

less than 200m

land below sea level

▲ highest peaks with heights in metres

Scale 1: 5 000 000

0   50   100   150km

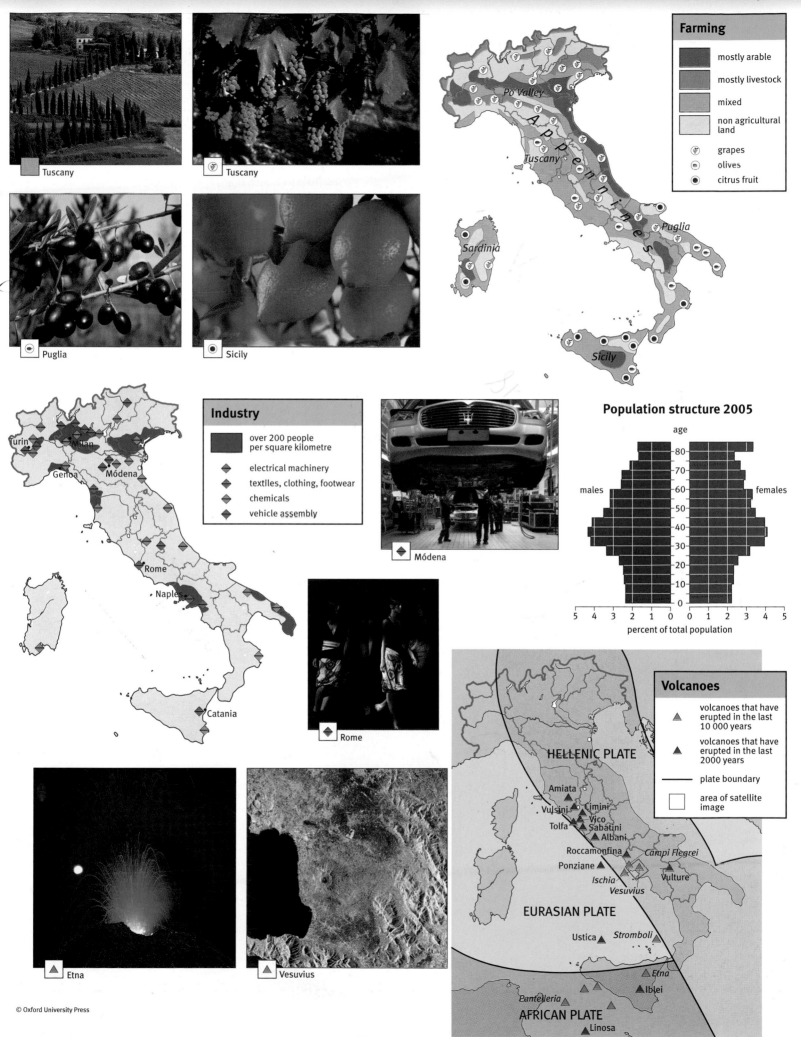

Tuscany

Tuscany

Puglia

Sicily

Farming

- mostly arable
- mostly livestock
- mixed
- non agricultural land
- ⊛ grapes
- ◎ olives
- ◉ citrus fruit

Po Valley

Appennines

Tuscany

Sardinia

Puglia

Sicily

Industry

- over 200 people per square kilometre
- ◆ electrical machinery
- ◆ textiles, clothing, footwear
- ◆ chemicals
- ◆ vehicle assembly

Turin
Milan
Genoa
Módena
Rome
Naples
Catania

Módena

Rome

Population structure 2005

age

males — females

80
70
60
50
40
30
20
10
0

5 4 3 2 1 0 0 1 2 3 4 5

percent of total population

Etna

Vesuvius

Volcanoes

- ▲ volcanoes that have erupted in the last 10 000 years
- ▲ volcanoes that have erupted in the last 2000 years
- — plate boundary
- ☐ area of satellite image

HELLENIC PLATE

Amiata
Vulsini   Cimini
Tolfa   Vico
Sabatini
Albani
Roccamonfina
Ponziane
Campi Flegrei
Ischia   Vulture
Vesuvius

EURASIAN PLATE

Ustica   Stromboli

Etna

Pantelleria   Iblei

AFRICAN PLATE   Linosa

© Oxford University Press

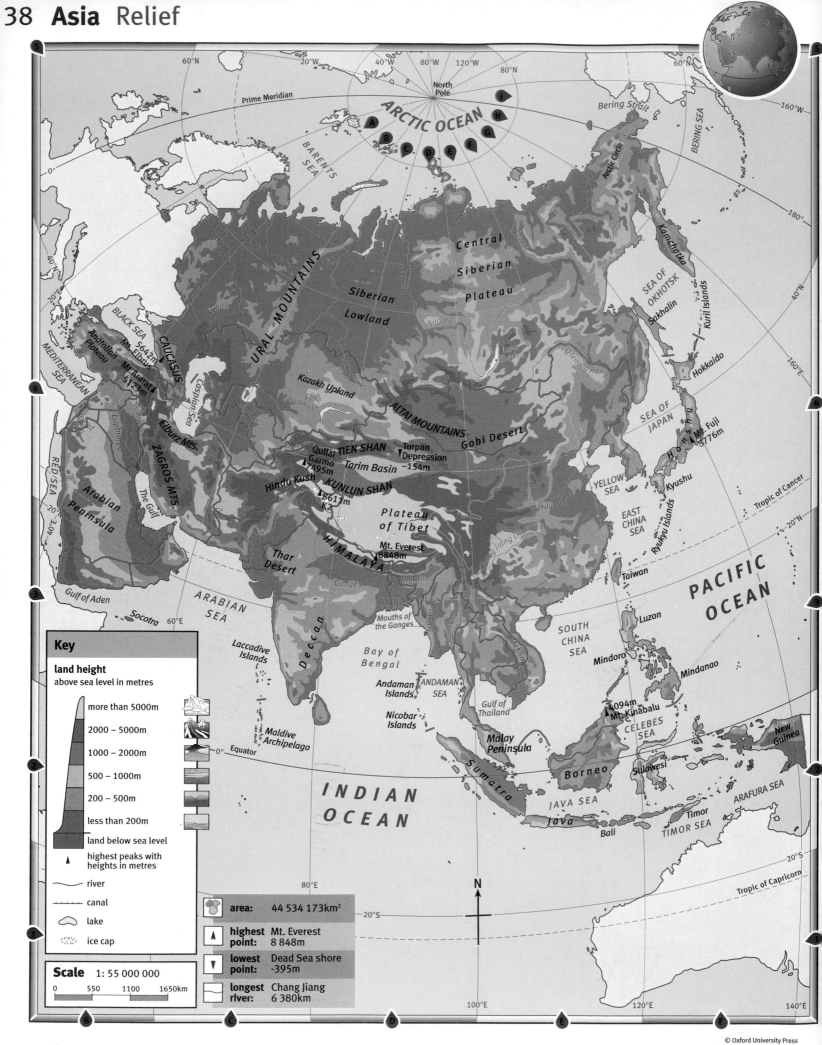

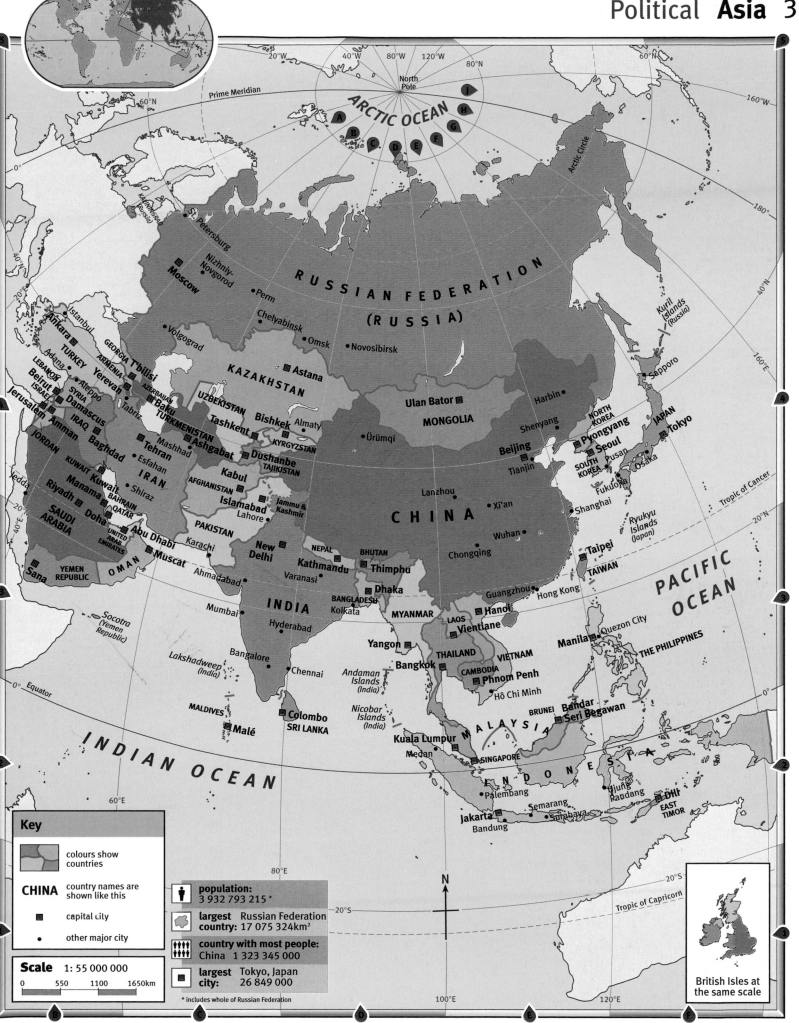

ARCTIC OCEAN

North Pole

R U S S I A N   F E D E R A T I O N

(R U S S I A)

Kaliningrad (Russia)

• St. Petersburg

• Moscow

• Nizhniy-Novgorod

• Perm

• Chelyabinsk

• Volgograd

• Omsk   • Novosibirsk

KAZAKHSTAN

☐ Astana

Kuril Islands (Russia)

Istanbul
TURKEY
Ankara ☐
Adana
GEORGIA T'bilisi ☐
ARMENIA Yerevan ☐
AZERBAIJAN
Baku ☐
Tabriz

LEBANON
Beirut ☐ Aleppo
ISRAEL **SYRIA**
Jerusalem ☐ Damascus ☐
JORDAN Amman ☐
Baghdad ☐ **IRAQ**
Mashhad •
UZBEKISTAN
Tashkent ☐ Bishkek ☐
Almaty •
KYRGYZSTAN

TURKMENISTAN
Ashgabat ☐ Dushanbe ☐
TAJIKISTAN

Tehran ☐
Esfahan •
IRAN
Shiraz •

Kabul ☐
AFGHANISTAN

Ulan Bator ☐
MONGOLIA

• Ürümqi

Harbin •
Shenyang •
NORTH KOREA
Pyongyang ☐
Beijing ☐
Tianjin •
SOUTH KOREA
Seoul ☐ Pusan •

JAPAN
Tokyo ☐
Sapporo •
Fukuoka • Osaka •

Lanzhou •

C H I N A

Xi'an •
Shanghai •

Ryukyu Islands (Japan)

Wuhan •
Chongqing •

Guangzhou • Hong Kong •

Taipei ☐
TAIWAN

PACIFIC OCEAN

KUWAIT
Kuwait ☐
Manama ☐ **BAHRAIN**
Doha ☐ **QATAR**
SAUDI ARABIA
Riyadh ☐
Jedda •
Abu Dhabi ☐
UNITED ARAB EMIRATES

Islamabad ☐
Lahore •
Jammu & Kashmir
PAKISTAN
Karachi •

New Delhi ☐
NEPAL **BHUTAN**
Kathmandu ☐ Thimphu ☐
Varanasi •

Ahmadabad •

Dhaka ☐

YEMEN REPUBLIC
Sana ☐
OMAN
Muscat ☐

Mumbai •
I N D I A
Hyderabad •

BANGLADESH
Kolkata •

MYANMAR

Hanoi ☐
LAOS
Vientiane ☐

Socotra (Yemen Republic)

Bangalore •
Lakshadweep (India)
Chennai •

Yangon ☐

Andaman Islands (India)

Bangkok ☐
THAILAND
CAMBODIA
Phnom Penh ☐
VIETNAM
Hô Chi Minh •

Manila ☐ Quezon City •
THE PHILIPPINES

INDIAN OCEAN

MALDIVES
Malé ☐

Colombo ☐
SRI LANKA

Nicobar Islands (India)

BRUNEI
Bandar Seri Begawan ☐

Kuala Lumpur ☐
Medan •
M A L A Y S I A
☐ SINGAPORE

I N D O N E S I A

• Palembang

• Jakarta • Semarang • Surabaya
Bandung •

Ujung Pandang •
Padang •

Dili ☐
EAST TIMOR

Key

colours show countries

CHINA country names are shown like this

☐ capital city

• other major city

Scale   1: 55 000 000

0   550   1100   1650km

population:
3 932 793 215 *

largest Russian Federation
country: 17 075 324km²

country with most people:
China 1 323 345 000

largest Tokyo, Japan
city: 26 849 000

* includes whole of Russian Federation

N

British Isles at the same scale

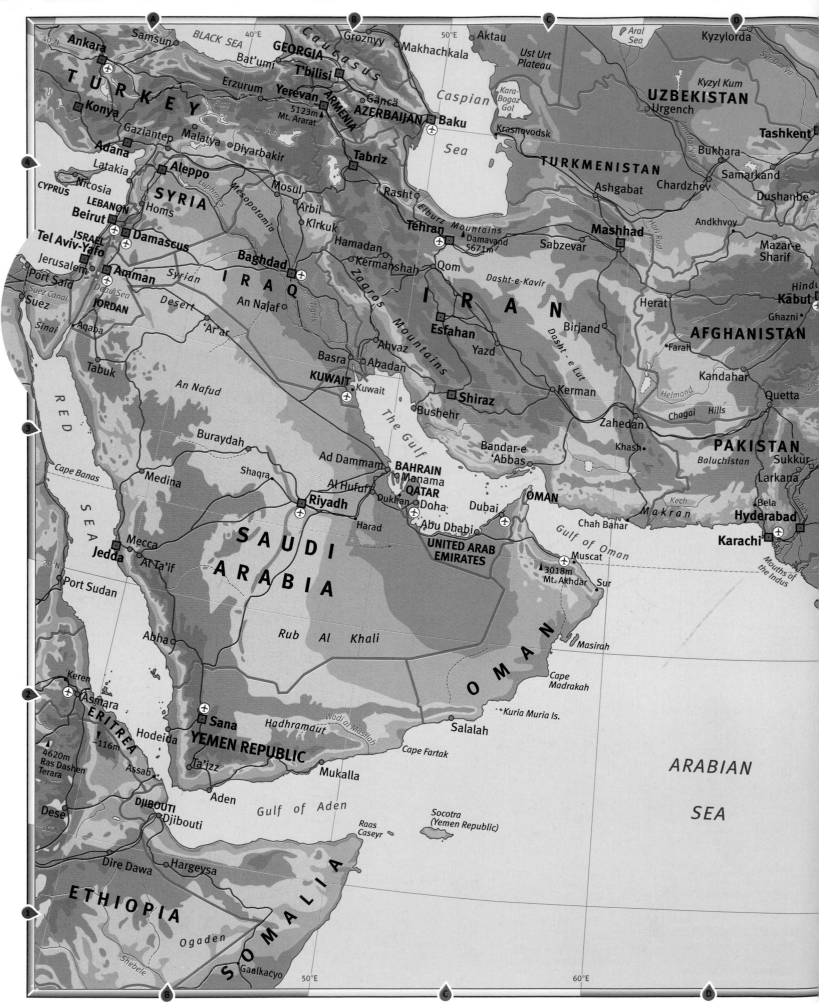

Key

———	country boundary
- - - -	disputed boundary
··········	ceasefire line
———	main road
———	railway
⊕	main airport
⌇	river
◡	lake
≈≈≈	marsh
❀	ice cap

settlements

▪	over 1 million people
●	100 000–1 000 000 people
•	under 100 000 people

land height
above sea level in metres

- more than 5000m
- 2000 – 5000m
- 1000 – 2000m
- 500 – 1000m
- 200 – 500m
- less than 200m
- land below sea level
- ▲ highest peaks with heights in metres

Scale   1: 16 000 000

One centimetre on the map represents 160 kilometres on the ground.

0   160   320   480km

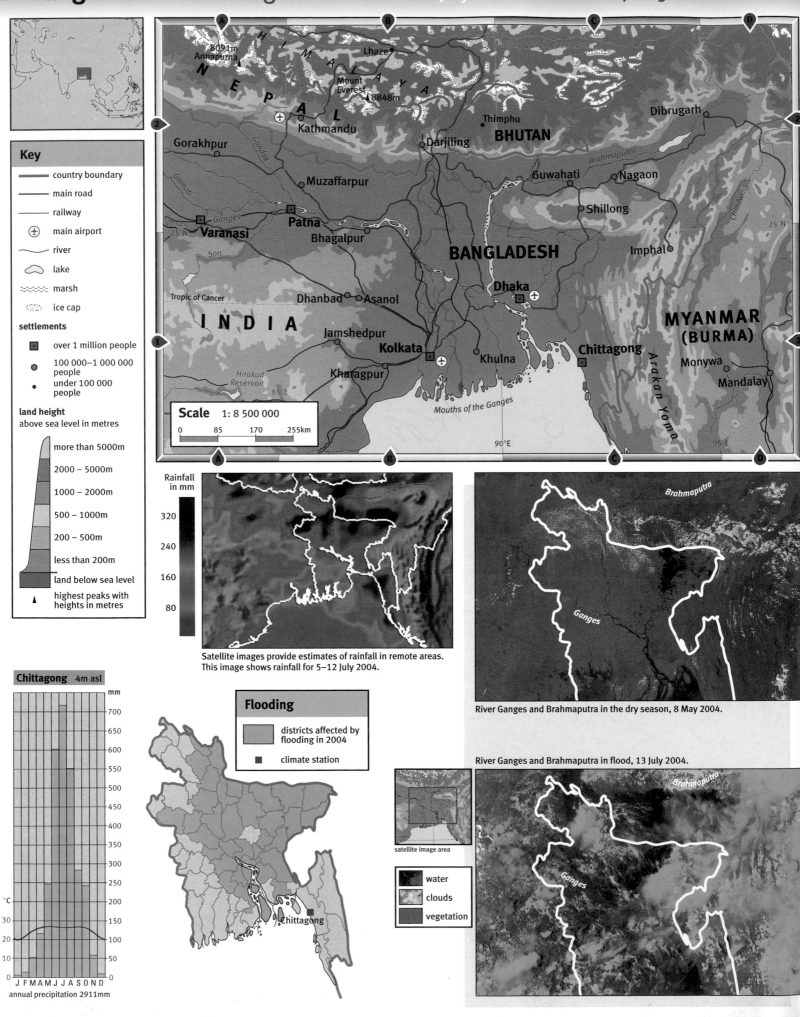

Key

- ━━━ country boundary
- ─── main road
- ── railway
- ⊕ main airport
- ∿ river
- ⌒ lake
- ∷ marsh
- ∷ ice cap

settlements

- ■ over 1 million people
- ● 100 000–1 000 000 people
- • under 100 000 people

land height
above sea level in metres

- more than 5000m
- 2000 – 5000m
- 1000 – 2000m
- 500 – 1000m
- 200 – 500m
- less than 200m
- land below sea level
- ▲ highest peaks with heights in metres

Scale   1: 8 500 000

0   85   170   255km

Mouths of the Ganges

Rainfall in mm

320
240
160
80

Satellite images provide estimates of rainfall in remote areas. This image shows rainfall for 5–12 July 2004.

River Ganges and Brahmaputra in the dry season, 8 May 2004.

River Ganges and Brahmaputra in flood, 13 July 2004.

satellite image area

- ■ water
- □ clouds
- ▨ vegetation

Flooding

- ▨ districts affected by flooding in 2004
- ■ climate station

Chittagong   4m asl

mm
700
650
600
550
500
450
400
350
300
250
200
150
100
50

°C
30
20
10
0

J F M A M J J A S O N D

annual precipitation 2911mm

Map labels

NEPAL · 8091m Annapurna · HIMALAYA · Lhaze · Mount Everest 8848m · Kathmandu · Thimphu · BHUTAN · Dibrugarh · Yarlung Zangbo Tsangpo · Gorakhpur · Darjiling · Brahmaputra · Muzaffarpur · Guwahati · Nagaon · Shillong · Gandak · Gomati · Ganges · Patna · Bhagalpur · BANGLADESH · Chindwin · Varanasi · 25 N · Son · Dhaka · Imphal · Tropic of Cancer · Dhanbad · Asanol · INDIA · MYANMAR (BURMA) · Monywa · Jamshedpur · Kolkata · Khulna · Chittagong · Mandalay · Hirakud Reservoir · Kharagpur · Arakan Yoma · 85 E · 90°E · 95 E

Chittagong

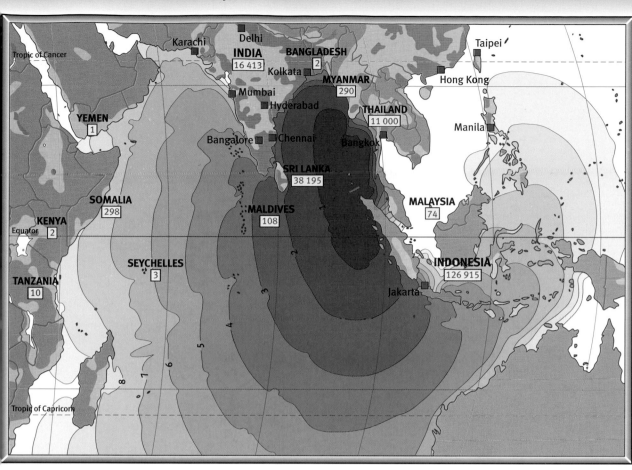

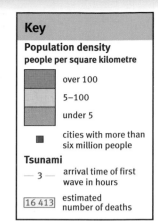

Key

Population density
people per square kilometre

- over 100
- 5–100
- under 5
- cities with more than six million people

Tsunami

— 3 — arrival time of first wave in hours

16 413   estimated number of deaths

Maximum wave height in metres

0   0.25   0.5   0.75   1.0   1.25   1.5   1.75   2.0   10.0

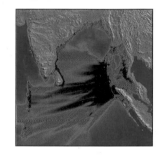

Map labels (population/deaths):

- YEMEN 1
- SOMALIA 298
- KENYA 2
- TANZANIA 10
- SEYCHELLES 3
- INDIA 16 413
- BANGLADESH 2
- MYANMAR 290
- THAILAND 11 000
- SRI LANKA 38 195
- MALDIVES 108
- MALAYSIA 74
- INDONESIA 126 915

Cities: Karachi, Delhi, Kolkata, Mumbai, Hyderabad, Bangalore, Chennai, Bangkok, Taipei, Hong Kong, Manila, Jakarta

Tropic of Cancer, Equator, Tropic of Capricorn

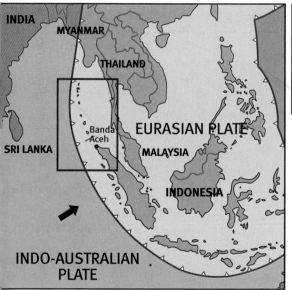

Plate boundary zone

- plate boundary (see also p78)
- direction of plate movement
- area of cross section

INDIA, MYANMAR, THAILAND, SRI LANKA, Banda Aceh, EURASIAN PLATE, MALAYSIA, INDONESIA, INDO-AUSTRALIAN PLATE

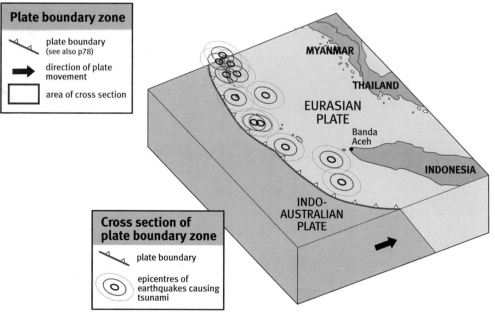

Cross section of plate boundary zone

- plate boundary
- epicentres of earthquakes causing tsunami

MYANMAR, THAILAND, EURASIAN PLATE, Banda Aceh, INDONESIA, INDO-AUSTRALIAN PLATE

Banda Aceh **before** the tsunami

Banda Aceh **after** the tsunami

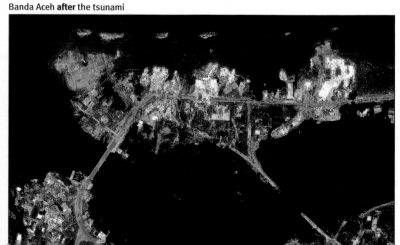

Eckert IV Projection

SEA OF OKHOTSK

RUSSIAN FEDERATION (RUSSIA)

Komsomol'sk-na-Amure
Yuzhno-Sakhalinsk
Sakhalin
Wakkanai
Asahikawa
Kushiro
Hakodate
Hokkaido
Aomori
Hachinohe
Morioka
Akita
Sendai
Niigata
Tokyo
Mt. Fuji 3776m
Yokohama
Nagoya
Kyoto
Osaka
Kobe
Kochi
Shikoku
Hiroshima
Fukuoka
Kyushu
Miyazaki
Nagasaki
Kagoshima
Okinawa

JAPAN

SEA OF JAPAN

Khabarovsk
Sikhote-Alin
Blagoveshchensk
Shuangyashan
Jiamusi
Jixi
Vladivostok
Khanka
Chongjin
Kimchaek
Hamhung
Kangnung

Bei'an
Hegang
Qiqihar
Harbin
Mudanjiang
Jilin
Daqing
Baicheng
Changchun
Siping
Fushun
Shenyang
Anshan
Tonghua
Dandong
Pyongyang
NORTH KOREA
Seoul
SOUTH KOREA
Inchon
Taejon
Taegu
Pusan
Kwangju
Kangnung
Pohang
Yantai
Qingdao

Nenjiang
Amur
Da Hinggan Ling
Argun (Ergun He)

Blagoveshchensk
Borzya
Manzhouli
Choybalsan
Erenhot

MONGOLIA

Ulan Bator
Saynshand
Saynshand

Gobi Desert

Ulan-Ude
Chita
Angarsk
Irkutsk
Lake Baykal
Hövsgöl Nuur
Selenge
Uliastay
Ust'-Kamenogorsk
Syryanovsk
Lake Zaysan

ALTAI MOUNTAINS

Altay
Hami
Ürümqi
Turpan
Turpan Depression -154m
Lop Nur

Anxi
Yumen
Qilian Shan
Golmud
Xining
Lanzhou
Yinchuan
Wuhai
Hohhot
Jining
Datong
Baotou
Taiyuan
Baoji
Xi'an
Luoyang
Handan
Dezhou
Shijiazhuang
Zibo
Jinan
Beijing
Tianjin
Tangshan
Zhangjiakou
Jining
Zhengzhou

YELLOW SEA

Dalian
Bo Hai
Lianyungang
Xuzhou
Suzhou
Bengbu
Hefei
Nanjing
Wuxi
Shanghai
Hangzhou
Ningbo

EAST CHINA SEA

Korea Strait
Cheju do
Korea Bay

RYUKYU ISLANDS

PACIFIC OCEAN

Tropic of Cancer

THE

Chengdu
Neijiang
Yibin
Zunyi
Chongqing
Guiyang
Kunming
Dali
Batang
Lhasa

CHINA

Plateau of Tibet

Hwang He
Chang Jiang (Yangtze)
Great Wall
Wei He

Wuhan
Changde
Changsha
Shaoyang
Nanchang
Jiujiang
Ji'an
Ganzhou
Hengyang
Zhuzhou
Shaoguan
Wuzhou
Guilin
Liuzhou
Nanning
Merzhou
Guangzhou
Macao
Hong Kong
Zhanjiang
Pingxiang
Hai Phong
Hanoi
Haikou
Hainan Dao
Sanya
Thanh Hoa
Vinh

Xi Jiang
Mekong
Salween

Taipei
Taichung
TAIWAN
Tainan
Kaohsiung
Luzon Strait
Laoag

Fuzhou
Nanping
Xiamen
Wenzhou
Taiwan Strait

LAOS
Vientiane
Louangphrabang
Phongsali
Lao Cai
Udon Thani
Nakhon

MYANMAR (BURMA)
Mandalay
Monywa
Chindwin
Irrawaddy
Arakan Yoma
Sittwe
Pye
Bassein
Yangon
Mouths of the

BANGLADESH
Dhaka
Chittagong
Shillong
Dibrugarh
Imphal
BHUTAN
Thimphu
Brahmaputra

Chiang Mai
Kengtung

© Oxford University Press
Conical Orthomorphic Projection

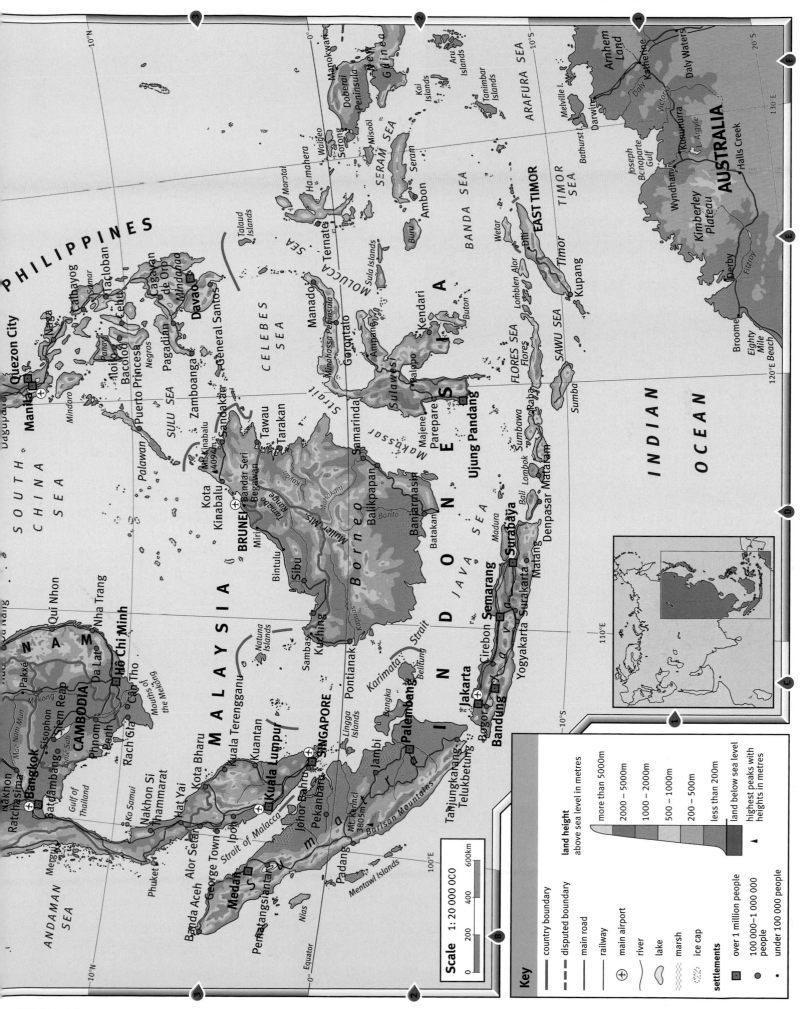

PHILIPPINES

Quezon City
Manila

SOUTH CHINA SEA

Dagupan
Baguio
Naga
Iloilo
Cebu
Bacolod
Panay
Negros
Catbalogan
Tacloban
Samar
Cagayan
de Oro
Mindanao
Davao
General Santos
Pagadian
Zamboanga
Puerto Princesa
Palawan
Mindoro

N A M
Quì Nhon
Nha Trang
Da Lat
Hồ Chí Minh
Rach Gia
Can Tho
Mouths of
the Mekong
Phnom
Penh
CAMBODIA
Battambang
Siem Reap
Sisophon
Mekong
Tonle Sap
Bac Lieu
Stem Reap
Nakhon
Ratchasima
Bangkok
Mae Nam Mun
Gulf of
Thailand
Ko Samui
Nakhon Si
Thammarat
Hat Yai
Phuket
Mergui
ANDAMAN
SEA
Kota Bharu
Kuala Terengganu
Kuantan
Alor Setar
George Town
Ipoh
M A L A Y S I A
Johor Bahru
Pekanbaru
Kuala Lumpur
SINGAPORE
Strait of Malacca
Medan
Banda Aceh
Pematangsiantar
Nias
Mentawi Islands
Padang
Mt. Kerinci
3805m
Barisan Mountains
S u m a t r a
Jambi
Palembang
Tanjungkarang
Telukbetung
Bangka
Belitung
Karimata Strait
Lingga
Islands
Natuna
Islands
Sambas
Kuching
Sibu
Bintulu
Miri
BRUNEI
Bandar Seri
Begawan
Kota
Kinabalu
Mt. Kinabalu
4094m
Sandakan
Tawau
Tarakan
Samarinda
Balikpapan
Banjarmasin
Batakan
B o r n e o
Muller Mts.
Tandjung Range
Mahakam
Barito
Kapuas
Kayan
Pontianak

SOUTH CHINA SEA

SULU SEA
CELEBES SEA
Manado
Gorontalo
Minahassa Peninsula
Talaud
Islands
MOLUCCA SEA
Ternate
Ha mahera
Morotai
Waigeo
Sorong
Misool
Buru
Ambon
Seram
SERAM SEA
New
Guinea
Manokwari
Doberai
Peninsula
Aru
Islands
Kai
Islands
Tanimbar
Islands
ARAFURA SEA
BANDA SEA
Sula Islands
Kendari
Buton
Parepare
Palopo
Majene
Ujung Pandang
Makassar
Sulawesi
Ampana
I N D O N E S I A
FLORES SEA
Flores
Lomblen Alor
Wetar
Timor
EAST TIMOR
Dili
Kupang
TIMOR SEA
Sumba
SAWU SEA
Raba
Sumbawa
Lombok
Bali
Denpasar Matalam
Madura
J A V A
SEA
Surakarta
Yogyakarta
Semarang
Surabaya
Cirebon
Bandung
Bogor
Jakarta
J a v a
Matang

AUSTRALIA
Arnhem
Land
Darwin
Melville I.
Bathurst I.
Daly Waters
Katherine
Daly
Victoria
Kununurra
L. Argyle
Halls Creek
Kimberley
Plateau
Wyndham
Joseph
Bonaparte
Gulf
Derby
Broome
Fitzroy
Eighty
Mile
Beach
INDIAN OCEAN

10°N
Equator
10°S
20°S
100°E
110°E
120°E
130°E

Scale 1:20 000 000

0   200   400   600km

Key

———	country boundary
– – –	disputed boundary
———	main road
———	railway
⊕	main airport
	river
	lake
	marsh
	ice cap

settlements

over 1 million people
100 000–1 000 000 people
under 100 000 people

land height
above sea level in metres

more than 5000m
2000 – 5000m
1000 – 2000m
500 – 1000m
200 – 500m
less than 200m

land below sea level

▲ highest peaks with heights in metres

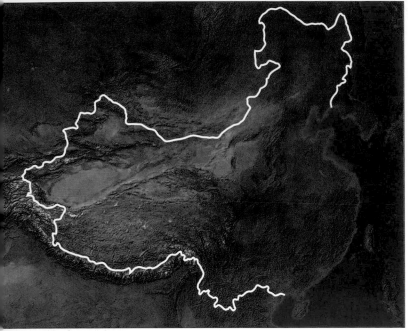

China from space.

Climate regions

Harbin

Hohhot

Golmud

Wuhan

Lhasa

Haikou

asl = metres above sea level

Arid   very dry

no reliable rain

Semi-arid   very dry

a little rain

Continental cold and wet

*warm summers
cold winters*

Mountain cold because
the land is high

heavy rain or snow

Temperate mild and wet

*warm summers
cool winters*

Tropical hot and wet

dry in winter

Golmud 2807m asl

°C   mm

30 / 300
20 / 250
10 / 200
0 / 150
-10 / 100
-20 / 50
-30 / 0

J F M A M J J A S O N D

annual precipitation 38mm

Hohhot 1063m asl

°C   mm

30 / 300
20 / 250
10 / 200
0 / 150
-10 / 100
-20 / 50
-30 / 0

J F M A M J J A S O N D

annual precipitation 426mm

Harbin 171m asl

°C   mm

30 / 300
20 / 250
10 / 200
0 / 150
-10 / 100
-20 / 50
-30 / 0

J F M A M J J A S O N D

annual precipitation 554mm

Lhasa 3658m asl

°C   mm

30 / 300
20 / 250
10 / 200
0 / 150
-10 / 100
-20 / 50
-30 / 0

J F M A M J J A S O N D

annual precipitation 454mm

Wuhan 23m asl

°C   mm

30 / 300
20 / 250
10 / 200
0 / 150
-10 / 100
-20 / 50
-30 / 0

J F M A M J J A S O N D

annual precipitation 1260mm

Haikou 14m asl

°C   mm

30 / 300
20 / 250
10 / 200
0 / 150
-10 / 100
-20 / 50
-30 / 0

J F M A M J J A S O N D

annual precipitation 1685mm

Population

people per square kilometre	cities and towns (people)
over 100	□ over 3 000 000
10–100	○ 1 000 000–3 000 000
1–10	◉ 500 000–1 000 000
under 1	

Shenyang

Beijing

Tianjin

Wuhan

Shanghai

Chongqing

Guangzhou

Hong Kong

Population structure 2005

age

males   females

80
70
60
50
40
30
20
10
0

5 4 3 2 1 0   0 1 2 3 4 5

percent of total population

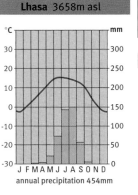

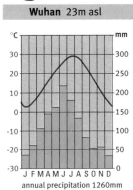

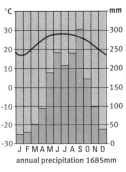

Beijing from space.
Blue/grey shows the
most densely
populated areas.

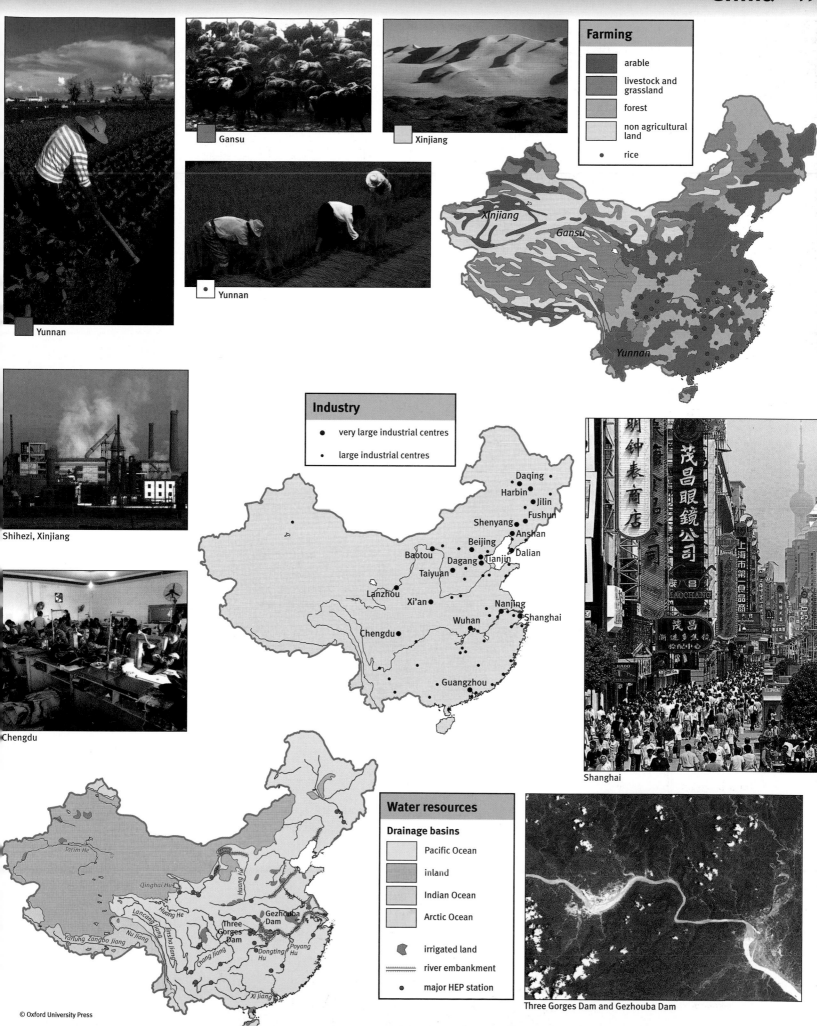

Farming

- arable
- livestock and grassland
- forest
- non agricultural land
- • rice

Gansu

Xinjiang

Yunnan

Yunnan

Xinjiang

Gansu

Yunnan

Shihezi, Xinjiang

Chengdu

Industry

- ● very large industrial centres
- • large industrial centres

Daqing
Harbin
Jilin
Fushun
Shenyang
Anshan
Beijing
Dalian
Baotou
Dagang
Tianjin
Taiyuan
Lanzhou
Xi'an
Nanjing
Wuhan
Shanghai
Chengdu
Guangzhou

Shanghai

Water resources

Drainage basins

- Pacific Ocean
- inland
- Indian Ocean
- Arctic Ocean

- ◄ irrigated land
- ⫘⫘ river embankment
- ● major HEP station

Tarim He

Qinghai Hu

Huang He

Huang He

Lancang Jiang

Nu Jiang

Jinsha Jiang

Yarlung Zangbo Jiang

Three Gorges Dam

Gezhouba Dam

Chang Jiang

Dongting Hu

Poyang Hu

Xi Jiang

Three Gorges Dam and Gezhouba Dam

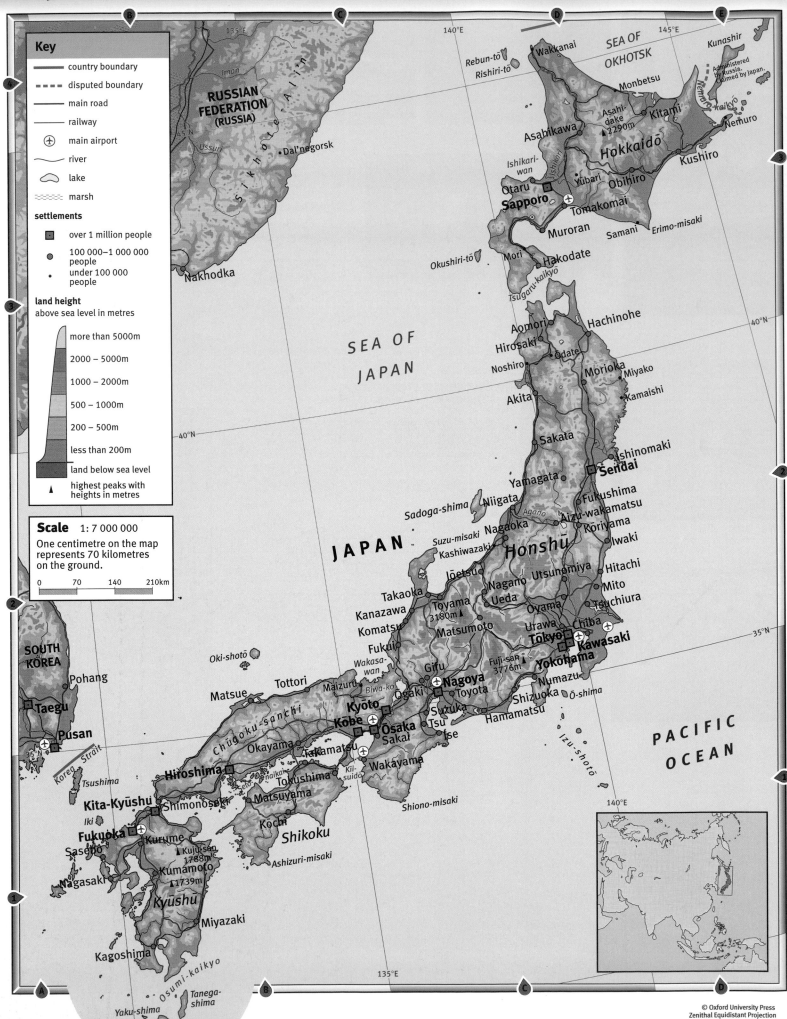

Key

——	country boundary
- - -	disputed boundary
——	main road
——	railway
⊕	main airport
～	river
⬭	lake
▓	marsh

settlements

▪	over 1 million people
●	100 000–1 000 000 people
•	under 100 000 people

land height
above sea level in metres

- more than 5000m
- 2000 – 5000m
- 1000 – 2000m
- 500 – 1000m
- 200 – 500m
- less than 200m
- land below sea level

▲ highest peaks with heights in metres

Scale 1: 7 000 000

One centimetre on the map represents 70 kilometres on the ground.

0   70   140   210km

RUSSIAN FEDERATION (RUSSIA)

Sikhote Alin'

Iman

Ussuri

Dal'negorsk

45 N

Nakhodka

SEA OF JAPAN

JAPAN

SEA OF OKHOTSK

Kunashir

Administered by Russia. Claimed by Japan.

Nemuro-kaikyo

Rebun-tō
Rishiri-tō
Wakkanai
Monbetsu
Kitami
Asahikawa
Asahi-dake 2290m
Hokkaidō
Nemuro
Kushiro
Ishikari-wan
Ishikari
Yubari
Obihiro
Otaru
Sapporo
Tomakomai
Muroran
Samani
Erimo-misaki
Okushiri-tō
Mori
Hakodate
Tsugaru-kaikyo
Aomori
Hachinohe
Hirosaki
Ōdate
Noshiro
Morioka
Miyako
Akita
Kamaishi
Sakata
Ishinomaki
Yamagata
Sendai
Sadoga-shima
Niigata
Fukushima
Agano
Aizu-wakamatsu
Nagaoka
Kōriyama
Suzu-misaki
Honshū
Iwaki
Kashiwazaki
Jōetsu
Utsunomiya
Hitachi
Takaoka
Toyama 3180m
Nagano
Ueda
Oyama
Mito
Kanazawa
Matsumoto
Tsuchiura
Komatsu
Urawa
Chiba
Fukui
Gifu
Tōkyō
Kawasaki
Wakasa-wan
Fuji-san 3776m
Yokohama
Oki-shotō
Tottori
Maizuru
Biwa-ko
Ogaki
Nagoya
Numazu
Matsue
Toyota
Shizuoka
Ō-shima
Okayama
Kyōto
Suzuka
Hamamatsu
Kōbe
Ōsaka
Tsu
Chūgoku-sanchi
Sakai
Ise
Takamatsu
Izu-shotō
Hiroshima
Wakayama
seto-naikai
Tokushima
Kii-suido
Shimonoseki
Matsuyama
Shiono-misaki
Kita-Kyūshu
Kōchi
Iki
Shikoku
Fukuoka
Kurume
Ashizuri-misaki
Sasebo
Kujū-san 1788m
Nagasaki
Kumamoto 1739m
Kyūshu
Miyazaki
Kagoshima
Osumi-kaikyo
Yaku-shima
Tanega-shima

SOUTH KOREA
Pohang
Taegu
Pusan
Korea Strait
Tsushima
35 N

PACIFIC OCEAN

140°E

135°E   140°E   145°E   40°N   35°N

© Oxford University Press
Zenithal Equidistant Projection

Population structure 2005

age
males / females
80
70
60
50
40
30
20
10
0
5 4 3 2 1 0 0 1 2 3 4 5
percent of total population

Population

people per square kilometre
- over 700
- 100–700
- 10–100
- under 10

cities and towns (people)
- ☐ over 2 000 000
- ○ 1 000 000–2 000 000
- ◉ 500 000–1 000 000

Sapporo
Sendai
Tōkyō
Kawasaki
Yokohama
Nagoya
Ōsaka Kyōto
Hiroshima
Kōbe
Kita Kyūshū
Fukuoka

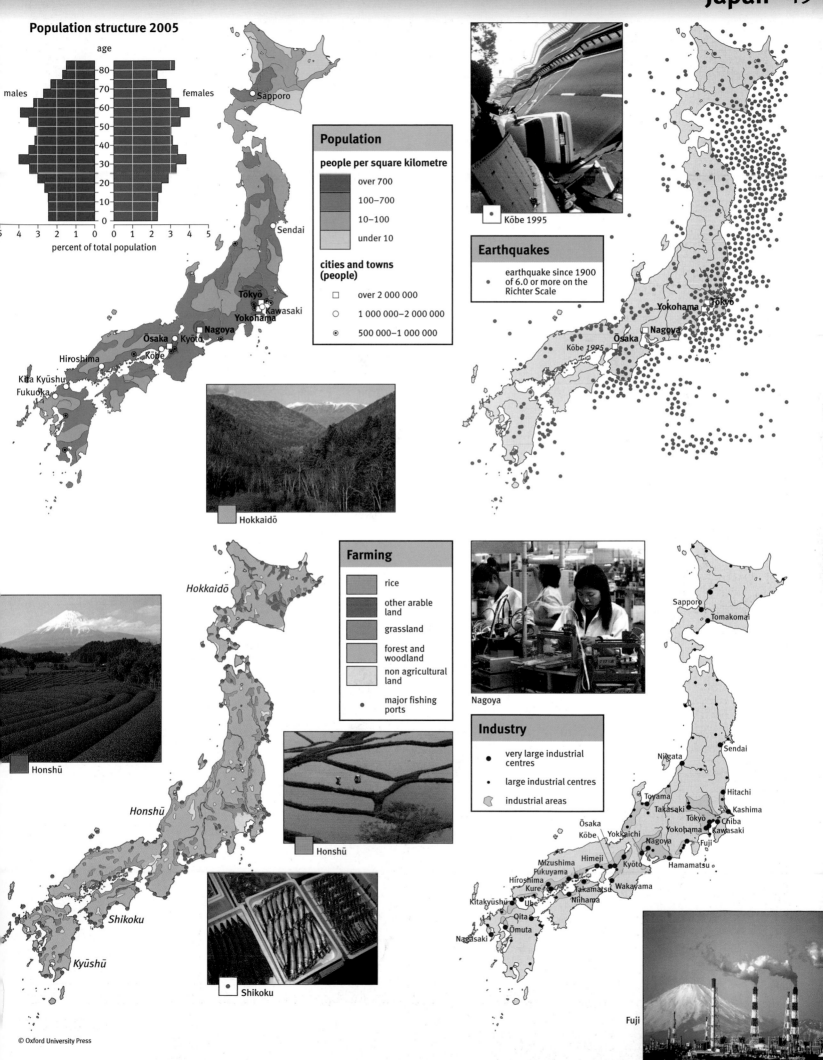

Hokkaidō

Kōbe 1995

Earthquakes

- • earthquake since 1900 of 6.0 or more on the Richter Scale

Yokohama Tōkyō
Ōsaka Nagoya
Kōbe 1995

Farming

- rice
- other arable land
- grassland
- forest and woodland
- non agricultural land
- • major fishing ports

Hokkaidō

Honshū

Honshū

Honshū

Shikoku

Kyūshū

Shikoku

Nagoya

Industry

- ● very large industrial centres
- • large industrial centres
- industrial areas

Sapporo
Tomakomai
Sendai
Niigata
Hitachi
Toyama
Kashima
Takasaki
Tōkyō
Chiba
Yokohama Kawasaki
Ōsaka
Kōbe
Yokkaichi
Nagoya
Fuji
Kyōto
Hamamatsu
Himeji
Mizushima
Fukuyama
Hiroshima
Kure
Takamatsu
Wakayama
Kitakyūshū
Ube
Niihama
Ōita
Ōmuta
Nagasaki

Fuji

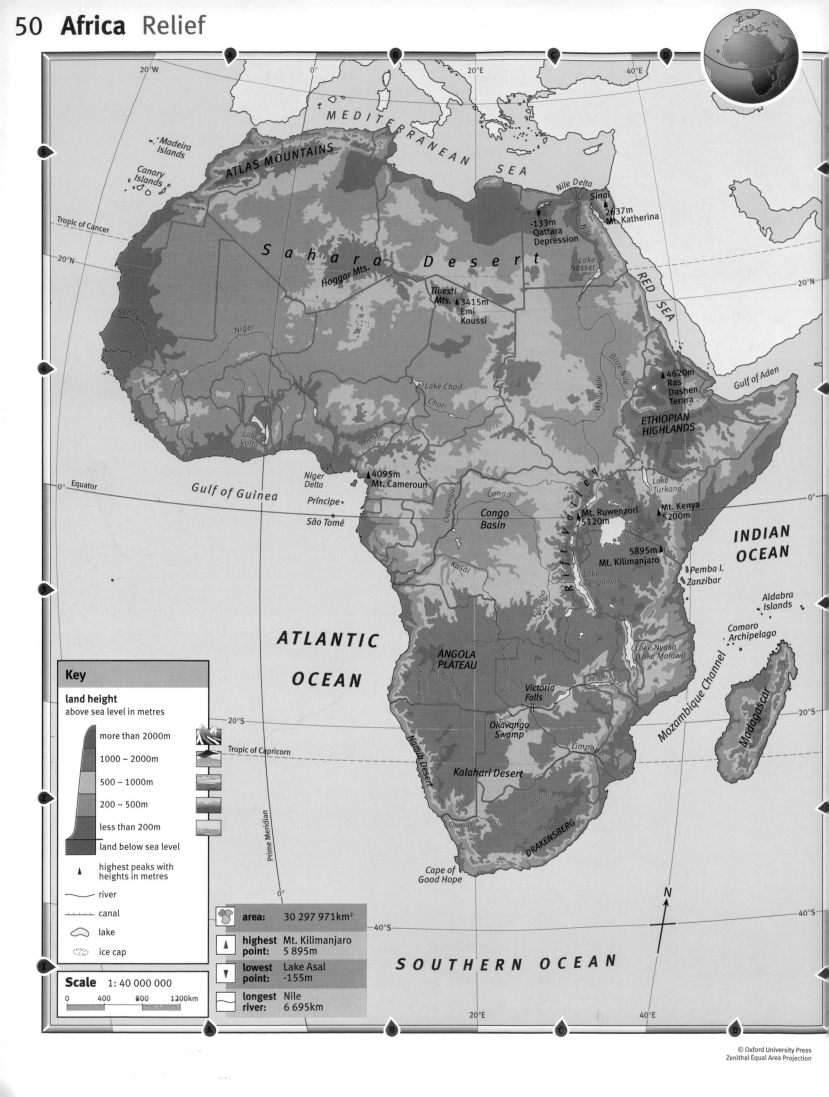

Key

land height
above sea level in metres

- more than 2000m
- 1000 – 2000m
- 500 – 1000m
- 200 – 500m
- less than 200m
- land below sea level

▲ highest peaks with heights in metres

〜 river

┼┼┼ canal

〰 lake

▒ ice cap

Scale 1: 40 000 000

0   400   800   1200km

	area:	30 297 971km²
▲	highest point:	Mt. Kilimanjaro 5 895m
▼	lowest point:	Lake Asal -155m
〰	longest river:	Nile 6 695km

MEDITERRANEAN SEA

Madeira Islands

ATLAS MOUNTAINS

Canary Islands

Tropic of Cancer

Nile Delta

Sinai

2637m
Mt. Katherina

-133m
Qattara
Depression

Sahara Desert

20°N

Hoggar Mts.

Lake Nasser

RED SEA

20°N

Tibesti Mts. ▲3415m
Emi Koussi

Senegal

Niger

4620m
Ras Dashen
Terara

Gulf of Aden

Lake Chad

Chari

White Nile

Blue Nile

ETHIOPIAN HIGHLANDS

Benue

Lake Volta

4095m
Mt. Cameroun

Niger Delta

Gulf of Guinea

Equator 0°

Príncipe

São Tomé

Oubangui

Congo

Congo Basin

Rift Valley

Mt. Ruwenzori
5120m

Lake Turkana

Mt. Kenya
5200m

Lake Victoria

0°

INDIAN OCEAN

Kasai

5895m▲
Mt. Kilimanjaro

Pemba I.
Zanzibar

ATLANTIC

Lualaba

Lake Tanganyika

Aldabra Islands

OCEAN

Comoro Archipelago

ANGOLA PLATEAU

Lake Nyasa
(Lake Malawi)

Lunene

Cubango

Zambezi

Mozambique Channel

Madagascar

20°S

Victoria Falls

20°S

Tropic of Capricorn

Okavango Swamp

Limpopo

Namib Desert

Kalahari Desert

Vaal

Prime Meridian

Orange

DRAKENSBERG

N

Cape of Good Hope

40°S

SOUTHERN OCEAN

20°E

40°E

20°W

0°

20°E

40°E

© Oxford University Press
Zenithal Equal Area Projection

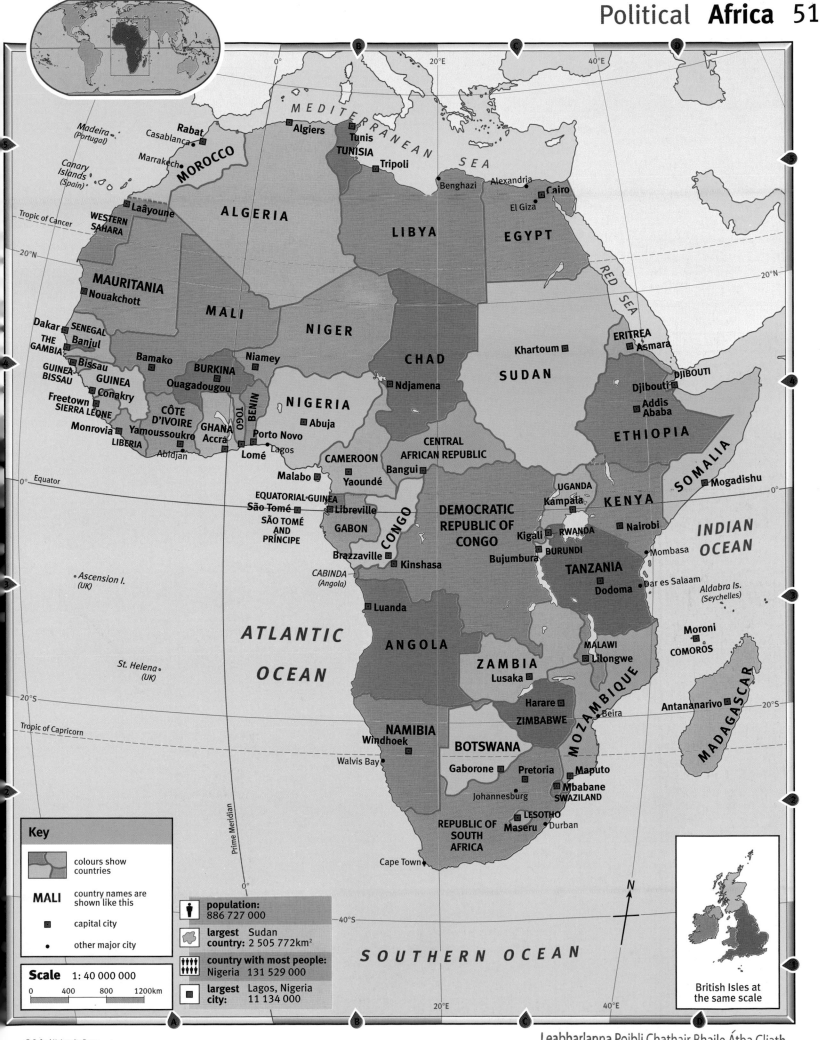

MEDITERRANEAN SEA

Madeira
(Portugal)

Rabat
Casablanca
Marrakech
MOROCCO

Algiers
Tunis
TUNISIA
Tripoli

Benghazi

Alexandria
Cairo
El Giza

*Canary
Islands*
(Spain)

Tropic of Cancer

Laâyoune

**WESTERN
SAHARA**

ALGERIA

LIBYA

EGYPT

RED SEA

20°N

MAURITANIA
Nouakchott

MALI

NIGER

CHAD

Khartoum

ERITREA
Asmara

Dakar **SENEGAL**
THE **Banjul**
GAMBIA
Bissau
GUINEA-
BISSAU **GUINEA**
Freetown **Conakry**
SIERRA LEONE

Bamako

Niamey

SUDAN

DJIBOUTI
Djibouti
**Addis
Ababa**

BURKINA
Ouagadougou

Ndjamena

NIGERIA

Abuja

**CENTRAL
AFRICAN REPUBLIC**

ETHIOPIA

Monrovia **Yamoussoukro**
LIBERIA **CÔTE
D'IVOIRE** **GHANA**
Accra
Abidjan

TOGO **BENIN**
Porto Novo
Lomé Lagos

Bangui

SOMALIA

CAMEROON
Malabo
Yaoundé

Mogadishu

EQUATORIAL·GUINEA
São Tomé
**SÃO TOMÉ
AND
PRÍNCIPE**

Libreville

UGANDA
Kampala

KENYA

INDIAN
OCEAN

Equator

GABON
Brazzaville
Kinshasa

CONGO

**DEMOCRATIC
REPUBLIC OF
CONGO**

Kigali **RWANDA**
Bujumbura **BURUNDI**

Nairobi

Mombasa

CABINDA
(Angola)

Ascension I.
(UK)

Luanda

TANZANIA
Dodoma Dar es Salaam

Aldabra Is.
(Seychelles)

ATLANTIC

St. Helena
(UK)

OCEAN

ANGOLA

ZAMBIA
Lusaka

MALAWI
Lilongwe

Moroni
COMOROS

20°S

Harare
ZIMBABWE

Beira

Antananarivo

MADAGASCAR

Tropic of Capricorn

Prime Meridian

NAMIBIA
Windhoek

BOTSWANA

Walvis Bay

Gaborone
Johannesburg

Pretoria
Maputo
Mbabane
SWAZILAND

MOZAMBIQUE

LESOTHO
Maseru Durban

**REPUBLIC OF
SOUTH
AFRICA**

Cape Town

N

SOUTHERN OCEAN

Key

	colours show countries
MALI	country names are shown like this
◼	capital city
•	other major city

Scale 1 : 40 000 000

0   400   800   1200km

👤 **population:**
886 727 000

🗺 **largest Sudan
country:** 2 505 772km²

👥 **country with most people:**
Nigeria 131 529 000

◼ **largest Lagos, Nigeria
city:** 11 134 000

British Isles at
the same scale

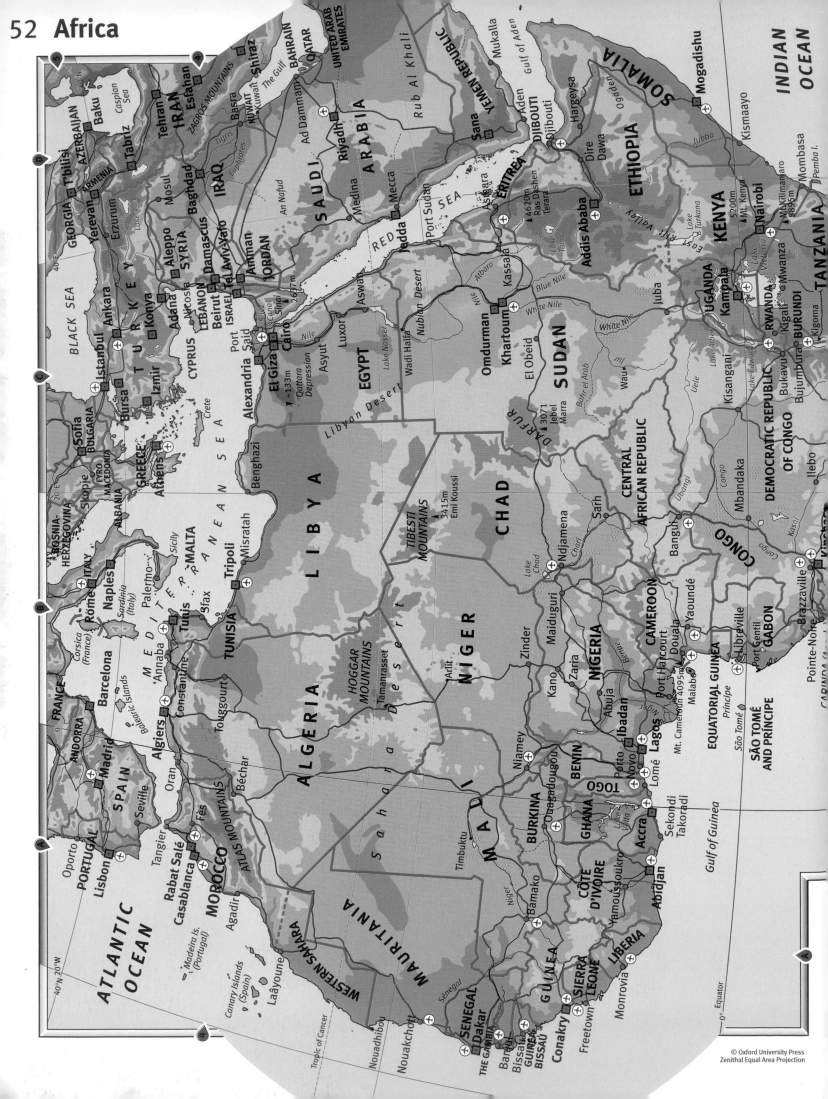

Key

- country boundary
- disputed boundary
- main road
- railway
- main airport
- river
- lake
- marsh

settlements

- ⊕ over 1 million people
- ● 100 000–1 000 000 people
- · under 100 000 people

land height
above sea level in metres

- more than 5000m
- 2000 – 5000m
- 1000 – 2000m
- 500 – 1000m
- 200 – 500m
- less than 200m
- land below sea level

▲ highest peaks with heights in metres

Scale 1: 26 000 000

One centimetre on the map represents 260 kilometres on the ground.

0   260   520   780km

© Oxford University Press

ATLANTIC OCEAN

Prime Meridian

Tropic of Capricorn

20°S

MADAGASCAR

COMOROS

Aldabra Is. (Seychelles)

Moroni

Antananarivo

Toamasina

Fianarantsoa

Mahajanga

Toliara

Mozambique Channel

Dar es Salaam

Mtwara

Dodoma

Mbeya

Lake Nyasa

Fuvuma

Nampula

Moçambique

MALAWI

Blantyre

Lilongwe

MOZAMBIQUE

Beira

Lake Tanganyika

Kalemie

Lake Mweru

Lubumbashi

Likasi

Kitwe

Kamina

Kamanga

Matadi

Luanda

Benguela

Huambo

Lubango

ANGOLA

Malanje

Cuanza

Cubango

Cunene

ZAMBIA

Lusaka

Zambezi

Harare

ZIMBABWE

Bulawayo

Lake Kariba

Livingstone

Victoria Falls

Okavango Swamp

Okavango

Kalahari Desert

BOTSWANA

Francistown

Gaborone

NAMIBIA

Windhoek

Namib Desert

Walvis Bay

Lüderitz

Cubango

Maputo

SWAZILAND

Mbabane

Pretoria

Johannesburg

Maseru

LESOTHO

Drakensberg

Kimberley

REPUBLIC OF SOUTH AFRICA

Durban

East London

Port Elizabeth

Cape Town

Cape of Good Hope

Orange

Limpopo

Zambezi

Luapula

20°E

40°E

AFRICAN BANKING CORPORATION

Key

——	country boundary
-----	disputed boundary
——	regional boundary
——	main road
——	railway
⊕	main airport
～	river
⋯	seasonal river
⬭	lake
▨	marsh

settlements

▣	over 1 million people
●	100 000–1 000 000 people
•	under 100 000 people

land height
above sea level in metres

more than 5000m
2000 – 5000m
1000 – 2000m
500 – 1000m
200 – 500m
less than 200m
land below sea level

▲ highest peaks with heights in metres

SUDAN

UNDER KENYAN ADMINISTRATION

ETHIOPIA

Yabelo

Lokitaung

Lake Turkana

Chew Bahir

Kalokol

Kitgum

Lodwar

Moyale

Mandera

Luuq

Gulu

Kotido

Moroto

3084m Mt. Moroto

▲2293m Mount Kulai

El Wak

Baardheere

UGANDA

Great Rift Valley

RIFT

Marsabit

NORTH-

SOMALIA

Soroti

Mount Elgon 4321m

VALLEY

EASTERN

EASTERN

Wajir

Mbale

KENYA

Kampala

Jinja

Tororo

WESTERN

Eldoret

Nanyuki

Meru

Hagadera

Equator

Entebbe

Kisumu

NYANZA

Nakuru

▲5200m Mount Kenya

Nyeri

CENTRAL

Embu

Garissa

Kismaayo

Homa Bay

Kisii

Aberdare Range

Narok

Nairobi

Thika

Machakos

Lake Baringo

Ewaso Ngiro

Lake Victoria

Musoma

NAIROBI

Magadi

Mwanza

Namanga

Garsen

Lamu

COAST

Serengeti Plain

Loolmalasin 3648m

Lake Natron

5895m Mount Kilimanjaro

Malindi

Shinyanga

Lake Eyasi

Moshi

Voi

Nzega

Arusha

TANZANIA

Mombasa

INDIAN OCEAN

Babati

Kondoa

Maasai Steppe

Mombo Tanga

Korogwe

Pemba Island

Pemba Channel

Scale   1 : 7 000 000

0   70   140   210km

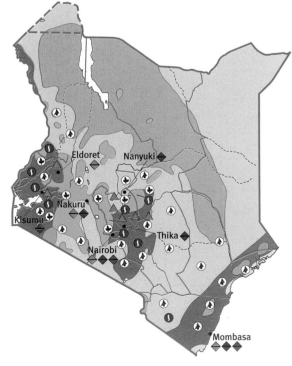

Eldoret

Nanyuki

Nakuru

Kisumu

Nairobi

Thika

Mombasa

Landscape and economy

☐	mangrove
▨	forest
▨	savannah
☐	bush
▨	desert
▨	mountain forest

☕	tea
☕	coffee
☕	maize
▲	hydro-electric power
◆	textiles
◆	chemicals
◆	vehicle assembly

mangrove

forest

savannah

bush

desert

mountain forest

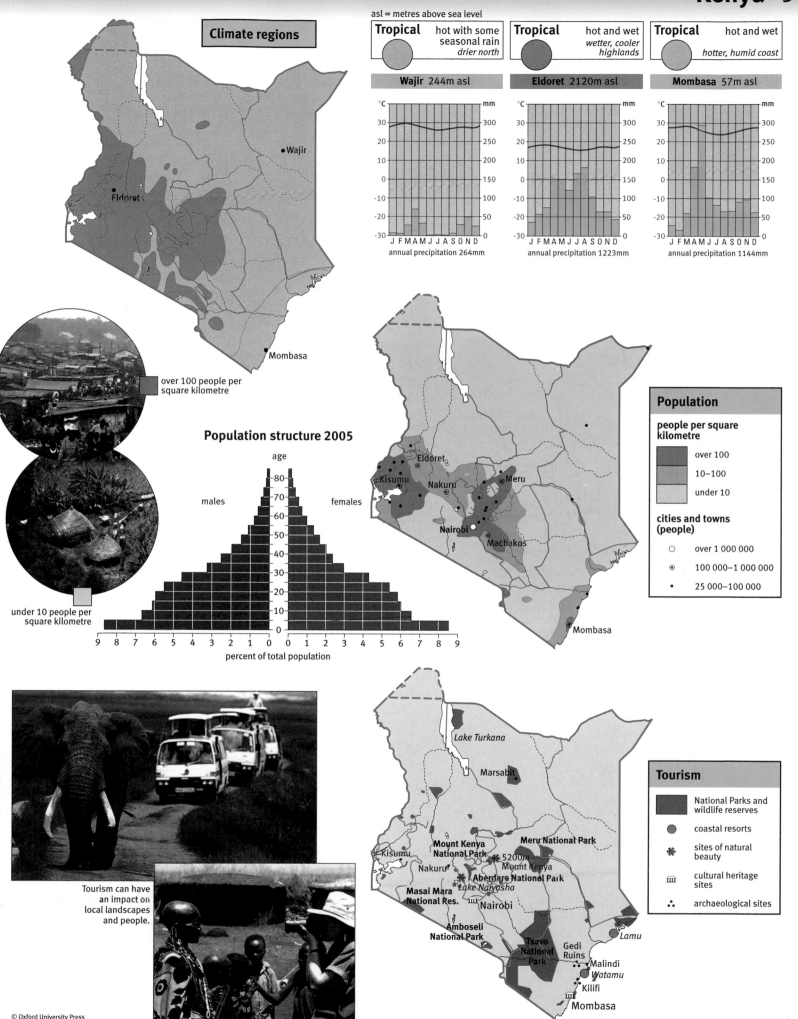

Climate regions

• Wajir

Eldoret

Mombasa

asl = metres above sea level

Tropical — hot with some seasonal rain *drier north*

Wajir 244m asl

°C / mm
30 / 300
20 / 250
10 / 200
0 / 150
-10 / 100
-20 / 50
-30 / 0
J F M A M J J A S O N D

annual precipitation 264mm

Tropical — hot and wet *wetter, cooler highlands*

Eldoret 2120m asl

°C / mm
30 / 300
20 / 250
10 / 200
0 / 150
-10 / 100
-20 / 50
-30 / 0
J F M A M J J A S O N D

annual precipitation 1223mm

Tropical — hot and wet *hotter, humid coast*

Mombasa 57m asl

°C / mm
30 / 300
20 / 250
10 / 200
0 / 150
-10 / 100
-20 / 50
-30 / 0
J F M A M J J A S O N D

annual precipitation 1144mm

over 100 people per square kilometre

under 10 people per square kilometre

Population structure 2005

age
males — females
80
70
60
50
40
30
20
10

percent of total population
9 8 7 6 5 4 3 2 1 0 | 0 1 2 3 4 5 6 7 8 9

Population

people per square kilometre
- over 100
- 10–100
- under 10

cities and towns (people)
- ○ over 1 000 000
- ◉ 100 000–1 000 000
- • 25 000–100 000

Eldoret
Kisumu
Nakuru
Meru
Nairobi
Machakos
Mombasa

Tourism can have an impact on local landscapes and people.

Lake Turkana
Marsabit
Kisumu
Mount Kenya National Park
Meru National Park
Nakuru
※ 5200m Mount Kenya
Aberdare National Park
Lake Naivasha
Masai Mara National Res.
Nairobi
Amboseli National Park
Tsavo National Park
Gedi Ruins
Lamu
Malindi
Watamu
Kilifi
Mombasa

Tourism

- National Parks and wildlife reserves
- ● coastal resorts
- ※ sites of natural beauty
- 🏛 cultural heritage sites
- ∴ archaeological sites

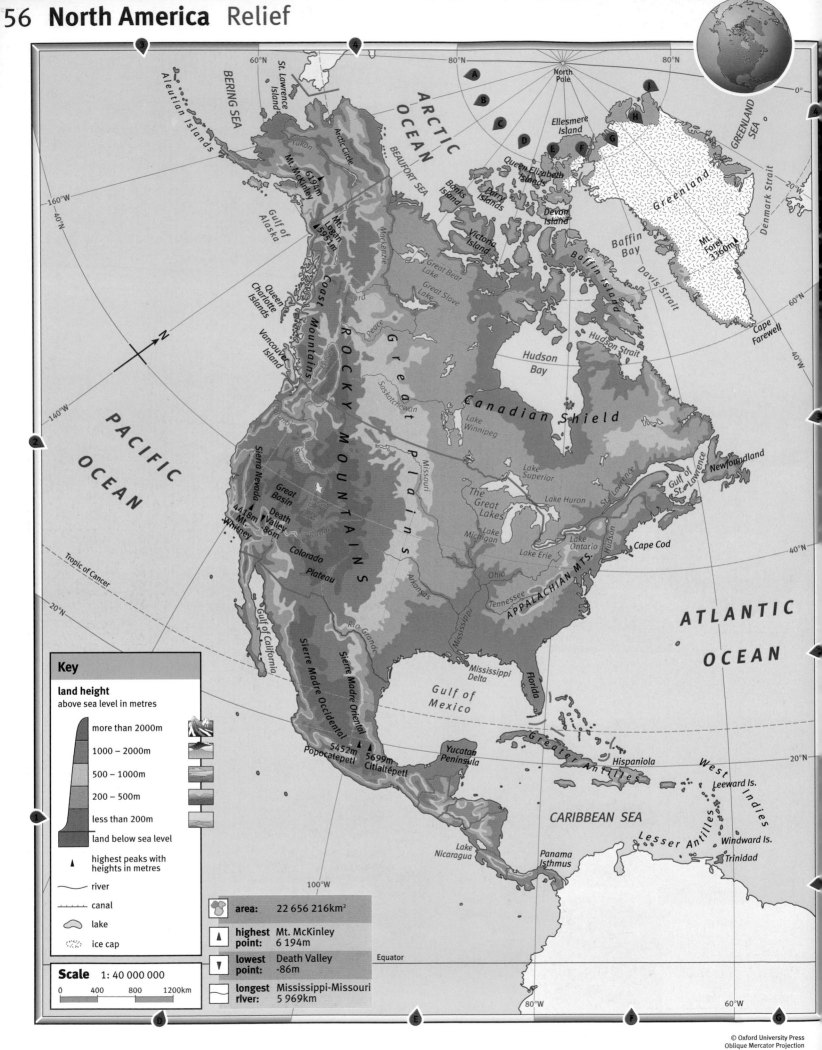

BERING SEA

Aleutian Islands

St. Lawrence Island

60°N

ARCTIC CIRCLE

ARCTIC OCEAN

North Pole

80°N

80°N

0°

GREENLAND SEA

Denmark Strait

Ellesmere Island

Queen Elizabeth Islands

Banks Island

Parry Islands

Victoria Island

Devon Island

Baffin Island

Baffin Bay

Davis Strait

Greenland

Mt. Forel 3360m

Cape Farewell

60°N

Gulf of Alaska

Mt. McKinley 6194m

Yukon

Mt. Logan 5951m

Coast Mountains

Mackenzie

Great Bear Lake

Great Slave Lake

ROCKY MOUNTAINS

Peace

Great Plains

Saskatchewan

Canadian Shield

Hudson Bay

Hudson Strait

Queen Charlotte Islands

Vancouver Island

Sierra Nevada

Great Basin

Fraser

Columbia

Lake Winnipeg

Lake Superior

Missouri

Lake Huron

Newfoundland

Gulf of St. Lawrence

St. Lawrence

PACIFIC OCEAN

4418m Mt. Whitney

Death Valley -86m

Colorado

Colorado Plateau

The Great Lakes

Lake Michigan

Lake Erie

Lake Ontario

Hudson

Cape Cod

ATLANTIC OCEAN

40°N

40°N

Tropic of Cancer

20°N

Gulf of California

Sierra Madre Occidental

Sierra Madre Oriental

Arkansas

Ohio

Tennessee

Mississippi

Rio Grande

APPALACHIAN MTS.

Florida

20°N

5452m Popocatepetl

5699m Citlaltépetl

Mississippi Delta

Gulf of Mexico

Yucatan Peninsula

Greater Antilles

Hispaniola

West Indies

Leeward Is.

CARIBBEAN SEA

Lesser Antilles

Windward Is.

Lake Nicaragua

Panama Isthmus

Trinidad

20°N

Equator

80°W

60°W

100°W

160°W

140°W

Key

land height
above sea level in metres

- more than 2000m
- 1000 – 2000m
- 500 – 1000m
- 200 – 500m
- less than 200m
- land below sea level

▲ highest peaks with heights in metres

—— river

┼┼┼ canal

lake

ice cap

	area:	22 656 216km²
▲	highest point	Mt. McKinley 6 194m
▼	lowest point	Death Valley -86m
	longest river	Mississippi-Missouri 5 969km

Scale 1: 40 000 000

0   400   800   1200km

A B C D E F G H J

ARCTIC OCEAN

ARCTIC OCEAN

A
B
C
D
E
F
G
H
I

GREENLAND
(Denmark)

Nuuk

USA
ALASKA

Anchorage

YUKON
TERRITORY

NORTHWEST TERRITORIES

NUNAVUT

BRITISH
COLUMBIA

ALBERTA

SASKATCHEWAN

MANITOBA

ONTARIO

QUÉBEC

NEWFOUNDLAND
LABRADOR

Arctic Circle

C A N A D A

Vancouver
Seattle
Portland
WASHINGTON
OREGON
IDAHO
MONTANA
NORTH
DAKOTA
SOUTH
DAKOTA
MINNESOTA
WISCONSIN
MICHIGAN

Calgary
Edmonton

Winnipeg

Ottawa
Québec
Montréal
St-Pierre
& Miquelon
(France)

NEW
BRUNSWICK
NOVA
SCOTIA
Halifax
MAINE

San
Francisco
Sacramento
NEVADA
Salt Lake
City
UTAH
WYOMING
COLORADO
NEBRASKA
IOWA
Chicago
Detroit
Toronto
Denver
Kansas
City
MISSOURI
ILLINOIS INDIANA OHIO
Pittsburgh
PENNSYLVANIA
N.H.
NEW YORK
VT.
Boston
MA.
CT.
New York
N.J.

Los Angeles
San Diego
CALIFORNIA

UNITED STATES OF AMERICA

ARIZONA
Phoenix
NEW
MEXICO
KANSAS
OKLAHOMA
ARKANSAS
St Louis
KENTUCKY
TENNESSEE
VIRGINIA
W.V.
NORTH CAROLINA
Washington D.C.
MD.
DE.
Philadelphia

TEXAS
Dallas
Houston
MS.
ALABAMA
GEORGIA
Atlanta
SOUTH
CAROLINA

Monterray

LOUISIANA
New
Orleans

FLORIDA
Miami

Gulf of
Mexico

Bermuda
(UK)

ATLANTIC
OCEAN

PACIFIC
OCEAN

Tropic of Cancer

Guadalajara
MEXICO
Mexico City
Puebla

Havana

CUBA

THE BAHAMAS
Nassau

Belmopan
Guatemala City
GUATEMALA
BELIZE
San Salvador
EL SALVADOR
HONDURAS
Tegucigalpa
NICARAGUA
Managua
San José
COSTA RICA
PANAMA
Panama
City

Kingston
JAMAICA
HAITI
Port-au-
Prince
DOMINICAN
REPUBLIC
Santo
Domingo
PUERTO RICO
(USA)
San
Juan

ST. KITTS AND NEVIS
ANTIGUA &
BARBUDA
DOMINICA
ST. LUCIA
BARBADOS
ST. VINCENT &
THE GRENADINES
GRENADA
Port of Spain
TRINIDAD &
TOBAGO

CARIBBEAN
SEA

Equator

CT.	CONNECTICUT
DE.	DELAWARE
MA.	MASSACHUSETTS
MD.	MARYLAND
MS.	MISSISSIPPI
N.H.	NEW HAMPSHIRE
N.J.	NEW JERSEY
R.I.	RHODE ISLAND
VT.	VERMONT
W.V.	WEST VIRGINIA

British Isles at
the same scale

Key

colours show
countries

CUBA country names are
shown like this

■ capital city

• other major city

Scale 1 : 40 000 000

0   400   800   1200km

population:
511 166 000

**largest Canada
country:** 9 970 601km²

country with most people:
USA 298 213 000

**largest Mexico City, Mexico
city:** 18 934 000

© Oxford University Press

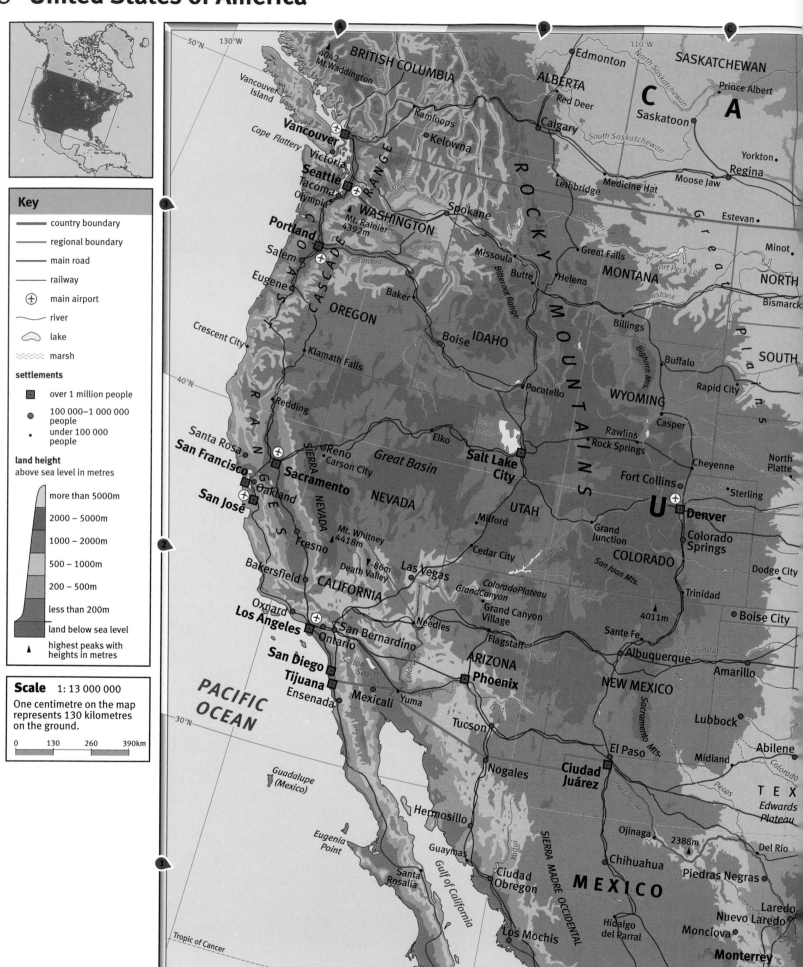

Key

- ━━━ country boundary
- ─── regional boundary
- ─── main road
- ─── railway
- ⊕ main airport
- ∿ river
- ⬭ lake
- ▒▒▒ marsh

settlements

- ▣ over 1 million people
- ● 100 000–1 000 000 people
- • under 100 000 people

land height
above sea level in metres

- more than 5000m
- 2000 – 5000m
- 1000 – 2000m
- 500 – 1000m
- 200 – 500m
- less than 200m
- land below sea level
- ▲ highest peaks with heights in metres

Scale 1: 13 000 000

One centimetre on the map represents 130 kilometres on the ground.

0   130   260   390km

PACIFIC OCEAN

Tropic of Cancer

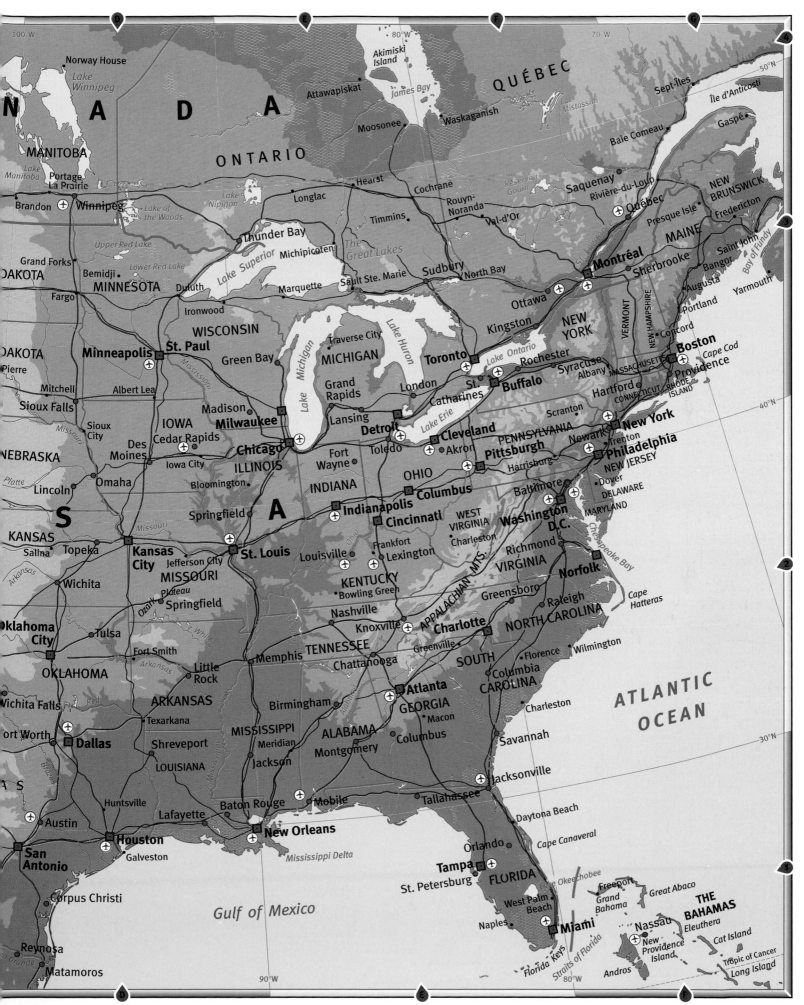

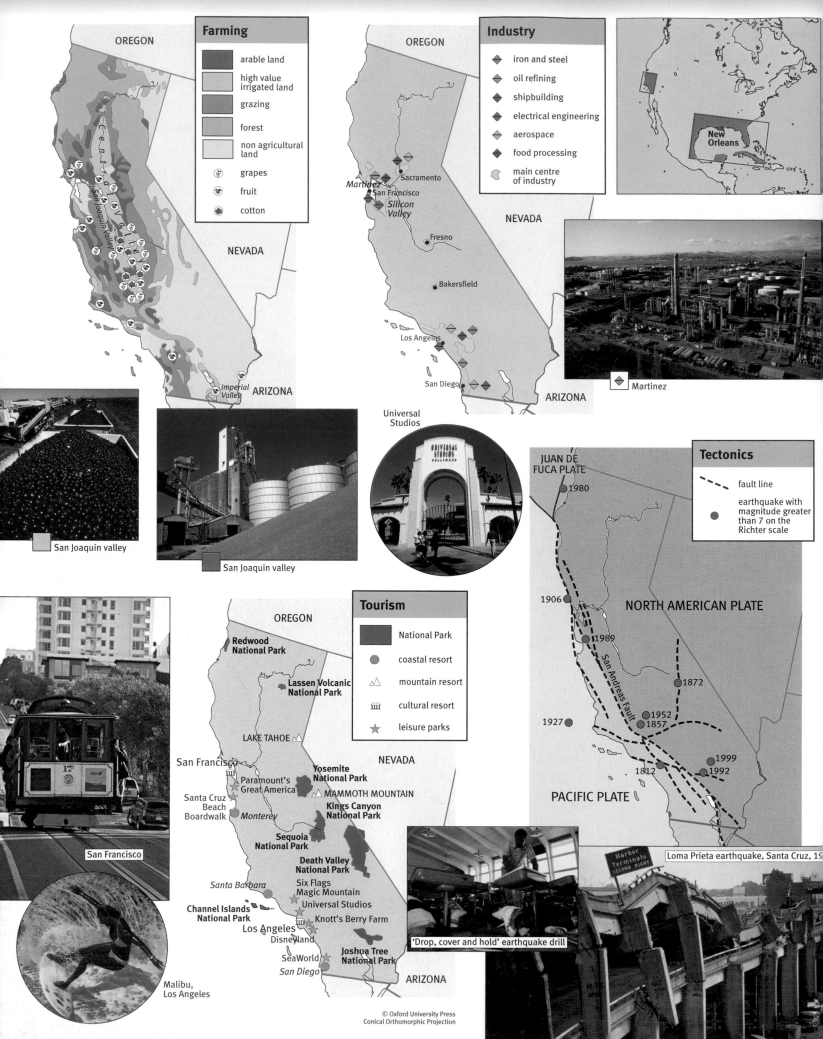

Farming

- arable land
- high value irrigated land
- grazing
- forest
- non agricultural land

- grapes
- fruit
- cotton

OREGON
NEVADA
Central Valley
San Joaquin Valley
Imperial Valley
ARIZONA

San Joaquin valley

San Joaquin valley

Industry

- iron and steel
- oil refining
- shipbuilding
- electrical engineering
- aerospace
- food processing
- main centre of industry

OREGON
NEVADA
Martinez
Sacramento
San Francisco
Silicon Valley
Fresno
Bakersfield
Los Angeles
San Diego
ARIZONA

Martinez

New Orleans

Universal Studios

Tectonics

- fault line
- earthquake with magnitude greater than 7 on the Richter scale

JUAN DE FUCA PLATE
1980
1906
1989
NORTH AMERICAN PLATE
1872
San Andreas Fault
1927
1952
1857
1999
1812
1992
PACIFIC PLATE

Loma Prieta earthquake, Santa Cruz, 19

Tourism

- National Park
- coastal resort
- mountain resort
- cultural resort
- leisure parks

OREGON
Redwood National Park
Lassen Volcanic National Park
LAKE TAHOE
NEVADA
San Francisco
Paramount's Great America
Yosemite National Park
Santa Cruz Beach Boardwalk
Monterey
MAMMOTH MOUNTAIN
Kings Canyon National Park
Sequoia National Park
Death Valley National Park
Santa Barbara
Six Flags Magic Mountain
Universal Studios
Channel Islands National Park
Knott's Berry Farm
Los Angeles
Disneyland
SeaWorld
Joshua Tree National Park
San Diego
ARIZONA

San Francisco

Malibu, Los Angeles

'Drop, cover and hold' earthquake drill

Harbor Terminals SECOND RIGHT

© Oxford University Press
Conical Orthomorphic Projection

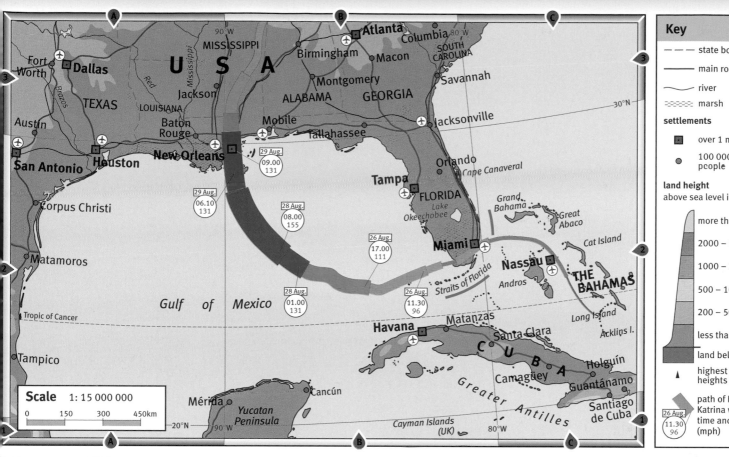

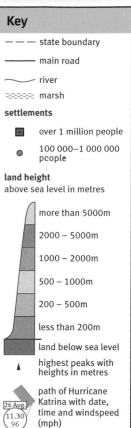

Key

- – – – state boundary
- ——— main road
- ～～～ river
- ∷∷∷ marsh

settlements

- ■ over 1 million people
- ● 100 000–1 000 000 people

land height
above sea level in metres

- more than 5000m
- 2000 – 5000m
- 1000 – 2000m
- 500 – 1000m
- 200 – 500m
- less than 200m
- land below sea level
- ▲ highest peaks with heights in metres
- path of Hurricane Katrina with date, time and windspeed (mph)
  - 26 Aug. / 11.30 / 96

Scale 1: 15 000 000
0 150 300 450km

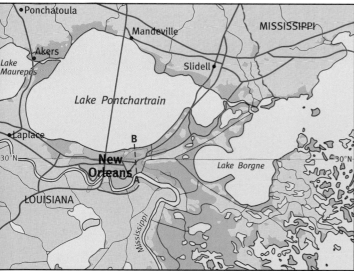

Flooding caused by Hurricane Katrina

- ▨ maximum extent of persistent flooding in New Orleans area
- A – – – B line of cross section

Cross-section through New Orleans

Mississippi River average annual highwater level

A Floodwall 7m asl

natural levee

Gentilly Ridge

Hurricane protection levee and floodwall 5.3m asl

Lake Pontchartrain normal lake level

B

metres
9
6
3
SL
-3
-6

sea level

The Isle of New Orleans

© Oxford University Press
Zenithal Equidistant Projection

29 August, 09.00

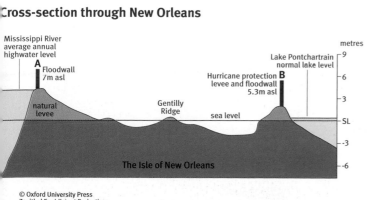

New Orleans before Hurricane Katrina

New Orleans after Hurricane Katrina

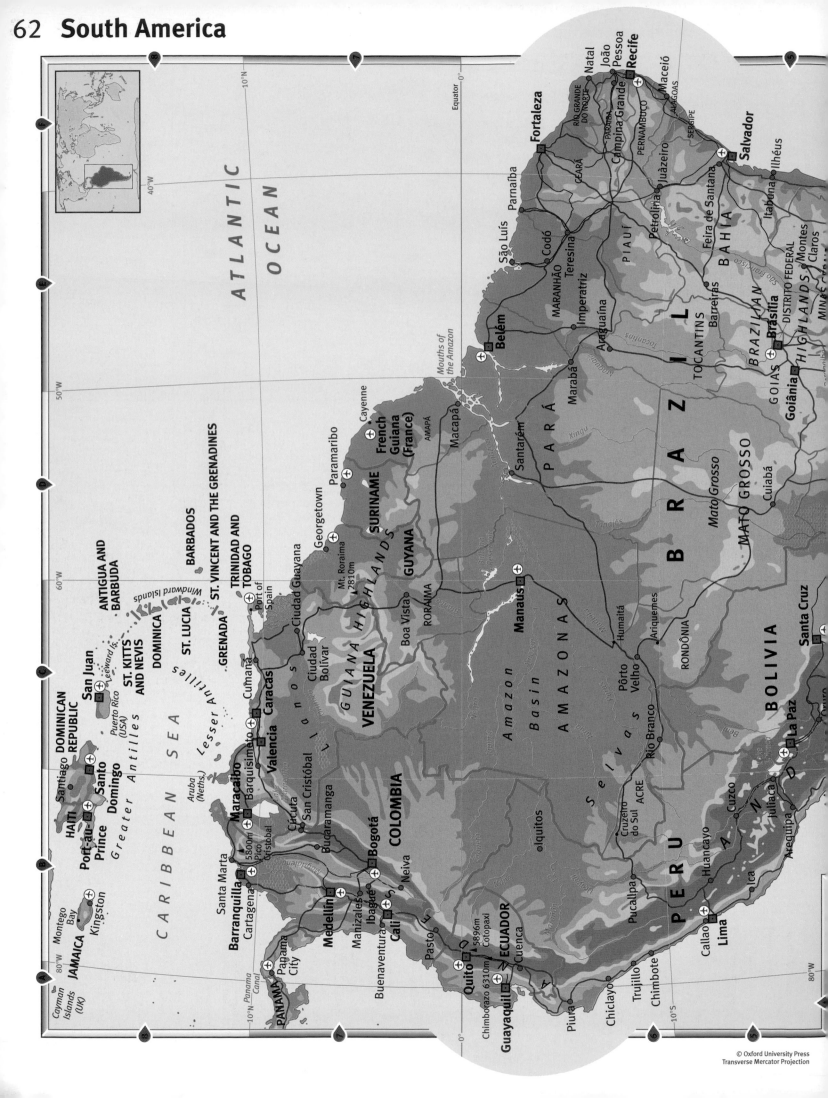

ATLANTIC OCEAN

CARIBBEAN SEA

Equator

40°W

50°W

60°W

80°W

80°W

10°N

0°

10°S

10°N

Cayman Islands (UK)

JAMAICA
Montego Bay
Kingston

HAITI
Port-au-Prince
Santiago
DOMINICAN REPUBLIC
Santo Domingo
San Juan
Puerto Rico (USA)
Greater Antilles
Leeward Is.
ST. KITTS AND NEVIS
ANTIGUA AND BARBUDA
DOMINICA
ST. LUCIA
BARBADOS
ST. VINCENT AND THE GRENADINES
GRENADA
TRINIDAD AND TOBAGO
Lesser Antilles
Windward Islands
Port of Spain

PANAMA
Panama City
Panama Canal

Santa Marta
Barranquilla
Cartagena
Pico Cristóbal 5800m
Maracaibo
Valencia
Caracas
Barquisimeto
Cumaná

VENEZUELA
Cúcuta
San Cristóbal
Bucaramanga
Medellín
Manizales
Ibagué
Bogotá
Cali
Buenaventura
Neiva

COLOMBIA
Pasto
Mahales

ECUADOR
Quito
Chimborazo 6310m
Cotopaxi 5896m
Guayaquil
Cuenca

Ciudad Bolívar
Ciudad Guayana
Georgetown
GUYANA
SURINAME
Paramaribo
French Guiana (France)
Cayenne

GUIANA HIGHLANDS
Mt. Roraima 2810m
Boa Vista
RORAIMA
Llanos

Orinoco

PERU
Iquitos
Piura
Chiclayo
Trujillo
Chimbote
Callao
Lima
Ica
Arequipa
Juliaca
Cuzco
Pucallpa
Cruzeiro do Sul
ACRE

Amazon Basin
AMAZONAS
Manaus
Humaitá
Pôrto Velho
Ariquemes
Rio Branco
RONDÔNIA
Selvas

BOLIVIA
La Paz
Santa Cruz
A N D E S

BRAZIL

Mouths of the Amazon
Belém
Macapá
AMAPÁ
Santarém
PARÁ
Marabá
Xingu
Tapajós

MARANHÃO
São Luís
Codó
Teresina
Imperatriz
Araguaína
Parnaíba

Fortaleza
CEARÁ
PIAUÍ

Natal
João Pessoa
Campina Grande
Recife
RIO GRANDE DO NORTE
PARAÍBA
PERNAMBUCO
Maceió
ALAGOAS
SERGIPE

Petrolina
Juàzeiro
Barreiras
Feira de Santana
Salvador
BAHIA
Itabuna
Ilhéus

BRAZILIAN HIGHLANDS
TOCANTINS
Tocantins
GOIÁS
Brasília
DISTRITO FEDERAL
Goiânia
Montes Claros
MINAS GERAIS
São Francisco

MATO GROSSO
Mato Grosso
Cuiabá

© Oxford University Press
Transverse Mercator Projection

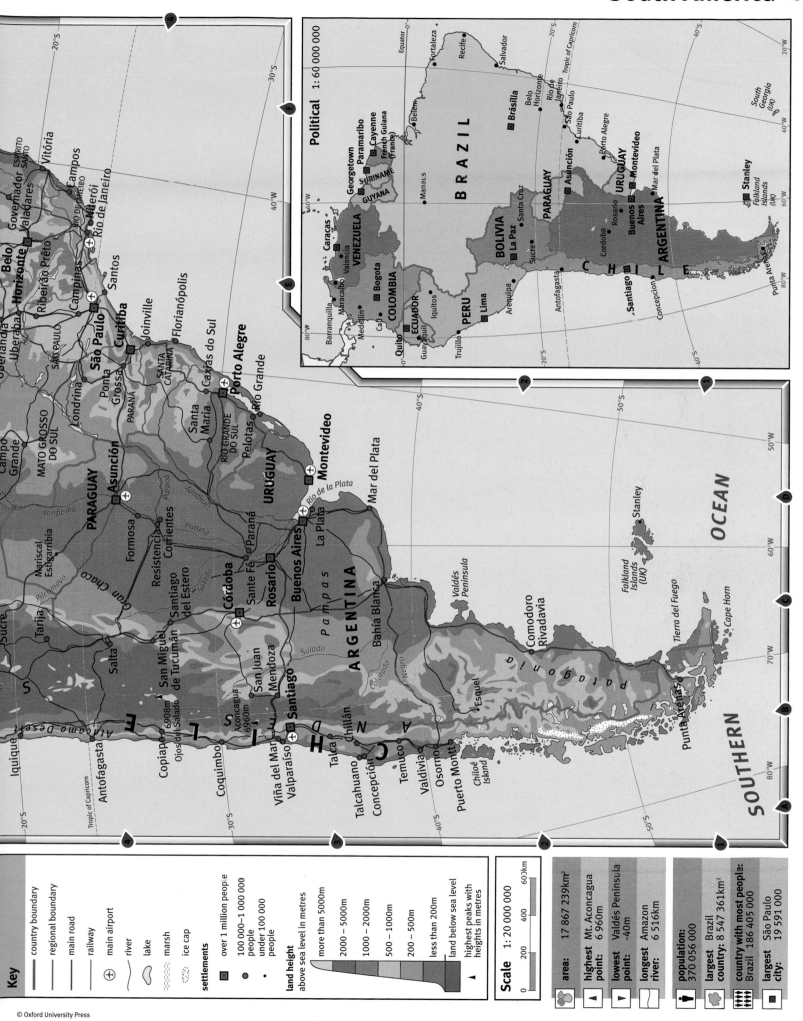

Political 1:60 000 000

Georgetown
Paramaribo
Cayenne
French Guiana (France)
SURINAME
GUYANA
VENEZUELA
Caracas
Valencia
Maracaibo
Barranquilla
Medellín
COLOMBIA
Bogota
Cali
ECUADOR
Quito
Guayaquil
Iquitos
Manaus
Belém
Fortaleza
Recife
Salvador
B R A Z I L
Brasília
Belo Horizonte
Rio de Janeiro
São Paulo
Curitiba
Pôrto Alegre
PARAGUAY
Asunción
URUGUAY
Montevideo
Mar del Plata
Trujillo
PERU
Lima
Arequipa
BOLIVIA
La Paz
Sucre
Santa Cruz
Antofagasta
CHILE
Santiago
Concepción
Córdoba
Rosario
Buenos Aires
ARGENTINA
Punta Arenas
Stanley
Falkland Islands (UK)
South Georgia (UK)

Equator 0°
Tropic of Capricorn
0° 20°S 40°S
80°W 60°W 40°W 20°W

Vitória
ESPÍRITO SANTO
Governador Valadares
Campos
Niterói
Rio de Janeiro
RIO DE JANEIRO
Belo Horizonte
Uberaba
Ribeirão Prêto
Campinas
Santos
São Paulo
SÃO PAULO
Curitiba
Joinville
Florianópolis
Ponta Grossa
Londrina
SANTA CATARINA
PARANÁ
Caxias do Sul
Santa Maria
RIO GRANDE DO SUL
Porto Alegre
Pelotas
Rio Grande
Uberlândia
MATO GROSSO DO SUL
Campo Grande
PARAGUAY
Asunción
Mariscal Estigarribia
Pilcomayo
Gran Chaco
Paraguay
Paraná
Iguaçu
Formosa
Resistencia
Corrientes
Paraná
Santiago del Estero
San Miguel de Tucumán
Salta
Tarija
Sucre
Salado
Córdoba
Santa Fé
Rosario
San Juan
Mendoza
Santiago
Aconcagua 6960m
Ojos del Salado 6908m
Copiapó
Atacama Desert
Antofagasta
Iquique
Coquimbo
Viña del Mar
Valparaíso
C H I L E
Talca
Chillán
Talcahuano
Concepción
Temuco
Valdivia
Osorno
Puerto Montt
Chiloé Island
Salado
A R G E N T I N A
Pampas
Buenos Aires
La Plata
URUGUAY
Montevideo
Río de la Plata
Mar del Plata
Bahía Blanca
Colorado
Negro
Valdés Peninsula
Comodoro Rivadavia
P a t a g o n i a
Esquel
Tierra del Fuego
Cape Horn
Punta Arenas
Stanley
Falkland Islands (UK)
S O U T H E R N   O C E A N

Tropic of Capricorn
20°S 30°S 40°S 50°S
80°W 70°W 60°W 50°W 40°W

Key

- country boundary
- regional boundary
- main road
- railway
- ⊕ main airport
- river
- lake
- marsh
- ice cap

settlements
- ◼ over 1 million people
- ● 100 000–1 000 000 people
- • under 100 000 people

land height
above sea level in metres
- more than 5000m
- 2000–5000m
- 1000–2000m
- 500–1000m
- 200–500m
- less than 200m
- land below sea level
- ▲ highest peaks with heights in metres

Scale 1:20 000 000

0   200   400   600km

area:	17 867 239km²
highest point:	Mt. Aconcagua 6 960m
lowest point:	Valdés Peninsula -40m
longest river:	Amazon 6 516km
population:	370 056 000
largest country:	Brazil 8 547 361km²
country with most people:	Brazil 186 405 000
largest city:	São Paulo 19 591 000

© Oxford University Press

asl = metres above sea level

Equatorial warm and wet
*rain all year or
as monsoon*

Tropical hot and wet
dry in winter

Temperate mild and wet
*warm summers
cool winters*

Climate regions

Manaus
Rio Branco
Porto Alegre

Rio Branco 143m asl

°C / mm

annual precipitation 1938mm

Manaus 44m asl

°C / mm

annual precipitation 2088mm

Porto Alegre 3m asl

°C / mm

annual precipitation 1333mm

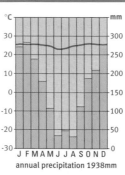

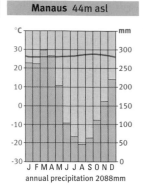
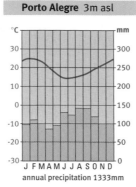

Belém
Manaus
Fortaleza
Recife
Salvador
Brasília
Goiânia
Belo Horizonte
Campinas
São Paulo
Guarulhos
Rio de Janeiro
Curitiba
Porto Alegre

over 100 people per
square kilometre

Population

people per square kilometre

- over 100
- 10–100
- 1–10
- under 1

**cities and towns
(people)**

- ☐ over 3 000 000
- ○ 1 000 000–3 000 000
- ◉ 500 000–1 000 000

under 1 person per
square kilometre

Population structure 2005

age

males

females

80
70
60
50
40
30
20
10
0

5 4 3 2 1 0   0 1 2 3 4 5

percent of total population

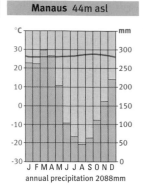

literacy and
life expectancy
are lowest in
the north east

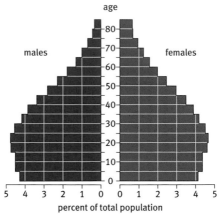

Quality of life

Literacy
percentage of people
over 15 years able to
read and write

- over 85%
- 75–85%
- 65–75%
- under 65%

Life expectancy
average number of
years a person can
expect to live

- ◉ over 70
- ◉ under 65

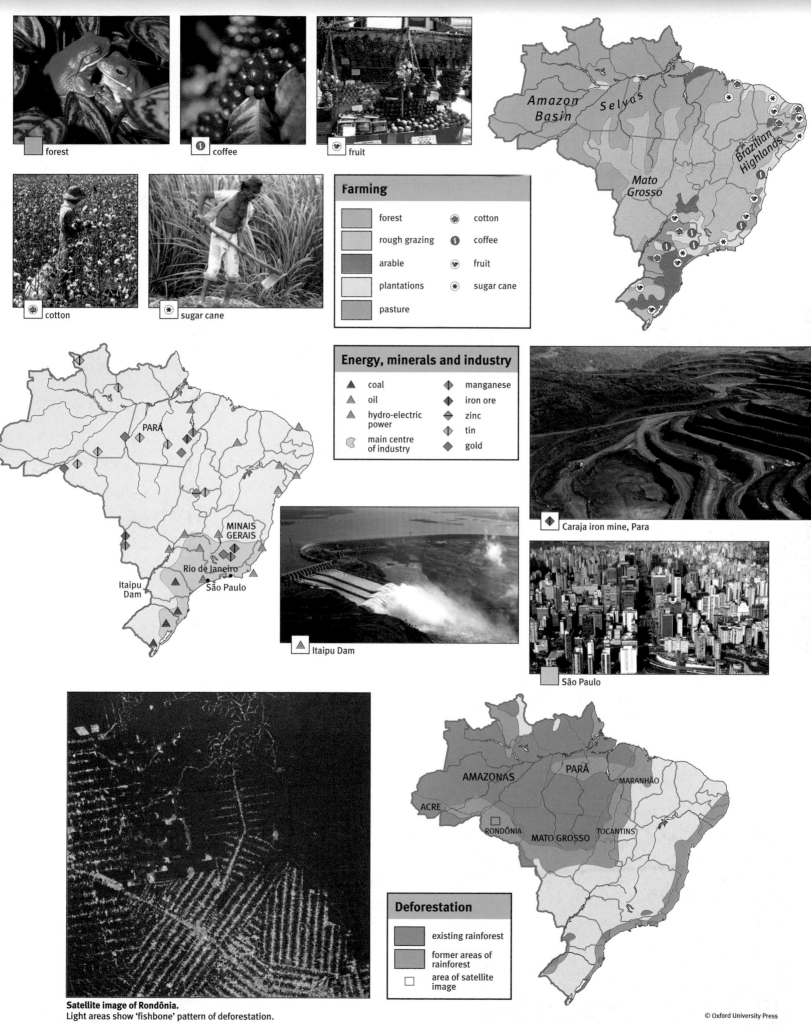

forest

coffee

fruit

cotton

sugar cane

Farming

	forest	✿	cotton
	rough grazing	❶	coffee
	arable	✤	fruit
	plantations	✱	sugar cane
	pasture		

Energy, minerals and industry

▲	coal	◈	manganese
▲	oil	◈	iron ore
▲	hydro-electric power	◈	zinc
⬠	main centre of industry	◈	tin
		◈	gold

PARÁ

MINAIS GERAIS

Rio de Janeiro

Itaipu Dam

São Paulo

Caraja iron mine, Para

Itaipu Dam

São Paulo

Satellite image of Rondônia.
Light areas show 'fishbone' pattern of deforestation.

AMAZONAS

PARÁ

MARANHÃO

ACRE

RONDÔNIA

MATO GROSSO

TOCANTINS

Deforestation

	existing rainforest
	former areas of rainforest
☐	area of satellite image

Amazon Basin

Selvas

Mato Grosso

Brazilian Highlands

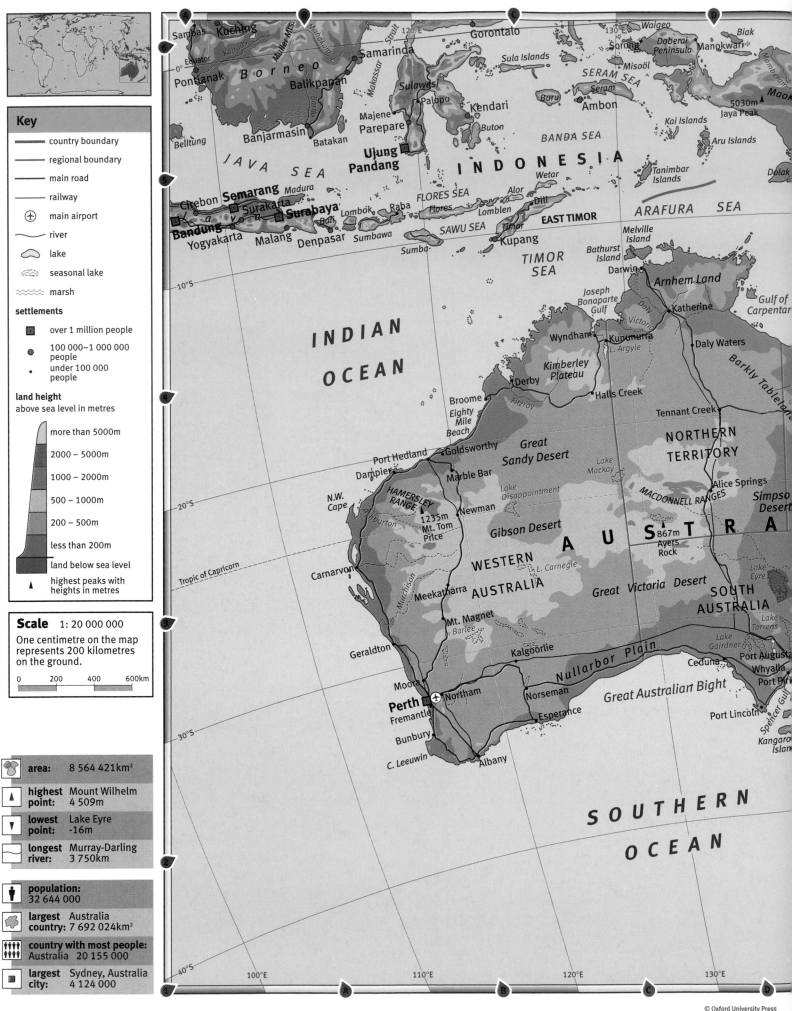

Key

———	country boundary
———	regional boundary
———	main road
—+—	railway
⊕	main airport
～	river
◡	lake
≈	seasonal lake
≋	marsh

settlements

▣	over 1 million people
●	100 000–1 000 000 people
•	under 100 000 people

land height
above sea level in metres

- more than 5000m
- 2000 – 5000m
- 1000 – 2000m
- 500 – 1000m
- 200 – 500m
- less than 200m
- land below sea level
- ▲ highest peaks with heights in metres

Scale 1: 20 000 000

One centimetre on the map represents 200 kilometres on the ground.

0   200   400   600km

area:	8 564 421km²	
highest point:	Mount Wilhelm 4 509m	
lowest point:	Lake Eyre -16m	
longest river:	Murray-Darling 3 750km	
population:	32 644 000	
largest country:	Australia 7 692 024km²	
country with most people:	Australia 20 155 000	
largest city:	Sydney, Australia 4 124 000	

Jayapura
Wewak
Sepik
Mountains
New
Guinea
4509m
Mt. Wilhelm
PAPUA NEW GUINEA
Lae
Kerema
Gulf of
Papua
Fly
Owen Stanley Range
Port
Moresby
Torres Strait
Cape York

Admiralty Is.
BISMARCK SEA
New
Ireland
Rabaul
Madang
New Britain
SOLOMON SEA
Woodlark I.
D'Entrecasteaux
Islands

Bougainville
Island
Choiseul
Santa Isabel
New
Georgia Is.
Honiara
Guadalcanal
Rennell
SOLOMON
ISLANDS
Malaita
San
Cristobal
Santa Cruz
Islands

NAURU
KIRIBATI

Tarawa
Gilbert Islands
Equator 0°

TUVALU
Funafuti
10°S

Espiritu Santo
Banks
Islands
VANUATU
Malakula
Vila Éfaté
Erromango

CORAL SEA

Cape Melville

GREAT
Barrier
Reef
Cooktown
Mitchell
Cairns
ormanton
Flinders
Townsville
Cloncurry
Mount
sa
Hughenden
Charters
Towers
Mackay
QUEENSLAND
Longreach
Barcaldine
Emerald
Rockhampton
DIVIDING
GREY RANGE
RANGE
Charleville
Roma
Toowoomba
Dalby
Cunnamula
I
A
Bundaberg
Maryborough
Gympie
Brisbane
Gold Coast
Lismore
Moree
Bourke
Grafton
RANGE
NEW SOUTH
WALES
Broken
Hill
Darling
Tamworth
Dubbo
Port Macquarie
Orange
DIVIDING
Newcastle
Sydney
Mildura
Murray
Lachlan
Albury
Wollongong
Adelaide
Murrumbidgee
ACT
Canberra
Murray
GREAT
SNOWY
2230m
Mt. Kosciuszko
Bendigo
VICTORIA
Ballarat
Melbourne
Cape Howe
Mount
ambier
Warrnambool
Geelong
Bass Strait
Devonport
Launceston
TASMANIA
Hobart
S.E. Cape

Îles
Chesterfield
Is. Loyauté
New
Caledonia
(Fr.)
Nouméa

Norfolk I.
(Aust.)

Lord Howe I.
(Aust.)

TASMAN
SEA

Tropic of Capricorn

20°S

Kermadec Is. (NZ)

30°S

Vanua Levu
Viti Levu
Suva
FIJI
Kadavu

North Cape
Auckland
Hamilton
New Plymouth
Rotorua
North
Island
Napier
Greymouth
Mt. Cook
3764
Southern Alps
Nelson
Cook Strait
Palmerston North
Wellington
NEW ZEALAND
South
Island
Christchurch
Cape Providence
Stewart I.
Invercargill
Dunedin
Chatham Is.
(NZ)

40°S

140°E
150°E
160°E
180°
170°W

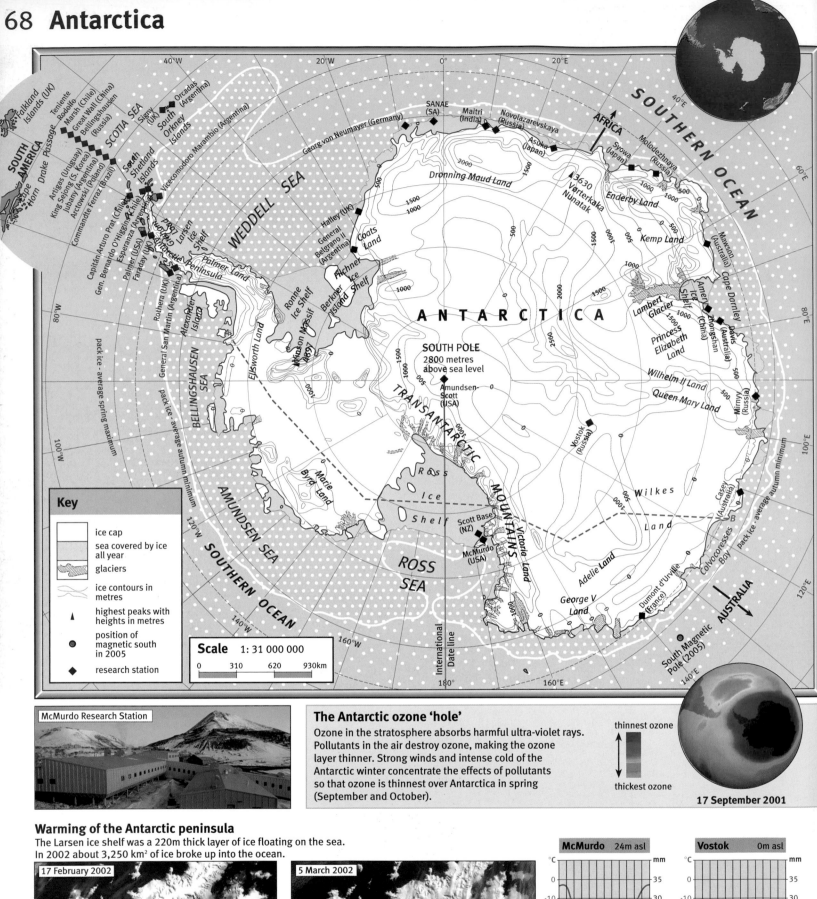

Key

- ice cap
- sea covered by ice all year
- glaciers
- ice contours in metres
- ▲ highest peaks with heights in metres
- ⊙ position of magnetic south in 2005
- ◆ research station

Scale 1 : 31 000 000

0   310   620   930km

SOUTH POLE
2800 metres
above sea level

McMurdo Research Station

The Antarctic ozone 'hole'

Ozone in the stratosphere absorbs harmful ultra-violet rays. Pollutants in the air destroy ozone, making the ozone layer thinner. Strong winds and intense cold of the Antarctic winter concentrate the effects of pollutants so that ozone is thinnest over Antarctica in spring (September and October).

thinnest ozone

thickest ozone

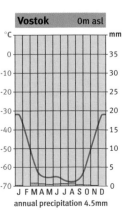

17 September 2001

Warming of the Antarctic peninsula

The Larsen ice shelf was a 220m thick layer of ice floating on the sea.
In 2002 about 3,250 km² of ice broke up into the ocean.

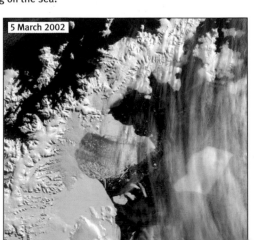

17 February 2002

5 March 2002

McMurdo 24m asl

annual precipitation 202.5mm

Vostok 0m asl

annual precipitation 4.5mm

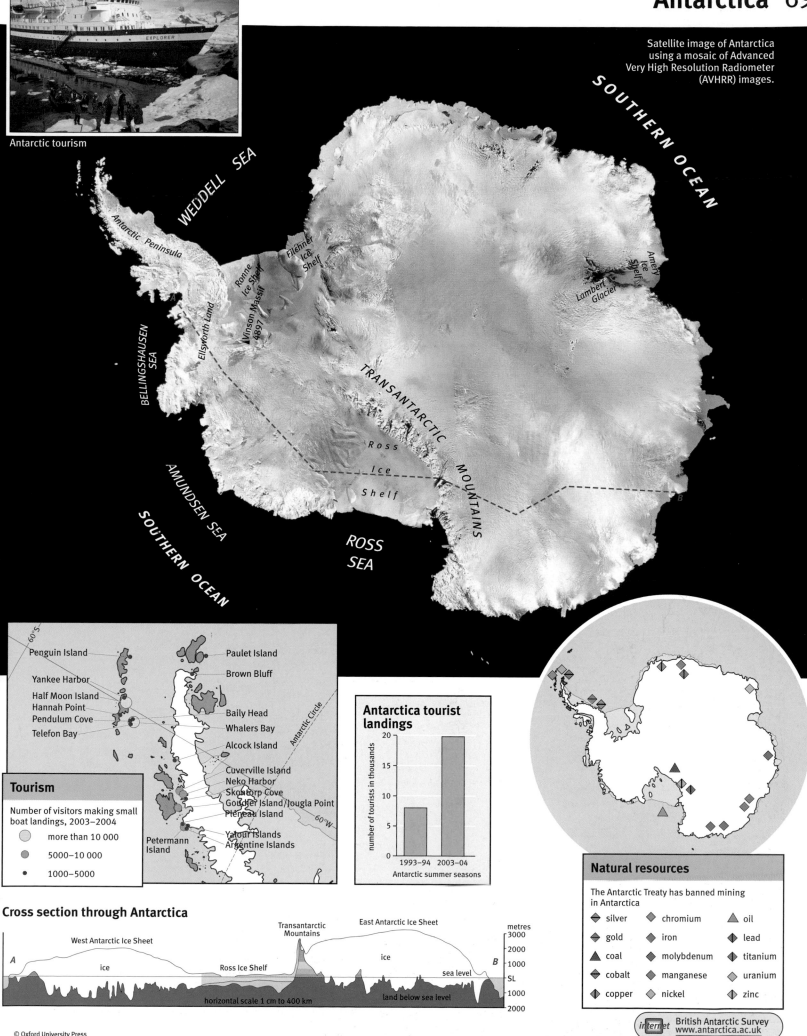

Antarctic tourism

Satellite image of Antarctica using a mosaic of Advanced Very High Resolution Radiometer (AVHRR) images.

SOUTHERN OCEAN

WEDDELL SEA

Antarctic Peninsula

Ronne Ice Shelf

Filchner Ice Shelf

Amery Ice Shelf

Lambert Glacier

BELLINGSHAUSEN SEA

Ellsworth Land

Vinson Massif 4897

TRANSANTARCTIC

Ross Ice Shelf

MOUNTAINS

AMUNDSEN SEA

SOUTHERN OCEAN

ROSS SEA

Tourism

60°S

Penguin Island
Yankee Harbor
Half Moon Island
Hannah Point
Pendulum Cove
Telefon Bay

Paulet Island
Brown Bluff

Baily Head
Whalers Bay
Alcock Island

Antarctic Circle

Cuverville Island
Neko Harbor
Skontorp Cove
Goudier Island/Jougla Point
Plenaeu Island

Petermann Island

Yalour Islands
Argentine Islands

60°W

Tourism

Number of visitors making small boat landings, 2003–2004

- more than 10 000
- 5000–10 000
- 1000–5000

Antarctica tourist landings

number of tourists in thousands

1993–94	2003–04
8	20

Antarctic summer seasons

Natural resources

The Antarctic Treaty has banned mining in Antarctica

- silver
- gold
- coal
- cobalt
- copper
- chromium
- iron
- molybdenum
- manganese
- nickel
- oil
- lead
- titanium
- uranium
- zinc

Cross section through Antarctica

Transantarctic Mountains

East Antarctic Ice Sheet

West Antarctic Ice Sheet

metres
3000
2000
1000

ice

Ross Ice Shelf

ice

sea level
SL

A

B

1000
2000

horizontal scale 1 cm to 400 km

land below sea level

British Antarctic Survey
www.antarctica.ac.uk
internet

Key

colours show countries

MALI   country names are labelled like this

■   capital cities

One centimetre on the map represents 1000 kilometres on the ground at the equator.

North America

South America

ARCTIC OCEAN

Arctic Circle

USA

Jan Maye (Norway)

Faeroes (Denmark)

Nuuk

Reykjavik
ICELAND

Greenland (Denmark)

UNITED KINGDO

REPUBLIC OF IRELAND
Dublin

Londo

C A N A D A

Ottawa

Azores (Portugal)

PORTUGAL
Lisbon

Madr

SPAI

UNITED STATES OF AMERICA

Washington D.C.

Bermuda (UK)

Madeira (Portugal)

Rabat

MOROCCO

Tropic of Cancer

Canary Islands (Spain)

Laayoune

Hawaiian Islands (USA)

MEXICO

Havana
CUBA

THE BAHAMAS

DOMINICAN
REPUBLIC

Puerto Rico (USA)

WESTERN SAHARA

Mexico City

BELIZE
Belmopan
GUATEMALA

JAMAICA
Kingston

HAITI

ST. KITTS
AND NEVIS

ANTIGUA AND BARBUDA

DOMINICA

MAURITANIA

Nouakchott

MA

Guatemala City
HONDURAS
San Salvador Tegucigalpa
EL SALVADOR NICARAGUA
Managua

ST. VINCENT AND
THE GRENADINES

ST. LUCIA
BARBADOS
GRENADA

CAPE VERDE

Dakar
SENEGAL
G

BU

GiB

P A C I F I C

San José COSTA RICA

TRINIDAD AND TOBAGO

GUINEA

Ouagadougo

Panama City Caracas
PANAMA VENEZUELA

Georgetown

Conakry

SIERRA LEONE

Freetown

CÔTE

Bogotá

GUYANA
Paramaribo

SURINAME

Cayenne
French Guiana
(France)

Yamoussoukro
Monrovia

D'IVOIRE

LIBERIA

ACC

O C E A N

COLOMBIA

QUITO
ECUADOR

A T L A N T I C

Equator

Galapagos Islands (Ecuador)

Quito

O C E A N

KIRIBATI

B R A Z I L

Ascension Island (UK)

American Samoa

PERU
Lima

French Polynesia (France)

SAMOA

Cook Islands (New Zealand)

La Paz

Brasília

St. Helena (UK)

BOLIVIA

TONGA

Tropic of Capricorn

PARAGUAY

Pitcairn Island (UK)

Asunción

Easter Island (Chile)

URUGUAY

Santiago

Buenos Aires
CHILE

Montevideo

Tristan da Cunha (UK)

ARGENTINA

Falkland Islands (UK)

South Georgia (UK)

Antarctic Circle

A N T A R C T I C A

Oslo
NORWAY

Stockholm

Helsinki

Tallinn
ESTONIA

RUSSIAN FEDERATION (RUSSIA)

SWEDEN

LATVIA
Riga

DENMARK
Copenhagen

LITHUANIA
Kaliningrad Vilnius
(Russia)

Minsk

NETHERLANDS
Amsterdam

Berlin

Warsaw

BELARUS

Brussels
BELGIUM

GERMANY

POLAND

Kiev

LUXEMBOURG
Luxembourg

Prague
CZECH REPUBLIC

SLOVAKIA

UKRAINE

Paris

LIECHTENSTEIN

Vienna
Bratislava

Chisinau

SWITZERLAND
Bern
Vaduz

AUSTRIA

Budapest

MOLDOVA

Ljubljana
SLOVENIA

HUNGARY

ROMANIA

FRANCE

ITALY

Zagreb
CROATIA

Belgrade

Bucharest

Monaco

San Marino

BOSNIA-
HERZEGOVINA
Sarajevo

SERBIA

MONACO
SAN MARINO

MONTENEGRO

BULGARIA

Podgorica

Sofia

Rome

SPAIN

Tirane
ALBANIA

Skopje
FYRO
MACEDONIA

GREECE

TURKEY

Athens

Abbreviations

A	ALBANIA	CZ	CZECH REPUBLIC	Q	QATAR
AR	ARMENIA	G	THE GAMBIA	R	ROMANIA
AU	AUSTRIA	G-B	GUINEA-BISSAU	S	SLOVAKIA
AZ	AZERBAIJAN	H	HUNGARY	SE	SERBIA
B	BELGIUM	IS	ISRAEL	SL	SLOVENIA
BE	BENIN	L	LEBANON	SW	SWITZERLAND
BH	BOSNIA-HERZEGOVINA	LI	LITHUANIA	T	TAJIKISTAN
BR	BRUNEI	LU	LUXEMBOURG	TU	TURKMENISTAN
BU	BURKINA	M	FORMER YUGOSLAV	U	UGANDA
C	CROATIA		REPUBLIC OF MACEDONIA	UAE	UNITED ARAB EMIRATES
CAR	CENTRAL AFRICAN	MT	MONTENEGRO	ZIM	ZIMBABWE
	REPUBLIC	N	NETHERLANDS		

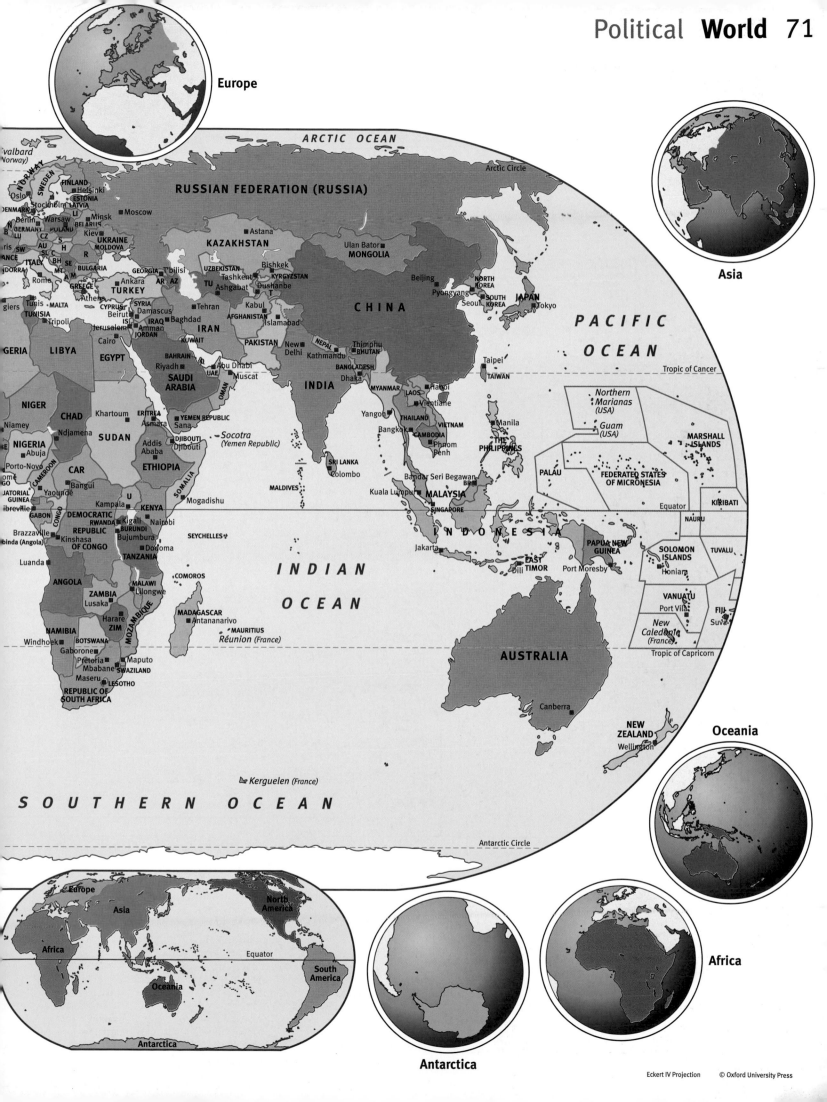

Europe

ARCTIC OCEAN

Asia

Arctic Circle

RUSSIAN FEDERATION (RUSSIA)

NORWAY
SWEDEN
FINLAND
Helsinki
Oslo ESTONIA
Stockholm LATVIA
DENMARK LI
Berlin Warsaw BELARUS Minsk Moscow
GERMANY POLAND Kiev
B LU Astana
CZ UKRAINE
ris AU S H MOLDOVA KAZAKHSTAN
ANCE ITALY CZ R
SW BH
SE Bishkek MONGOLIA Ulan Bator
DORRA MT SC BULGARIA GEORGIA T'bilisi UZBEKISTAN KYRGYZSTAN Beijing NORTH KOREA
Rome AM GREECE TURKEY AR AZ Tashkent Dushanbe T JAPAN
giers Tunis MALTA Ankara Athens TU Ashgabat T Pyongyang SOUTH KOREA Tokyo
TUNISIA CYPRUS SYRIA Damascus Tehran Kabul Seoul
Tripoli Beirut IS IRAQ Baghdad AFGHANISTAN Islamabad CHINA
Jerusalem Amman JORDAN IRAN PAKISTAN PACIFIC
GERIA LIBYA EGYPT Cairo KUWAIT New Delhi NEPAL Thimphu OCEAN
BAHRAIN Riyadh Q Abu Dhabi Kathmandu BHUTAN Taipei
UAE Muscat BANGLADESH Tropic of Cancer
NIGER SAUDI OMAN INDIA Dhaka TAIWAN
CHAD ARABIA MYANMAR LAOS Hanoi Northern
Niamey Khartoum ERITREA Marianas
Ndjamena SUDAN Asmara YEMEN REPUBLIC Vientiane (USA)
NIGERIA Addis Sana Socotra Yangon THAILAND VIETNAM Guam MARSHALL
Abuja CAR Ababa DJIBOUTI (Yemen Republic) Bangkok CAMBODIA Manila (USA) ISLANDS
Porto-Novo Djibouti Phnom THE
omè Bangui ETHIOPIA SRI LANKA Penh PHILIPPINES PALAU FEDERATED STATES
GO CAMEROON SOMALIA Colombo Bandar Seri Begawan OF MICRONESIA KIRIBATI
JATORIAL Yaoundé U KENYA MALDIVES BR Equator
GUINEA Kampala Kuala Lumpur MALAYSIA
ibreville GABON DEMOCRATIC RWANDA Kigali Nairobi SINGAPORE NAURU
CONGO REPUBLIC BURUNDI Bujumbura Mogadishu I N D O N E S I A TUVALU
Brazzaville OF CONGO Dodoma PAPUA NEW SOLOMON
binda (Angola) Kinshasa TANZANIA SEYCHELLES Jakarta GUINEA ISLANDS
Luanda EAST Port Moresby Honiara
ANGOLA MALAWI COMOROS INDIAN DILI TIMOR
ZAMBIA Lilongwe OCEAN VANUATU FIJI
Lusaka MADAGASCAR Port Vila Suva
NAMIBIA Harare ZIM Antananarivo New
Windhoek BOTSWANA MAURITIUS Caledonia
Gaborone MOZAMBIQUE Réunion (France) (France) Tropic of Capricorn
Pretoria Maputo AUSTRALIA
Mbabane SWAZILAND
Maseru LESOTHO Canberra
REPUBLIC OF
SOUTH AFRICA
NEW
ZEALAND Oceania
Wellington

Kerguelen (France)

S O U T H E R N   O C E A N

Antarctic Circle

Europe
Asia
North America
Africa
Equator
Oceania South America
Antarctica

Antarctica

Africa

Eckert IV Projection   © Oxford University Press

Equatorial scale 1: 100 000 000

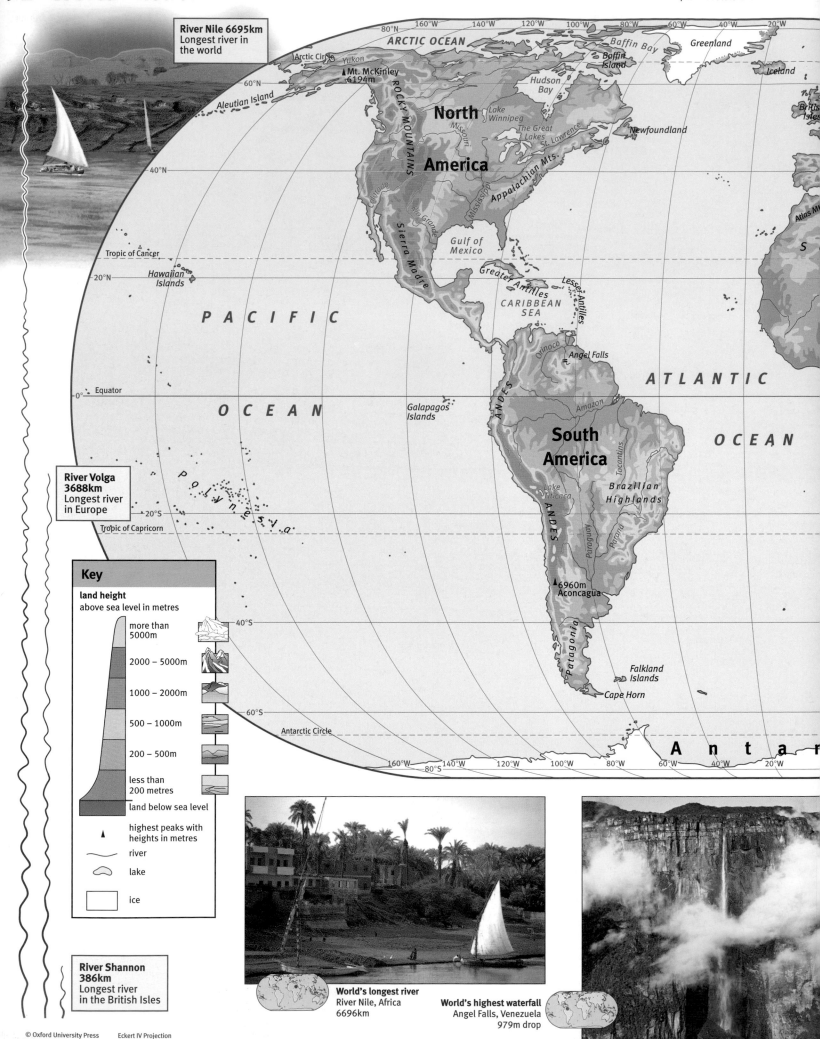

River Nile 6695km
Longest river in
the world

**River Volga
3688km**
Longest river
in Europe

**River Shannon
386km**
Longest river
in the British Isles

ARCTIC OCEAN

Arctic Circle

Yukon

Mt. McKinley
6194m

Aleutian Island

ROCKY MOUNTAINS

**North
America**

Missouri

Lake
Winnipeg

The Great
Lakes

St. Lawrence

Hudson
Bay

Baffin Bay

Baffin
Island

Greenland

Iceland

Newfoundland

British
Isles

Appalachian Mts.

Sierra Madre

Rio Grande

Mississippi

Colorado

Gulf of
Mexico

Greater Antilles

Lesser Antilles

CARIBBEAN
SEA

Atlas Mt

S

Hawaiian
Islands

Tropic of Cancer

20°N

P A C I F I C

Galapagos
Islands

Orinoco

Angel Falls

A T L A N T I C

Equator

O C E A N

O C E A N

P o l y n e s i a

South
America

ANDES

Amazon

Tocantins

Lake
Titicaca

Brazilian
Highlands

Paraguay

Paraná

20°S

Tropic of Capricorn

ANDES

6960m
Aconcagua

Patagonia

Falkland
Islands

Cape Horn

40°S

60°S

Antarctic Circle

A n t a r

Key

land height
above sea level in metres

more than
5000m

2000 – 5000m

1000 – 2000m

500 – 1000m

200 – 500m

less than
200 metres

land below sea level

▲ highest peaks with
heights in metres

river

lake

ice

World's longest river
River Nile, Africa
6696km

World's highest waterfall
Angel Falls, Venezuela
979m drop

© Oxford University Press   Eckert IV Projection

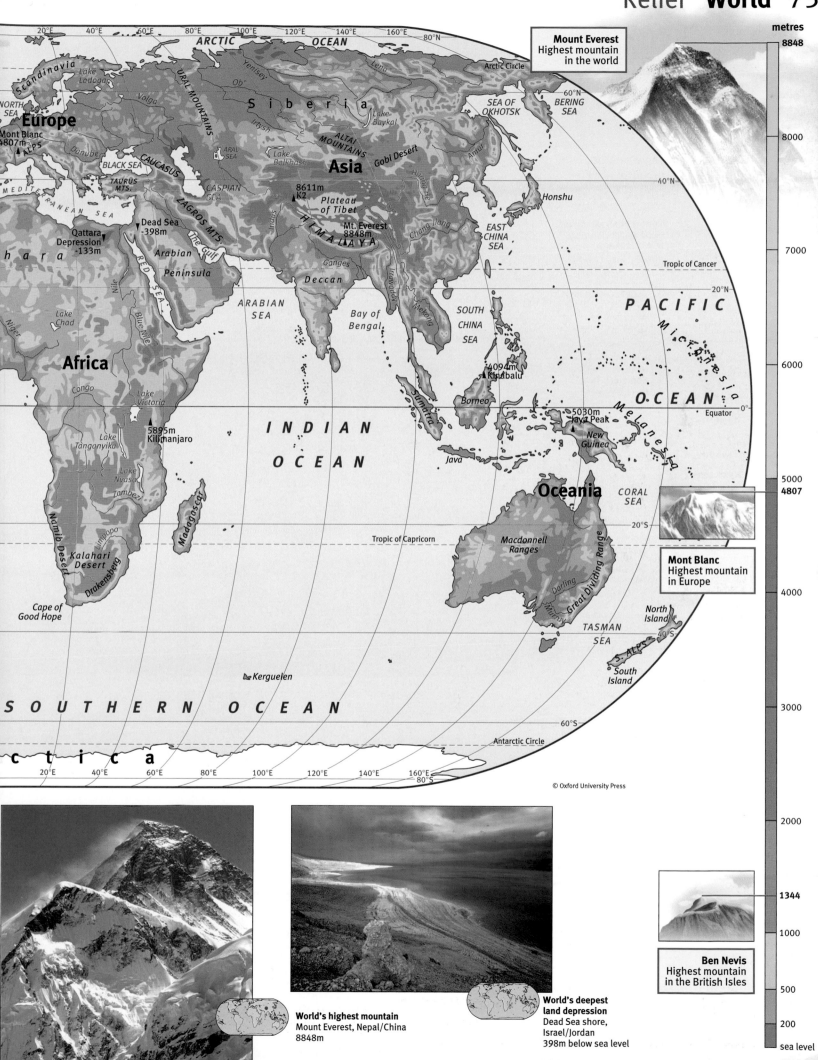

metres

8848

8000

Mount Everest
Highest mountain
in the world

ARCTIC OCEAN

20°E 40°E 60°E 80°E 100°E 120°E 140°E 160°E 80°N

Scandinavia

Lake Ladoga

URAL MOUNTAINS

Ob'

Yenisey

Lena

Arctic Circle

60°N

BERING SEA

SEA OF OKHOTSK

NORTH SEA

Europe

Mont Blanc 4807m

ALPS

Danube

Volga

Irtysh

S i b e r i a

ALTAI MOUNTAINS

Lake Baykal

Amur

40°N

Honshu

BLACK SEA

CAUCASUS

ARAL SEA

Lake Balkhash

Asia

Gobi Desert

Huang He

CASPIAN SEA

8611m K2

TAURUS MTS.

ZAGROS MTS.

Dead Sea -398m

Qattara
Depression
-133m

h a r a

Nile

The Gulf

Arabian
Peninsula

RED SEA

Blue Nile

Indus

Plateau
of Tibet

H I M A L A Y A

Mt. Everest
8848m

Ganges

Chang Jiang

EAST
CHINA
SEA

Tropic of Cancer

20°N

PACIFIC

8000

7000

Africa

Niger

Congo

Lake
Chad

Lake
Victoria

ARABIAN
SEA

Deccan

Irrawaddy

Bay of
Bengal

Mekong

SOUTH
CHINA
SEA

Micronesia

OCEAN

Equator 0°

6000

Lake
Tanganyika

5895m
Kilimanjaro

I N D I A N

O C E A N

Sumatra

Borneo

4094m
Kinabalu

5030m
Java Peak

New
Guinea

Melanesia

Lake
Nyasa

Zambezi

Madagascar

Java

Oceania

CORAL
SEA

20°S

5000

4807

Namib Desert

Kalahari
Desert

Limpopo

Drakensberg

Tropic of Capricorn

Macdonnell
Ranges

Great Dividing Range

Mont Blanc
Highest mountain
in Europe

4000

Cape of
Good Hope

Darling

Murray

North
Island

40°S

TASMAN
SEA

S. ALPS

S O U T H E R N   O C E A N

Kerguelen

South
Island

3000

60°S

c t i c a

Antarctic Circle

20°E 40°E 60°E 80°E 100°E 120°E 140°E 160°E 80°S

© Oxford University Press

2000

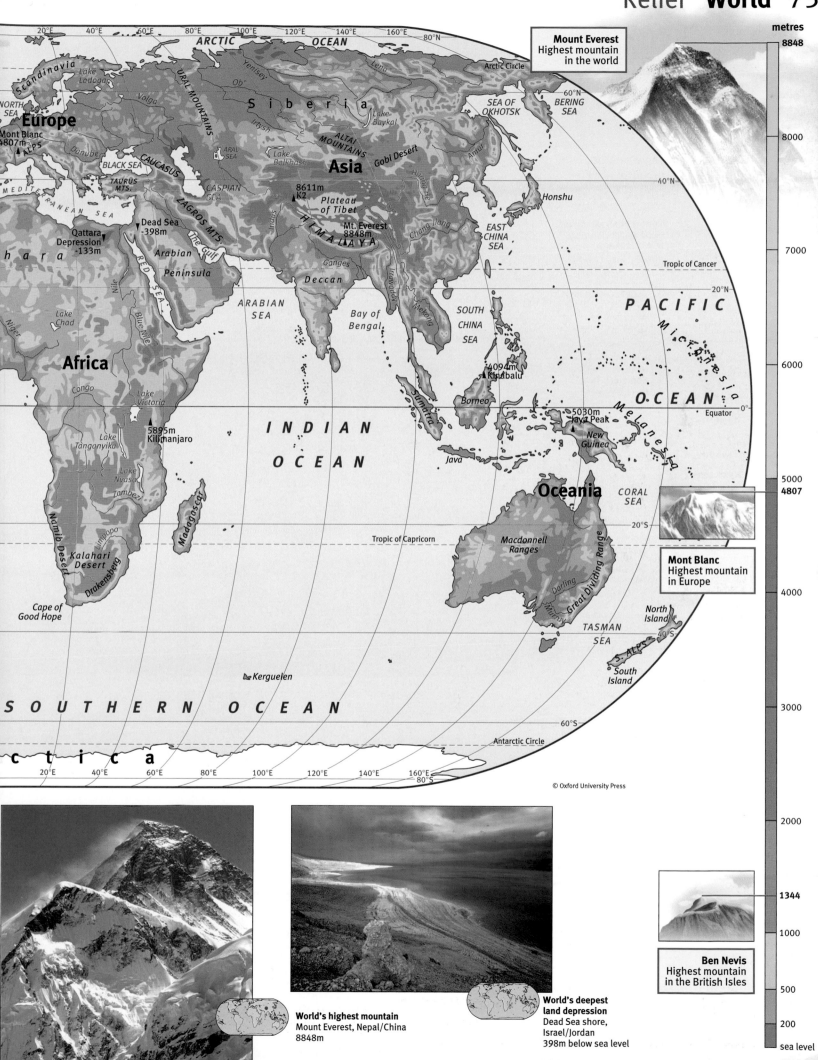

World's highest mountain
Mount Everest, Nepal/China
8848m

**World's deepest
land depression**
Dead Sea shore,
Israel/Jordan
398m below sea level

1344

Ben Nevis
Highest mountain
in the British Isles

1000

500

200

sea level

Equatorial scale 1: 240 000 000

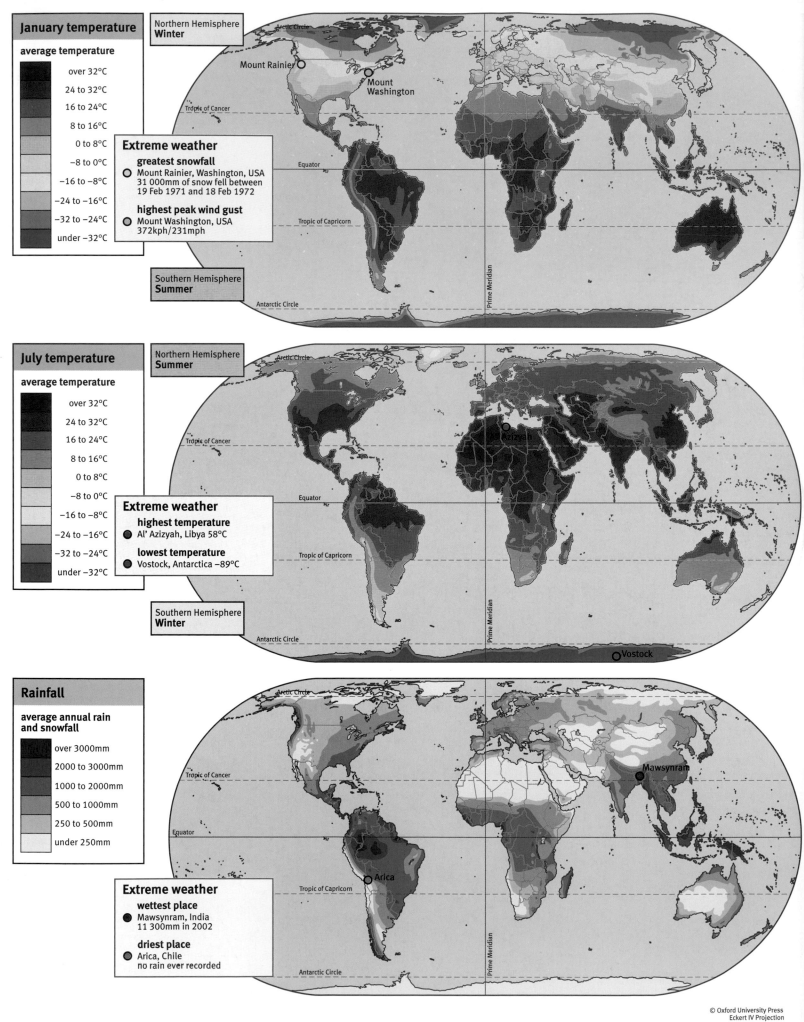

January temperature

average temperature

	over 32°C
	24 to 32°C
	16 to 24°C
	8 to 16°C
	0 to 8°C
	−8 to 0°C
	−16 to −8°C
	−24 to −16°C
	−32 to −24°C
	under −32°C

Northern Hemisphere **Winter**

Extreme weather
greatest snowfall
○ Mount Rainier, Washington, USA
31 000mm of snow fell between
19 Feb 1971 and 18 Feb 1972

highest peak wind gust
○ Mount Washington, USA
372kph/231mph

Southern Hemisphere **Summer**

Mount Rainier
Mount Washington

Arctic Circle
Tropic of Cancer
Equator
Tropic of Capricorn
Antarctic Circle
Prime Meridian

July temperature

average temperature

	over 32°C
	24 to 32°C
	16 to 24°C
	8 to 16°C
	0 to 8°C
	−8 to 0°C
	−16 to −8°C
	−24 to −16°C
	−32 to −24°C
	under −32°C

Northern Hemisphere **Summer**

Extreme weather
highest temperature
● Al' Azizyah, Libya 58°C

lowest temperature
● Vostock, Antarctica −89°C

Southern Hemisphere **Winter**

Al' Azizyah
Vostock

Arctic Circle
Tropic of Cancer
Equator
Tropic of Capricorn
Antarctic Circle
Prime Meridian

Rainfall

average annual rain and snowfall

	over 3000mm
	2000 to 3000mm
	1000 to 2000mm
	500 to 1000mm
	250 to 500mm
	under 250mm

Extreme weather
wettest place
● Mawsynram, India
11 300mm in 2002

driest place
● Arica, Chile
no rain ever recorded

Mawsynram
Arica

Arctic Circle
Tropic of Cancer
Equator
Tropic of Capricorn
Antarctic Circle
Prime Meridian

© Oxford University Press
Eckert IV Projection

Equatorial scale 1: 186 000 000

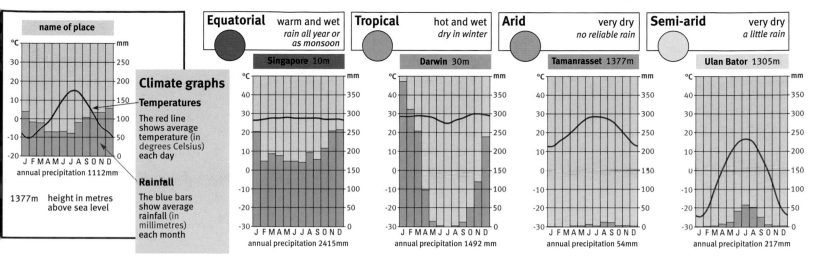

Climate graphs

name of place

°C / mm

annual precipitation 1112mm

1377m height in metres above sea level

Temperatures

The red line shows average temperature (in degrees Celsius) each day

Rainfall

The blue bars show average rainfall (in millimetres) each month

Equatorial	warm and wet *rain all year or as monsoon*
Tropical	hot and wet *dry in winter*
Arid	very dry *no reliable rain*
Semi-arid	very dry *a little rain*

Singapore 10m
annual precipitation 2415mm

Darwin 30m
annual precipitation 1492 mm

Tamanrasset 1377m
annual precipitation 54mm

Ulan Bator 1305m
annual precipitation 217mm

internet World Meteorological Organization
www.wmo.ch

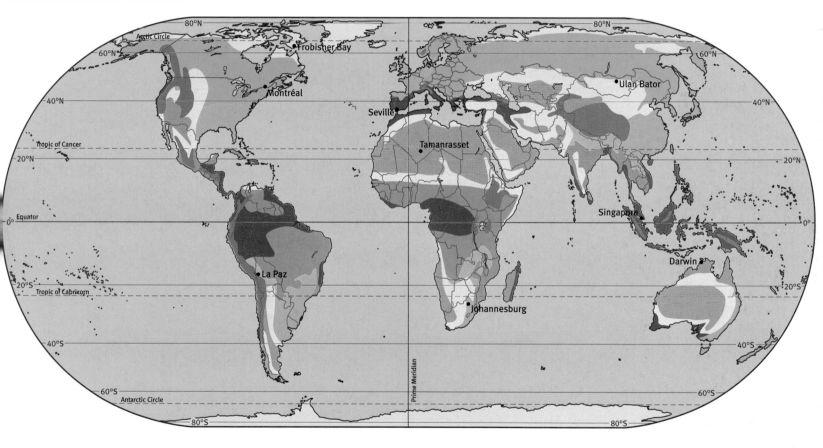

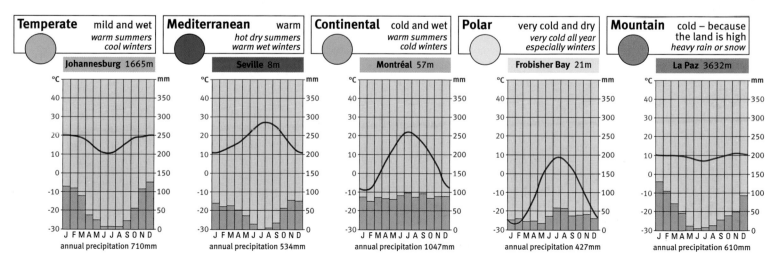

Temperate	mild and wet *warm summers cool winters*
Mediterranean	warm *hot dry summers warm wet winters*
Continental	cold and wet *warm summers cold winters*
Polar	very cold and dry *very cold all year especially winters*
Mountain	cold – because the land is high *heavy rain or snow*

Johannesburg 1665m
annual precipitation 710mm

Seville 8m
annual precipitation 534mm

Montréal 57m
annual precipitation 1047mm

Frobisher Bay 21m
annual precipitation 427mm

La Paz 3632m
annual precipitation 610mm

© Oxford University Press

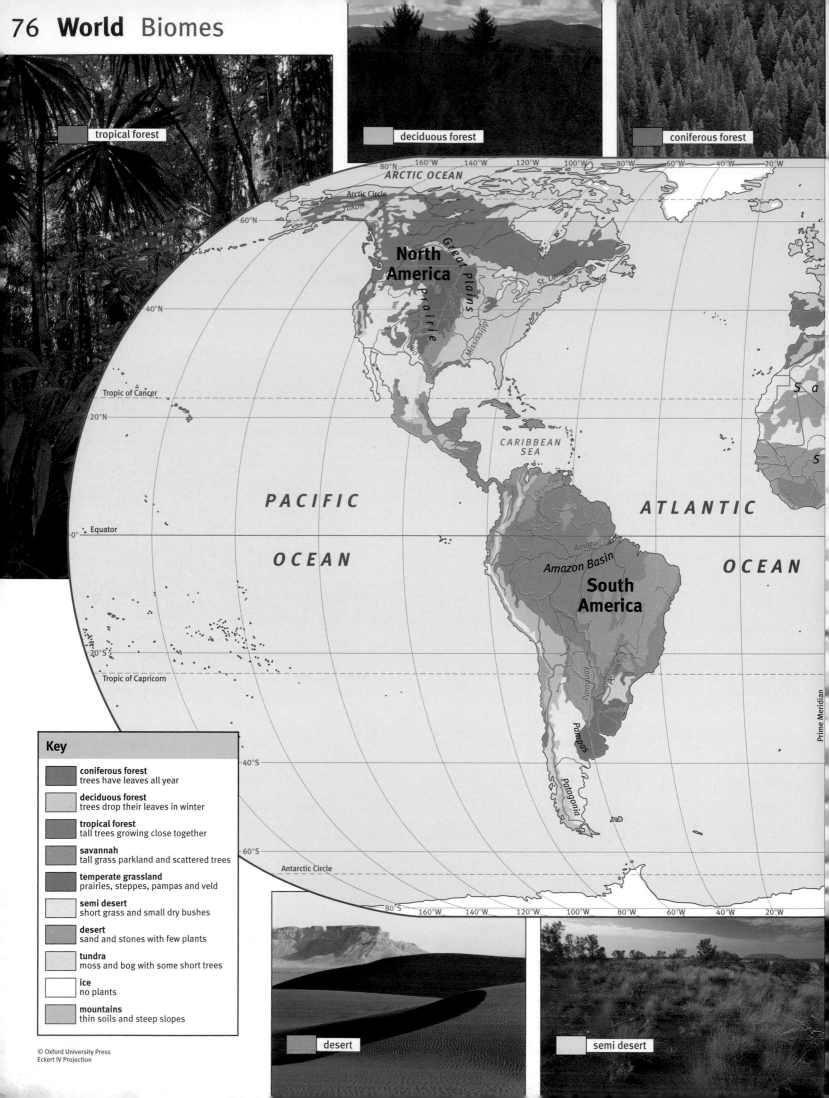

tropical forest

deciduous forest

coniferous forest

ARCTIC OCEAN

Arctic Circle

Yukon

60°N

North
America

Great Plains

prairie

St. Lawrence

40°N

Missouri

Mississippi

Rio Grande

Tropic of Cancer

20°N

CARIBBEAN
SEA

S a

S

PACIFIC

Orinoco

ATLANTIC

Equator

Amazon

OCEAN

Amazon Basin

South
America

OCEAN

20°S

Paraguay

Parana

Tropic of Capricorn

Pampas

Patagonia

Prime Meridian

40°S

60°S

Antarctic Circle

80°S

160°W   140°W   120°W   100°W   80°W   60°W   40°W   20°W

Key

- **coniferous forest**
  trees have leaves all year
- **deciduous forest**
  trees drop their leaves in winter
- **tropical forest**
  tall trees growing close together
- **savannah**
  tall grass parkland and scattered trees
- **temperate grassland**
  prairies, steppes, pampas and veld
- **semi desert**
  short grass and small dry bushes
- **desert**
  sand and stones with few plants
- **tundra**
  moss and bog with some short trees
- **ice**
  no plants
- **mountains**
  thin soils and steep slopes

desert

semi desert

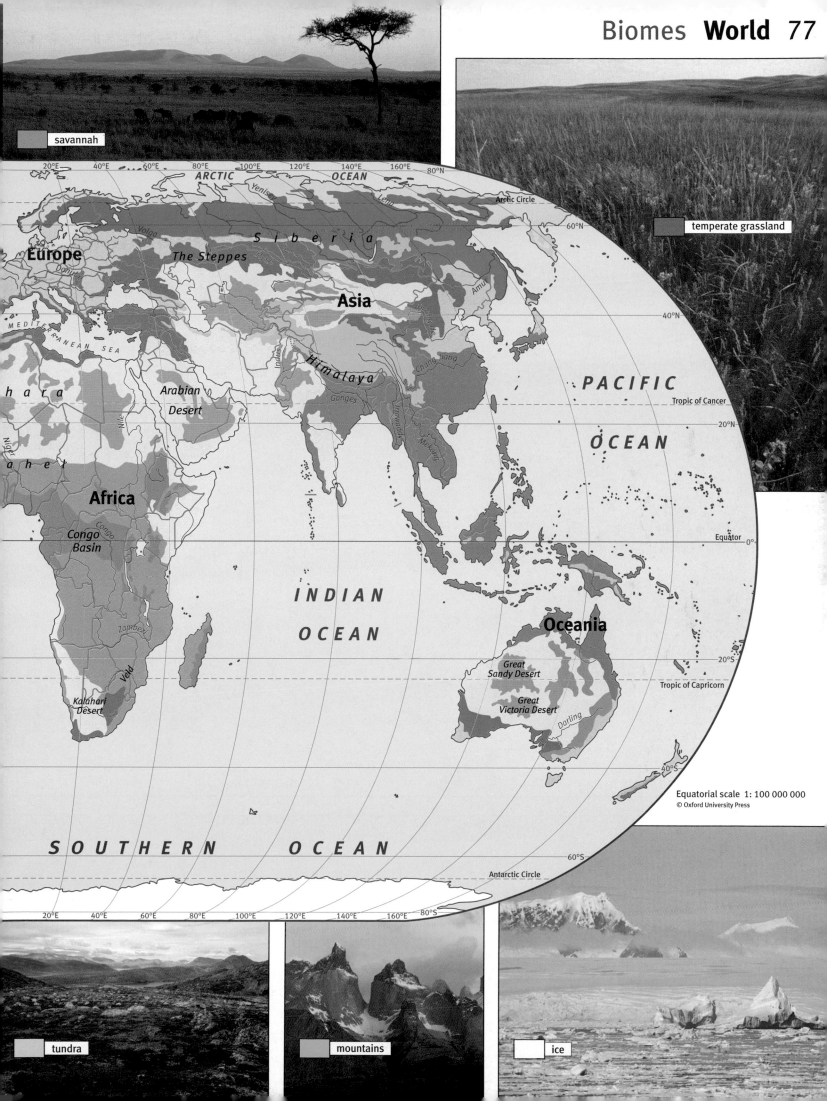

savannah

temperate grassland

ARCTIC   OCEAN

80°N

Arctic Circle

Yenisey

Lena

60°N

Europe

S i b e r i a

Volga

The Steppes

Ob

Asia

Amur

40°N

MEDITE
RRANEAN SEA

Danube

h a r a

Nile

Arabian
Desert

Indus

Himalaya

Ganges

Chang Jiang

Huang He

PACIFIC

Tropic of Cancer

a h e t

Niger

Irrawaddy

Mekong

20°N

OCEAN

Africa

Congo
Basin

Congo

Equator   0°

INDIAN

Oceania

OCEAN

Zambezi

Great
Sandy Desert

20°S

Veld

Great
Victoria Desert

Tropic of Capricorn

Kalahari
Desert

Darling

40°S

Equatorial scale 1: 100 000 000
© Oxford University Press

S O U T H E R N   O C E A N

60°S

Antarctic Circle

20°E   40°E   60°E   80°E   100°E   120°E   140°E   160°E   80°S

tundra

mountains

ice

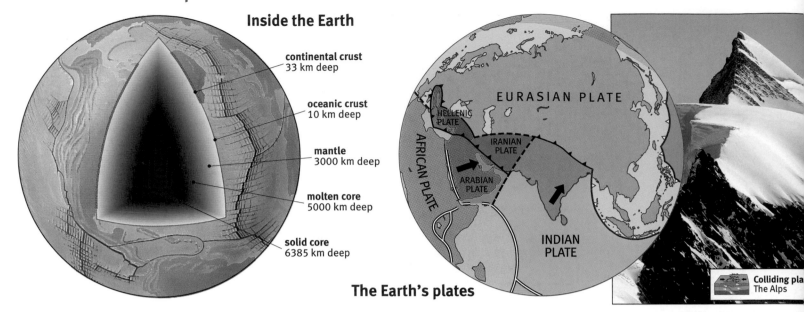

Inside the Earth

continental crust
33 km deep

oceanic crust
10 km deep

mantle
3000 km deep

molten core
5000 km deep

solid core
6385 km deep

Colliding pla
The Alps

The Earth's plates

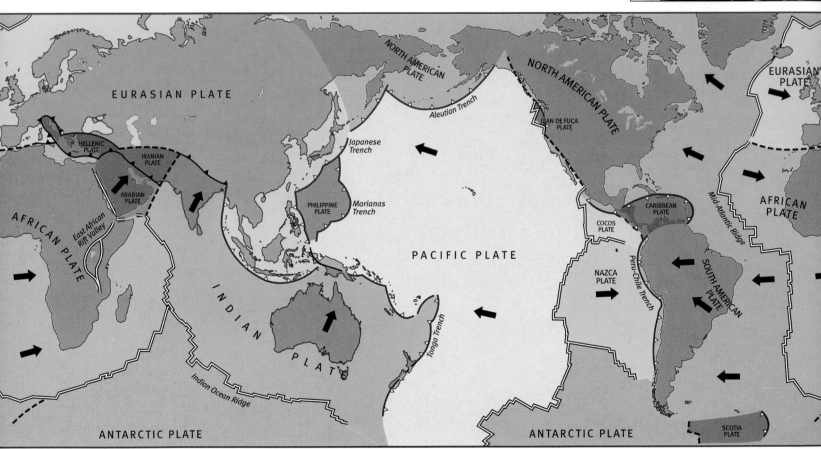

EURASIAN PLATE

NORTH AMERICAN PLATE

Aleutian Trench

Japanese Trench

Marianas Trench

HELLENIC PLATE

IRANIAN PLATE

ARABIAN PLATE

East African Rift Valley

AFRICAN PLATE

INDIAN PLATE

PHILIPPINE PLATE

PACIFIC PLATE

Tonga Trench

Indian Ocean Ridge

ANTARCTIC PLATE

JUAN DE FUCA PLATE

Mid-Atlantic Ridge

EURASIAN PLATE

AFRICAN PLATE

CARIBBEAN PLATE

COCOS PLATE

NAZCA PLATE

Peru-Chile Trench

SOUTH AMERICAN PLATE

ANTARCTIC PLATE

SCOTIA PLATE

The Earth's plates

plate boundaries

diverging plates	Ocean plates move apart. Magma rises to form new crust. Mid-ocean ridges are formed.	

colliding plates	Continental plates meet head-on. Land is folded upwards to make high mountains.	

subducting plates	An ocean plate collides with a continental plate. The ocean plate is forced down into the mantle. Volcanoes erupt along the boundary.	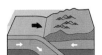

sliding plates	Plates slide past each other. Earthquakes occur where they rub together.	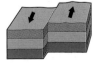

← direction of plate movement

Sliding plates
San Andreas Fault

Diverging plates
Surtsey, Iceland

Deadliest earthquakes
force measured on the Richter scale

Year	Place	Force	Deaths
1993	Maharashtra, India	6.3	9800
1994	Cauca, Colombia	6.8	1000
1995	Kobe, Japan	7.2	5500
1995	Sakhalin, Russia	7.6	2000
1997	Ardabil, Iran	unknown	>1000
1997	Khorash, Iran	7.1	>1600
1998	Takhar, Afghanistan	6.1	>3800
1998	NE Afghanistan	7.1	>3000
1999	Western Colombia	6.0	1124
1999	Izmit, Turkey	7.4	>17 000
1999	Central Taiwan	7.6	2295
1999	Ducze, Turkey	7.2	>700
2001	Gujarat, India	6.9	>20 000
2002	Baghlan, Afghanistan	6.0	>2000
2003	Northern Algeria	6.8	2266
2003	Bam, SE Iran	6.6	31 000
2004	Sumatra, Indonesia	9.0	283 106
2005	Kashmir, Pakistan	7.6	80 361

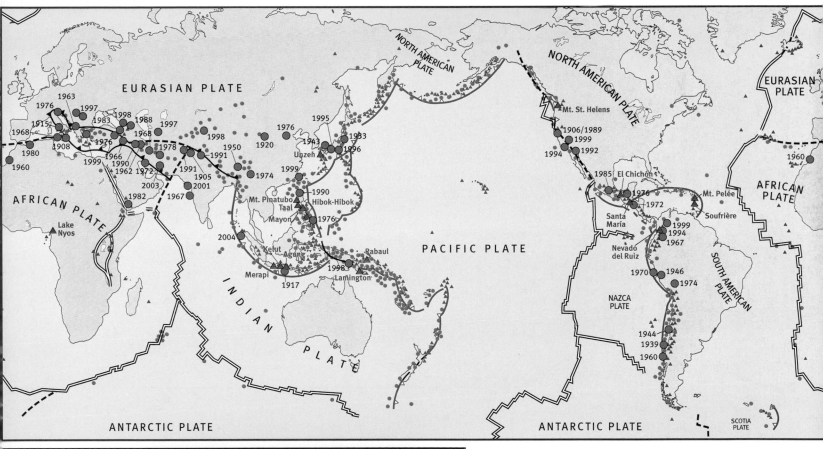

Subducting plates
Costa Rica

Major volcanic eruptions

Year	Volcano	Location
1980	Mt. St. Helens	USA
1982	El Chichón	Mexico
1984	Krafla	Iceland
1985	Nevada del Ruiz	Colombia
1989	Redoubt	USA
1991	Unzen	Japan
1991	Pinatubo	Luzon, Philippines
1991	Cerro Hudson	Chile
1992	Spurr	Alaska, USA
1993	Galeras	Colombia
1994	Rabaul	Papua New Guinea
1995	Fogo	Cape Verde Islands
1996	Manam	Papua New Guinea
1997	Soufrière Hills	Montserrat
2001	Mt. Etna	Italy
2002	Nyiragongo	Congo, Dem Rep.

Earthquakes and volcanoes

earthquakes since 1900

●   catastrophic earthquakes

•   magnitude greater than 7 on the Richter scale

volcanic eruptions since 1900

▲   major eruptions

▴   active volcanoes

 USGS Earthquake Hazards Program
http://neic.usgs.gov/

 USGS Volcano Hazards Program
http://volcanoes.usgs.gov/

© Oxford University Press

Equatorial scale 1: 105 000 000

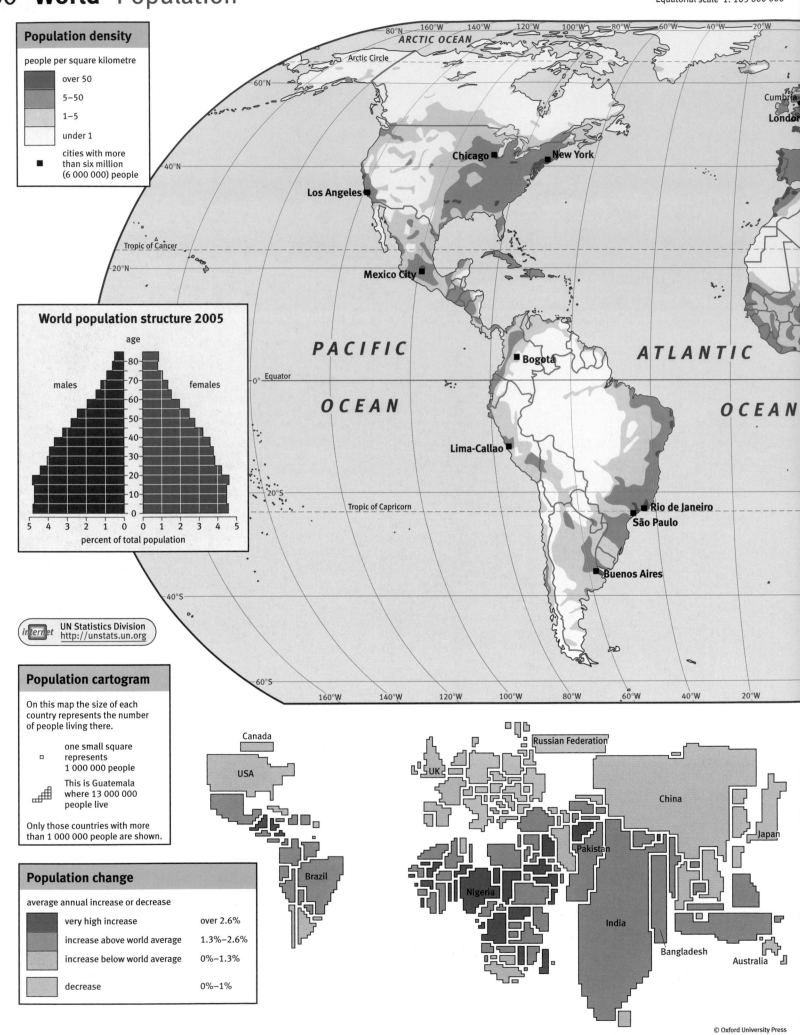

Population density

people per square kilometre

- over 50
- 5–50
- 1–5
- under 1
- ■ cities with more than six million (6 000 000) people

World population structure 2005

age

males | females

percent of total population

ARCTIC OCEAN

Arctic Circle

Cumbria
London

Chicago · New York

Los Angeles

Tropic of Cancer

Mexico City

PACIFIC

OCEAN

Bogotá

ATLANTIC

Equator

Lima-Callao

OCEAN

Tropic of Capricorn

Rio de Janeiro
São Paulo

Buenos Aires

UN Statistics Division
http://unstats.un.org

Population cartogram

On this map the size of each country represents the number of people living there.

- □ one small square represents 1 000 000 people
- This is Guatemala where 13 000 000 people live

Only those countries with more than 1 000 000 people are shown.

Canada

USA

Russian Federation

UK

China

Japan

Pakistan

Brazil

Nigeria

India

Bangladesh

Australia

Population change

average annual increase or decrease

very high increase	over 2.6%
increase above world average	1.3%–2.6%
increase below world average	0%–1.3%
decrease	0%–1%

© Oxford University Press
Eckert IV Projection

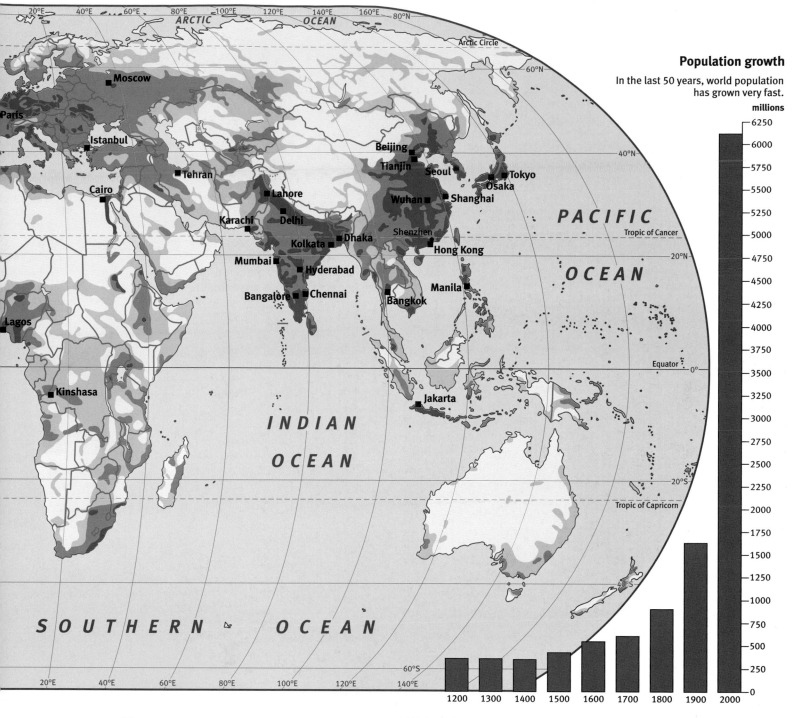

Population growth

In the last 50 years, world population has grown very fast.

millions

	6250
	6000
	5750
	5500
	5250
	5000
	4750
	4500
	4250
	4000
	3750
	3500
	3250
	3000
	2750
	2500
	2250
	2000
	1750
	1500
	1250
	1000
	750
	500
	250
	0

1200 1300 1400 1500 1600 1700 1800 1900 2000

over 50 people per square kilometre

under 1 person per square kilometre

In 2005 the total world population was approximately 6 485 000 000.

Natural population increase 2005

☺ represents 10 million births

☹ represents 10 million deaths

In 2005
130 013 274   people were born
☺☺☺☺☺☺☺
☺☺☺☺☺☺

and
56 130 242   people died
☹☹☹☹☹☹

so
73 883 032   people were added to the world's population
☺☺☺☺☺☺☺

Equatorial scale 1: 288 000 000

GDP 2004

GDP per person, adjusted for the local cost of living, in US dollars

- over 10 000
- 2000–10 000
- under 2000
- no data

GDP (Gross Domestic Product) is the value of all the goods and services produced in a country in one year.

Richest: Luxembourg	$69 207
United Kingdom	$36 039
Poorest: Sierra Leone	$90

Luxembourg

Sierra Leone

Equator

Many people in rich countries are poor. Some people in poor countries are rich.

internet The World Bank www.worldbank.org

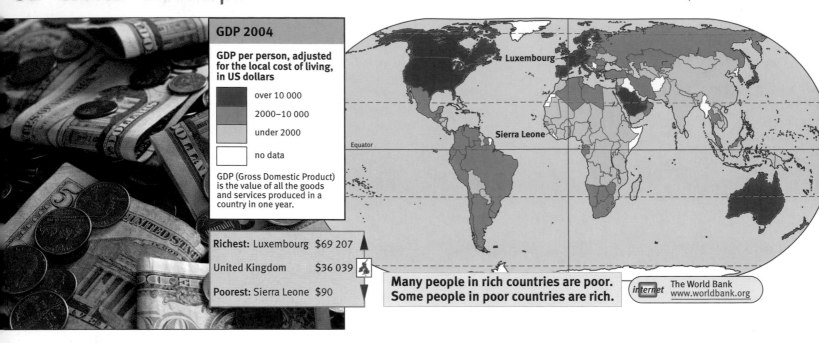

Adult literacy 2003

percentage of people aged 15 and over who can read and write

- over 90%
- 60–90%
- under 60%
- no data

Highest:	Georgia	100%
	United Kingdom	99%
Lowest:	Burkina	13%

Georgia

Burkina

Equator

One fifth of the world's adult population do not have basic literacy skills.

internet UNESCO Institute for Statistics www.uis.unesco.org

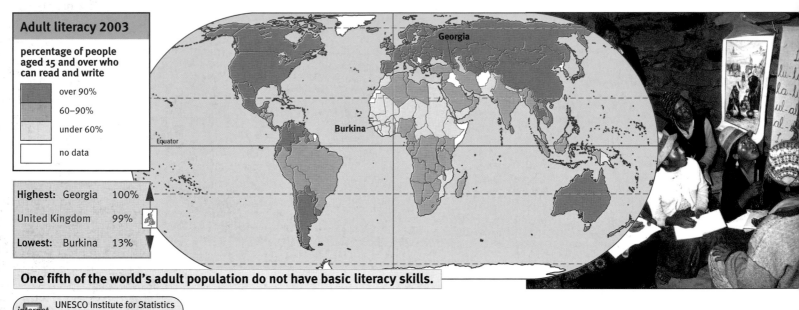

Life expectancy 2003

average number of years a baby can expect to live

- over 75 years
- 55–75 years
- under 55 years
- no data

Highest:	Japan	82 years
	United Kingdom	78 years
Lowest:	Swaziland	33 years

Japan

Equator

Swaziland

People in richer countries live longer than those in poorer countries.

internet UN Statistics Division http://unstats.un.org

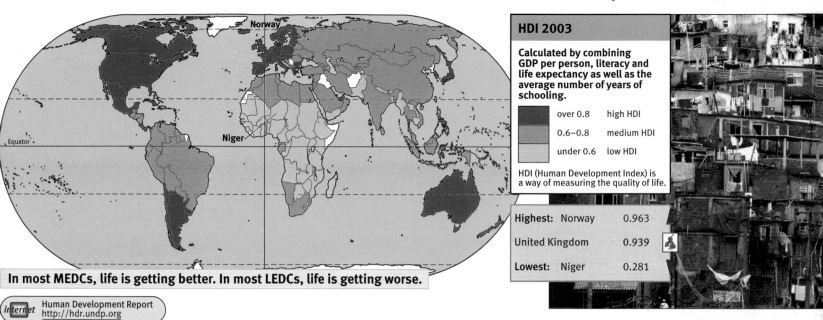

HDI 2003

Calculated by combining GDP per person, literacy and life expectancy as well as the average number of years of schooling.

■	over 0.8	high HDI
■	0.6–0.8	medium HDI
□	under 0.6	low HDI

HDI (Human Development Index) is a way of measuring the quality of life.

Highest:	Norway	0.963
	United Kingdom	0.939
Lowest:	Niger	0.281

In most MEDCs, life is getting better. In most LEDCs, life is getting worse.

internet Human Development Report
http://hdr.undp.org

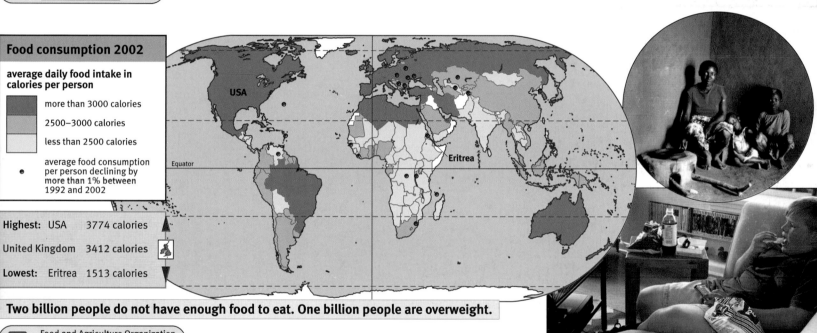

Food consumption 2002

average daily food intake in calories per person

■	more than 3000 calories
■	2500–3000 calories
□	less than 2500 calories
•	average food consumption per person declining by more than 1% between 1992 and 2002

Highest:	USA	3774 calories
	United Kingdom	3412 calories
Lowest:	Eritrea	1513 calories

Two billion people do not have enough food to eat. One billion people are overweight.

internet Food and Agriculture Organization
http://faostat.fao.org

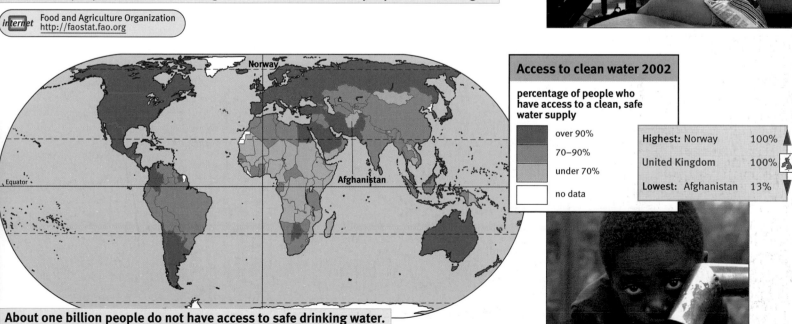

Access to clean water 2002

percentage of people who have access to a clean, safe water supply

■	over 90%
■	70–90%
■	under 70%
□	no data

Highest:	Norway	100%
	United Kingdom	100%
Lowest:	Afghanistan	13%

About one billion people do not have access to safe drinking water.

internet UN Statistics Division
http://millenniumindicators.un.org

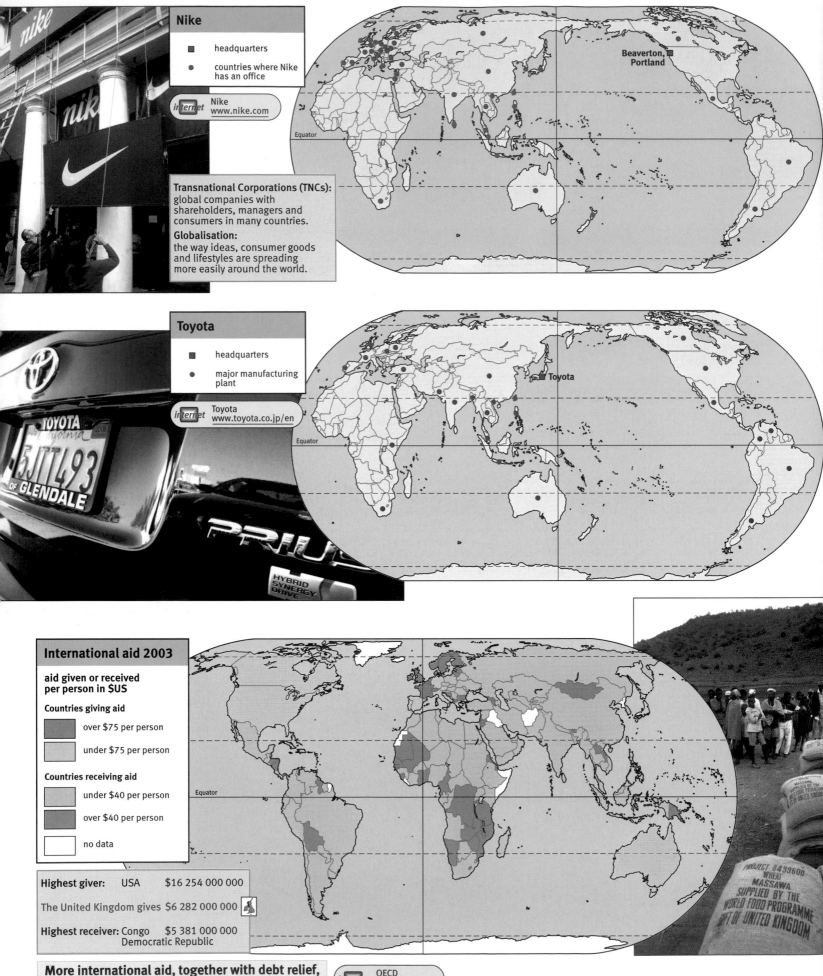

Nike

- ■ headquarters
- ● countries where Nike has an office

internet Nike www.nike.com

Transnational Corporations (TNCs):
global companies with shareholders, managers and consumers in many countries.

Globalisation:
the way ideas, consumer goods and lifestyles are spreading more easily around the world.

Equator

Beaverton, Portland

Toyota

- ■ headquarters
- ● major manufacturing plant

internet Toyota www.toyota.co.jp/en

Equator

Toyota

International aid 2003

aid given or received per person in $US

Countries giving aid

- over $75 per person
- under $75 per person

Countries receiving aid

- under $40 per person
- over $40 per person
- no data

Equator

Highest giver: USA $16 254 000 000

The United Kingdom gives $6 282 000 000

Highest receiver: Congo $5 381 000 000 Democratic Republic

More international aid, together with debt relief, would make poverty history.

internet OECD www.oecd.org

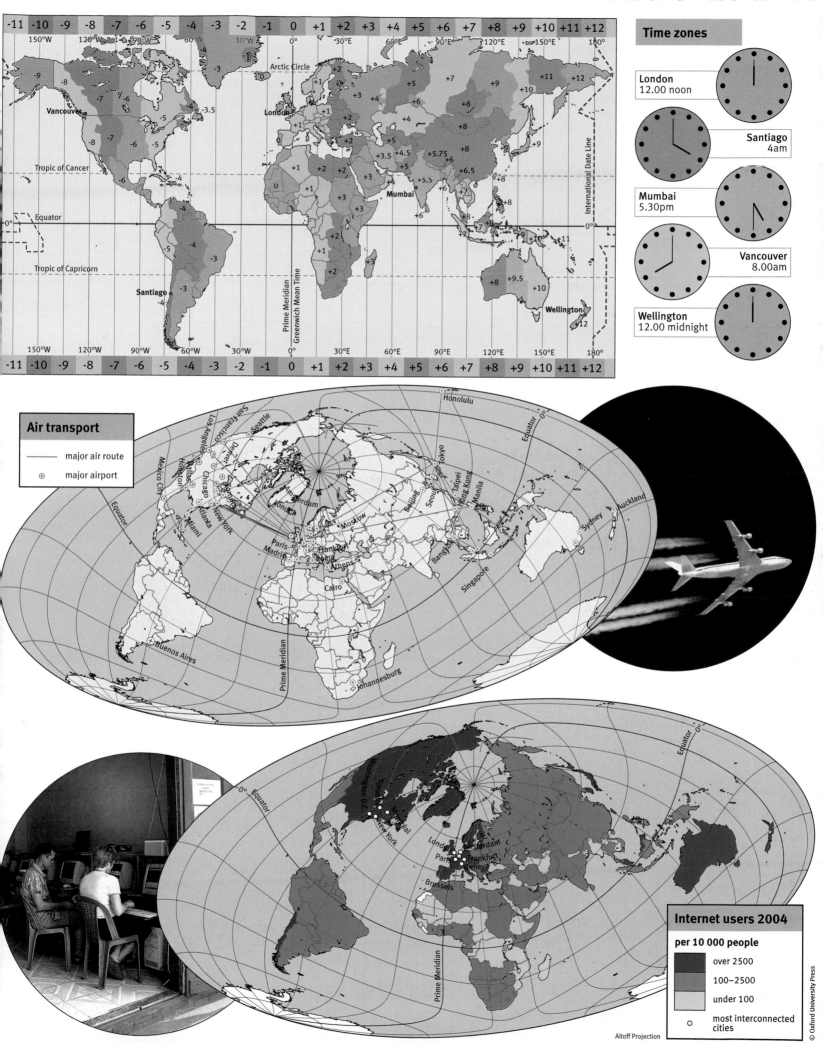

Time zones

| -11 | -10 | -9 | -8 | -7 | -6 | -5 | -4 | -3 | -2 | -1 | 0 | +1 | +2 | +3 | +4 | +5 | +6 | +7 | +8 | +9 | +10 | +11 | +12 |

150°W · 120°W · 90°W · 60°W · 30°W · 0° · 30°E · 60°E · 90°E · 120°E · 150°E · 180°

Arctic Circle
Tropic of Cancer
Equator
Tropic of Capricorn

Vancouver
London
Mumbai
Santiago
Wellington

International Date Line
Prime Meridian
Greenwich Mean Time

London 12.00 noon

Santiago 4am

Mumbai 5.30pm

Vancouver 8.00am

Wellington 12.00 midnight

Air transport

— major air route

⊕ major airport

Honolulu · San Francisco · Seattle · Los Angeles · Denver · Houston · Mexico City · Chicago · Dallas · Atlanta · New York · Miami · Amsterdam · London · Paris · Madrid · Frankfurt · Rome · Athens · Moscow · Beijing · Seoul · Tokyo · Taipei · Hong Kong · Manila · Bangkok · Singapore · Sydney · Auckland · Cairo · Buenos Aires · Johannesburg

Equator · Prime Meridian

Internet users 2004

per 10 000 people

- over 2500
- 100–2500
- under 100
- ○ most interconnected cities

Washington D.C. · Toronto · Montreal · New York · London · Amsterdam · Paris · Frankfurt · Geneva · Brussels

Equator · Prime Meridian

Aitoff Projection

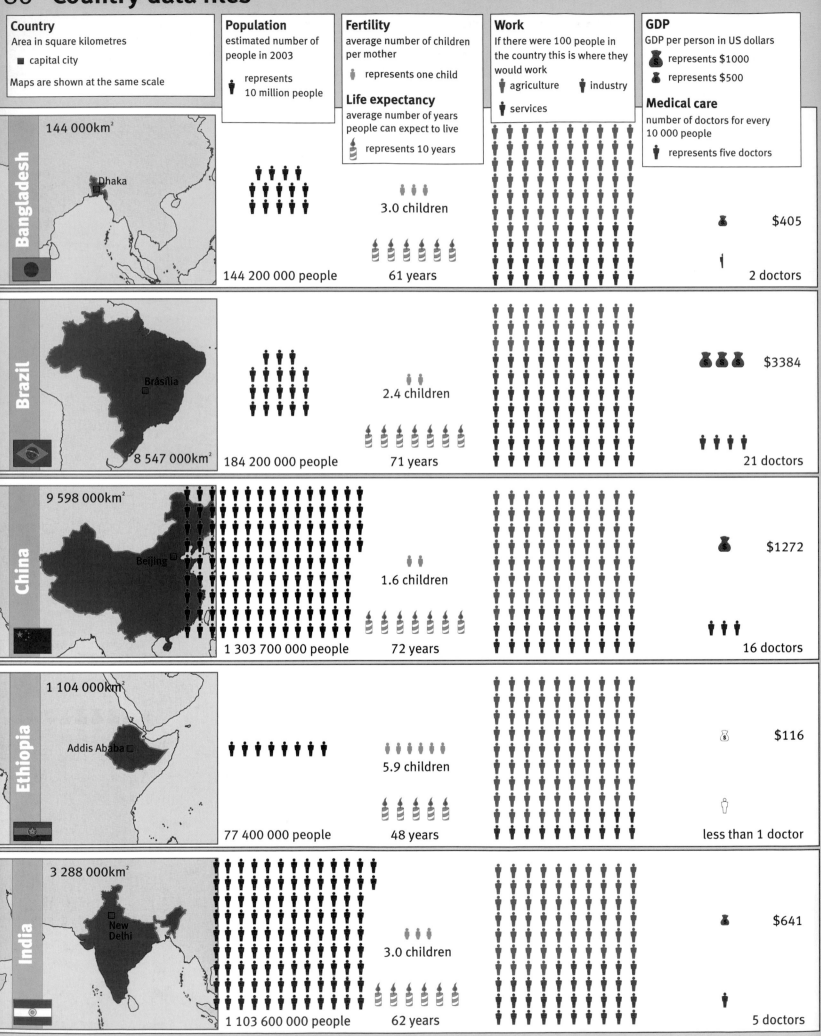

Country
Area in square kilometres

■ capital city

Maps are shown at the same scale

Population
estimated number of people in 2003

👤 represents 10 million people

Fertility
average number of children per mother

👤 represents one child

Life expectancy
average number of years people can expect to live

🕯 represents 10 years

Work
If there were 100 people in the country this is where they would work

👤 agriculture   👤 industry

👤 services

GDP
GDP per person in US dollars

💰 represents $1000

💰 represents $500

Medical care
number of doctors for every 10 000 people

👤 represents five doctors

Bangladesh
144 000km²
Dhaka

144 200 000 people

3.0 children

61 years

$405

2 doctors

Brazil
Brasília
8 547 000km²

184 200 000 people

2.4 children

71 years

$3384

21 doctors

China
9 598 000km²
Beijing

1 303 700 000 people

1.6 children

72 years

$1272

16 doctors

Ethiopia
1 104 000km²
Addis Ababa

77 400 000 people

5.9 children

48 years

$116

less than 1 doctor

India
3 288 000km²
New Delhi

1 103 600 000 people

3.0 children

62 years

$641

5 doctors

Country
Area in thousand square kilometres

■ capital city

Maps are shown at the same scale

Population
estimated number of people in 2003

👤 represents 10 million people

Fertility
average number of children per mother

👤 represents one child

Life expectancy
average number of years people can expect to live

🕯 represents 10 years

Work
If there were 100 people in the country this is where they would work

👤 agriculture   👤 industry

👤 services

GDP
GDP per person in US dollars

💰 represents $1000

💰 represents $500

Medical care
number of doctors for every 10 000 people

👤 represents five doctors

Italy
301 000 km²   ■ Rome

58 700 000 people

1.3 children

80 years

$29 047

61 doctors

Japan
378 000 km²   ■ Tokyo

1 27 700 000 people

1.3 children

82 years

$36 187

20 doctors

Kenya
580 000 km²   ■ Nairobi

33 800 000 people

4.9 children

47 years

$480

1 doctor

United Kingdom
245 000 km²   ■ London

60 100 000 people

1.7 children

78 years

$36 039

17 doctors

USA
9 629 000 km²   ■ Washington D.C.

296 500 000 people

2.0 children

78 years

$39 752

55 doctors

ooo no data

Country	Land	Population						2005	Employment			Quality of life		2004
	Area thousand km²	Total millions	Births per 1000 people	Deaths per 1000 people	Life expectancy years	Population change 1995–2005 per cent	Urban per cent		Primary per cent	Secondary per cent	Tertiary per cent	GDP ($US) per capita explanation: see p82	Health Doctors per 10 000 people	HDI explanation see p83
Afghanistan	652	29.9	48	22	42	43.3	22		ooo	ooo	ooo	ooo	ooo	ooo
Albania	29	3.2	15	6	74	4.8	42		55	23	22	2381	14	0.780
Algeria	2382	32.8	20	4	73	15.8	49		26	31	43	2615	9	0.722
Andorra	0.5	0.1	10	3	ooo	9.8	92		ooo	ooo	ooo	ooo	ooo	ooo
Angola	1247	15.4	49	24	40	25.5	33		75	8	17	1440	1	0.545
Antigua and Barbuda	0.4	0.1	20	6	71	8.0	37		ooo	ooo	ooo	10 038	2	0.797
Argentina	2780	38.6	18	8	74	12.0	89		12	32	56	3963	30	0.863
Armenia	30	3.0	12	9	71	-2.8	65		18	43	39	1164	35	0.759
Australia	7741	20.4	13	7	80	10.9	91		6	26	68	31 375	25	0.955
Austria	84	8.2	10	9	79	1.7	54		8	38	54	35 750	32	0.936
Azerbaijan	87	8.4	16	6	72	3.7	51		31	29	40	1029	35	0.729
Bahamas, The	14	0.3	17	6	70	9.6	89		5	16	79	16 438	11	0.832
Bahrain	0.7	0.7	21	3	74	20.2	87		2	30	68	13 251	16	0.846
Bangladesh	144	144.2	27	8	61	21.1	23		65	16	19	405	2	0.520
Barbados	0.4	0.3	15	8	72	4.1	50		14	30	56	9658	12	0.878
Belarus	208	9.8	9	15	69	-1.0	72		20	40	40	2324	45	0.786
Belgium	33	10.5	11	10	79	2.1	97		3	28	69	33 621	42	0.945
Belize	23	0.3	27	5	70	29.5	49		33	19	48	3866	11	0.753
Benin	113	8.4	42	13	54	34.2	40		63	8	29	591	1	0.431
Bhutan	47	1.0	34	9	63	24.5	21		94	2	4	751	1	0.536
Bolivia	1099	8.9	29	8	64	20.1	63		47	18	35	976	7	0.687
Bosnia-Herzegovina	51	3.8	9	8	74	19.5	43		ooo	ooo	ooo	2117	13	0.786
Botswana	582	1.6	25	28	35	11.8	54		46	20	34	5014	3	0.565
Brazil	8547	184.2	21	7	71	13.8	81		23	23	54	3384	21	0.792
Brunei	6	0.4	22	3	74	25.2	74		2	24	74	ooo	10	0.866
Bulgaria	111	7.7	9	14	72	-9.8	70		13	48	39	3102	34	0.808
Burkina	274	13.9	44	19	44	38.1	17		92	2	6	389	<1	0.317
Burundi	28	7.8	43	15	49	28.3	9		92	3	5	90	1	0.378
Cambodia	181	13.3	31	9	56	20.9	15		74	8	18	337	2	0.571
Cameroon	475	16.4	38	15	48	25.8	48		70	9	21	898	1	0.497
Canada	9971	32.2	10	7	80	10.8	79		3	25	72	30 712	21	0.949
Central African Republic	623	4.2	37	19	44	19.7	41		80	3	17	337	<1	0.355
Chad	1284	9.7	45	17	47	35.9	24		83	4	13	486	<1	0.341
Chile	757	16.1	16	5	76	12.5	87		19	25	56	5898	11	0.854
China	9598	1303.7	12	6	72	7.4	37		72	15	13	1272	16	0.755
Colombia	1139	46.0	22	5	72	18.4	75		27	23	50	2150	14	0.785
Comoros	2	0.7	40	10	60	35.1	33		78	9	13	598	1	0.547
Congo	342	4.0	44	13	52	36.0	52		49	15	36	1137	3	0.512
Congo, Dem. Rep.	2345	60.8	45	14	50	31.1	30		68	13	19	120	1	0.385
Costa Rica	51	4.3	17	4	79	18.7	59		26	27	47	4530	17	0.838
Côte d'Ivoire	322	18.2	39	17	47	23.7	46		60	10	30	892	1	0.420
Croatia	57	4.4	9	12	75	0.0	56		16	34	50	7587	24	0.841
Cuba	111	11.3	11	7	77	4.1	76		19	30	51	ooo	59	0.817
Cyprus	9	1.0	11	7	77	6.4	65		14	30	56	19 869	30	0.891
Czech Republic	79	10.2	10	11	75	-0.8	77		11	45	44	10 512	34	0.874

Country	Land — Area thousand km²	Population — Total millions	Births per 1000	Deaths per 1000	Life expectancy years	Population change 1995–2005 per cent	Urban per cent in 2005	Employment — Primary per cent	Secondary per cent	Tertiary per cent	Quality of life 2004 — GDP ($US) per capita explanation: see p82	Health Doctors per 10 000 people	HDI explanation: see p83
Denmark	43	5.4	12	10	77	3.8	72	6	28	66	45 033	37	0.941
Djibouti	23	0.8	32	13	52	16.4	82	ooo	ooo	ooo	926	1	0.495
Dominica	0.8	0.1	15	7	74	-5.4	71	ooo	ooo	ooo	3789	5	0.783
Dominican Republic	49	8.9	24	7	68	17.1	64	25	29	46	2107	19	0.749
Ecuador	284	13.0	28	6	74	16.8	61	33	19	48	2292	15	0.759
Egypt	1001	74.0	26	6	70	22.4	43	40	22	38	1093	21	0.659
El Salvador	21	6.9	26	6	70	20.4	59	36	21	43	2377	12	0.722
Equatorial Guinea	28	0.5	43	20	45	26.4	45	66	11	23	6393	3	0.655
Eritrea	118	4.7	39	13	58	21.0	19	80	5	15	207	<1	0.444
Estonia	45	1.3	10	13	72	-7.9	69	14	41	45	8036	32	0.853
Ethiopia	1104	77.4	41	16	48	29.0	15	86	2	12	116	<1	0.367
Fiji	18	0.8	21	6	68	15.1	46	46	15	39	3098	34	0.752
Finland	338	5.2	11	9	79	2.3	62	8	31	61	35 781	31	0.941
France	552	60.7	13	8	80	4.3	76	5	29	66	33 381	33	0.938
French Guiana	91	0.2	31	4	75	34.8	75	ooo	ooo	ooo	ooo	ooo	ooo
Gabon	268	1.4	33	12	56	30.5	81	51	16	33	5261	3	0.635
Gambia, The	11	1.6	41	13	53	38.7	26	82	8	10	286	<1	0.470
Georgia	70	4.5	11	11	72	-6.7	52	26	31	43	1126	39	0.732
Germany	357	82.5	9	10	79	1.0	88	4	38	58	32 850	36	0.930
Ghana	239	22.0	33	10	58	24.2	44	59	13	28	409	1	0.520
Greece	132	11.1	9	10	79	2.0	60	23	27	50	18 366	44	0.912
Guatemala	109	12.7	34	6	66	29.7	39	52	17	31	2174	9	0.663
Guinea	246	9.5	43	16	49	23.0	33	87	2	11	434	1	0.466
Guinea-Bissau	36	1.6	50	20	44	23.7	32	85	2	13	183	2	0.348
Guyana	215	0.8	22	9	63	2.3	36	22	25	53	1018	5	0.720
Haiti	28	8.3	33	14	52	21.7	36	68	9	23	411	3	0.475
Honduras	112	7.2	33	5	71	29.2	47	41	20	39	1032	8	0.667
Hungary	93	10.1	9	13	73	-2.8	65	15	38	47	9900	32	0.862
Iceland	103	0.3	15	6	81	10.9	94	ooo	ooo	ooo	42 690	35	0.956
India	3288	1103.6	25	8	62	17.2	28	64	16	20	641	5	0.602
Indonesia	1905	221.9	22	6	68	17.7	42	55	14	31	1184	2	0.697
Iran	1633	69.5	18	6	70	10.4	67	39	23	38	2431	11	0.736
Iraq	438	28.8	37	10	59	33.3	68	16	18	66	ooo	ooo	ooo
Ireland	70	4.1	16	7	78	11.1	60	14	29	57	45 673	24	0.946
Israel	21	7.1	21	6	80	18.3	92	4	29	67	17 292	39	0.915
Italy	301	58.7	9	10	80	1.4	90	9	31	60	29 047	61	0.934
Jamaica	11	2.7	19	6	73	10.8	52	25	23	52	3013	9	0.738
Japan	378	127.7	9	8	82	1.7	79	7	34	59	36 187	20	0.943
Jordan	89	5.8	29	5	72	37.1	79	15	23	62	2058	21	0.753
Kazakhstan	2717	15.1	17	11	66	-4.4	57	22	32	46	2724	33	0.761
Kenya	580	33.8	38	15	47	25.0	36	80	7	13	480	1	0.474
Kiribati	0.7	0.1	26	8	63	26.6	43	ooo	ooo	ooo	ooo	ooo	ooo
Kuwait	18	2.6	19	2	78	44.1	96	1	25	74	16 971	15	0.844
Kyrgyzstan	199	5.2	21	8	68	13.5	35	32	27	41	432	27	0.702
Laos	237	5.9	36	13	54	28.3	19	78	6	16	416	6	0.545

Country	Land	Population					2005	Employment			Quality of life		2004
	Area thousand km²	Total millions	Births per 1000 people	Deaths per 1000 people	Life expectancy years	Population change 1995–2005 per cent	Urban per cent	Primary per cent	Secondary per cent	Tertiary per cent	GDP ($US) per capita explanation: see p82	Health Doctors per 10 000 people	HDI explanation: see p83
Latvia	65	2.3	9	14	72	-7.9	68	16	40	44	5918	29	0.836
Lebanon	10	3.8	22	6	74	14.7	87	7	31	62	4780	33	0.759
Lesotho	30	1.8	26	28	35	5.8	13	40	28	32	760	1	0.497
Liberia	111	3.3	50	22	42	46.9	45	ooo	ooo	ooo	ooo	ooo	ooo
Libya	1760	5.8	27	4	76	23.9	86	11	23	66	5132	13	0.799
Lithuania	65	3.4	9	12	72	-2.1	67	18	41	41	6474	40	0.852
Luxembourg	3	0.5	12	8	78	14.4	91	ooo	ooo	ooo	69 207	26	0.949
Macedonia, FYRO	26	2.0	13	9	73	4.7	59	21	40	39	2544	ooo	0.797
Madagascar	587	17.3	40	129	55	35.2	26	78	7	15	252	1	0.499
Malawi	118	12.3	50	19	45	28.2	14	87	5	8	162	‹1	0.404
Malaysia	330	26.1	26	5	73	22.1	62	27	23	50	4672	7	0.796
Mali	1240	13.5	50	18	48	27.3	30	86	2	12	407	‹1	0.333
Malta	0.3	0.4	10	8	78	5.7	91	ooo	ooo	ooo	13 439	29	0.867
Mauritania	1026	3.1	42	15	52	31.8	40	55	10	35	467	1	0.477
Mauritius	2	1.2	16	7	72	9.0	42	17	43	40	4908	9	0.791
Mexico	1958	107.0	23	5	75	14.3	75	28	24	48	6518	17	0.814
Moldova	34	4.2	10	12	68	-0.1	45	33	30	37	615	27	0.671
Mongolia	1567	2.6	23	7	64	15.3	57	32	22	46	606	27	0.679
Montenegro	14	0.7	13	9	ooo	ooo	ooo	ooo	ooo	ooo	ooo	ooo	ooo
Morocco	447	30.7	21	6	70	19.2	57	45	25	30	1637	5	0.631
Mozambique	802	19.4	42	20	42	23.6	32	83	8	9	290	‹1	0.379
Myanmar	677	50.5	22	10	60	11.4	29	73	10	17	ooo	3	0.578
Namibia	824	2.0	27	17	46	20.4	33	49	15	36	2684	3	0.627
Nepal	147	25.4	31	9	62	26.3	14	94	0	6	266	1	0.526
Netherlands	41	16.3	12	8	79	6.1	62	5	26	69	35 524	33	0.943
New Zealand	271	4.1	14	7	79	13.2	86	10	25	65	24 547	22	0.933
Nicaragua	130	5.8	32	5	69	24.7	59	28	26	46	777	16	0.690
Niger	1267	14.0	56	22	43	33.1	21	90	4	6	255	‹1	0.281
Nigeria	924	131.5	43	19	44	27.5	44	43	7	50	516	3	0.453
North Korea	121	22.9	16	7	71	6.3	60	38	32	30	14 118	ooo	ooo
Norway	324	4.6	12	9	80	5.4	78	6	25	69	54 598	36	0.963
Oman	213	2.4	22	4	74	40.9	76	44	24	32	8160	13	0.781
Pakistan	796	162.4	34	10	62	26.2	34	52	19	29	632	7	0.527
Panama	76	3.2	23	5	75	19.4	62	26	16	58	4555	17	0.804
Papua New Guinea	463	5.9	32	11	55	27.6	13	79	7	14	695	1	0.523
Paraguay	407	6.2	22	5	71	30.1	54	39	22	39	1233	12	0.755
Peru	1285	27.9	22	6	70	17.1	73	36	18	46	2483	12	0.762
Philippines	300	84.8	28	5	70	22.5	48	46	15	39	1042	12	0.758
Poland	323	38.2	9	10	75	-0.1	62	27	36	37	6337	22	0.858
Portugal	92	10.6	11	10	77	5.0	53	18	34	48	16 125	32	0.904
Qatar	11	0.8	21	3	70	40.8	92	3	32	65	32 066	22	0.849
Romania	238	21.6	10	12	71	-1.6	53	24	47	29	3347	19	0.792
Russian Federation	17 075	143.0	11	16	66	-3.4	73	14	42	44	4078	42	0.795
Rwanda	26	8.7	41	18	44	47.9	17	92	3	5	219	‹1	0.450
St. Lucia	0.6	0.2	16	6	74	13.0	30	ooo	ooo	ooo	4445	52	0.772

Country data sets 91

Country	Land	Population					2005	Employment			Quality of life		2004
	Area thousand km²	Total millions	Births per 1000	Deaths per 1000	Life expectancy years	Population change 1995–2005 per cent	Urban per cent in 2005	Primary per cent	Secondary per cent	Tertiary per cent	GDP ($US) per capita explanation: see p82	Health Doctors per 10 000 people	HDI explanation: see p83
Samoa	3	0.2	29	6	73	-2.4	22	ooo	ooo	ooo	2028	7	0.776
São Tomé and Príncipe	1	0.2	34	9	63	36.7	38	ooo	ooo	ooo	385	5	0.604
Saudi Arabia	2150	24.6	30	3	72	32.3	86	19	20	61	10 793	14	0.772
Senegal	197	11.7	37	12	56	29.7	43	77	8	15	733	1	0.458
Serbia	88	10.1	13	12	ooo	ooo	ooo	ooo	ooo	ooo	ooo	ooo	ooo
Seychelles	0.5	0.1	18	8	71	5.5	50	ooo	ooo	ooo	8282	13	0.821
Sierra Leone	72	5.5	47	24	40	33.9	37	68	15	17	198	1	0.298
Singapore	1	4.3	10	4	79	24.9	100	0	36	64	24 641	14	0.907
Slovakia	49	5.4	10	10	74	1.3	56	12	32	56	7624	33	0.849
Slovenia	20	2.0	9	10	77	0.4	51	6	46	48	16 131	22	0.904
Solomon Islands	29	0.5	34	8	62	35.4	16	77	7	16	514	1	0.594
Somalia	638	8.6	46	18	47	36.6	33	ooo	ooo	ooo	ooo	ooo	ooo
South Africa	1221	46.9	23	16	52	6.1	53	14	32	54	4668	7	0.658
South Korea	99	48.3	10	5	77	7.5	80	18	35	47	ooo	18	0.901
Spain	506	43.5	11	9	80	1.5	76	12	33	55	24 014	32	0.928
Sri Lanka	66	19.7	19	6	73	9.6	30	48	21	31	1031	4	0.751
Sudan	2506	40.2	37	10	57	31.5	36	70	8	22	569	2	0.512
Suriname	163	0.4	21	7	69	5.8	74	21	18	61	2503	5	0.755
Swaziland	17	1.1	29	26	35	13.3	25	40	22	38	2155	2	0.498
Sweden	450	9.0	11	10	81	1.4	84	ooo	ooo	ooo	38 554	31	0.949
Switzerland	41	7.4	10	8	80	4.6	68	3	35	59	48 695	35	0.947
Syria	185	18.4	30	4	72	28.9	50	33	24	43	1301	14	0.721
Taiwan	36	22.7	9	6	76	7.6	78	ooo	ooo	ooo	ooo	ooo	ooo
Tajikistan	143	6.8	31	8	63	22.2	27	41	23	36	323	22	0.652
Tanzania	945	36.5	42	18	44	24.8	32	84	5	11	297	‹1	0.418
Thailand	513	65.0	14	7	71	9.1	31	64	14	22	2621	3	0.778
Togo	57	6.1	40	12	54	36.2	33	66	10	24	415	1	0.512
Tonga	0.8	0.1	25	7	71	18.1	33	ooo	ooo	ooo	2088	3	0.810
Trinidad and Tobago	5	1.3	14	8	71	-7.2	74	11	31	58	9482	8	0.801
Tunisia	164	10.0	17	6	73	12.3	65	28	33	39	2815	7	0.753
Turkey	775	72.9	21	7	69	13.8	65	53	18	29	4210	12	0.750
Turkmenistan	488	5.2	24	8	63	20.7	47	37	23	40	1251	32	0.738
Uganda	241	26.9	47	15	48	35.7	12	85	5	10	264	1	0.508
Ukraine	604	47.1	9	16	68	-8.3	68	20	40	40	1357	30	0.766
United Arab Emirates	84	4.6	15	1	77	17.9	78	8	27	65	16 564	20	0.849
United Kingdom	245	60.1	12	10	78	3.4	89	2	29	69	36 039	17	0.939
United States of America	9631	296.5	14	8	78	10.9	79	3	28	69	39 752	55	0.944
Uruguay	177	3.4	16	10	75	6.2	93	14	27	59	3865	37	0.840
Uzbekistan	447	26.4	23	7	67	17.5	37	34	25	41	461	29	0.694
Vanuatu	12	0.2	31	6	67	19.4	21	ooo	ooo	ooo	1470	1	0.659
Venezuela	912	26.7	23	5	73	17.7	87	12	27	61	4184	19	0.772
Vietnam	332	83.3	19	6	72	13.2	26	71	14	15	550	5	0.704
Yemen	528	20.7	43	10	61	39.5	26	61	17	22	649	2	0.489
Zambia	753	11.2	41	23	37	25.1	35	75	8	17	511	1	0.394
Zimbabwe	391	13.0	31	20	41	9.4	34	68	8	24	1350	1	0.505

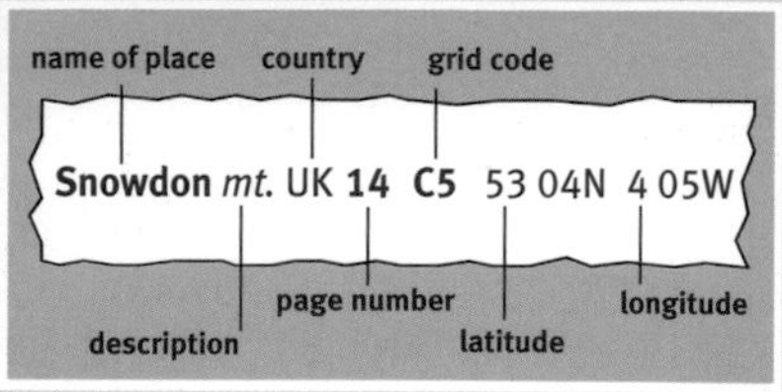
name of place
country
grid code
Snowdon mt. UK 14 C5 53 04N 4 05W
page number
longitude
description
latitude

A

Abadan Iran 40 B4 30 20N 48 15E
Aberaeron UK 14 C4 52 49N 44 43W
Aberdare UK 14 D3 51 43N 3 27W
Aberdeen UK 11 F3 57 10N 2 04W
Aberfeldy UK 11 E2 56 37N 3 54W
Abergavenny UK 14 D3 51 50N 3 00W
Abertillery UK 14 D3 51 45N 3 09W
Aberystwyth UK 14 C4 52 25N 4 05W
Abidjan Côte d'Ivoire 52 A3 5 19N 4 01W
Abingdon UK 15 F3 51 41N 1 17W
Aboyne UK 11 F3 57 05N 2 50W
Abu Dhabi UAE 40 C3 24 28N 54 25E
Abuja Nigeria 52 B3 9 10N 7 11E
Accra Ghana 52 A3 5 33N 0 15W
Achill Island RoI 16 A3/B3 53 55N 10 05W
A Coruña Spain 34 B3 43 22N 8 24W
Adana Turkey 35 F2 37 00N 35 19E
Addis Ababa Ethiopia 52 C3 9 03N 38 42E
Adelaide Australia 67 D2 34 55S 138 36E
Aden Yemen Rep. 40 B2 12 50N 45 03E
AFGHANISTAN 40/41 D4/E4
Agra India 41 E3 27 09N 78 00E
Ahmadabad India 41 E3 23 03N 72 40E
Ahvaz Iran 40 B4 31 17N 48 43E
Airdrie UK 11 E1 55 52N 3 59W
Ajaccio Corsica 36 A2 41 55N 8 43E
Akita Japan 48 D2 39 44N 140 05E
Alabama *state* USA 59 E2 32 00N 87 00W
ALBANIA 35 D3/E3
Albany Australia 66 B2 35 00S 117 53E
Ålborg Denmark 32 D2 57 05N 9 50E
Albuquerque USA 58 C2 35 05N 106 38W
Aldeburgh UK 15 J4 52 09N 1 35E
Aldershot UK 15 G3 51 15N 0 47W
Aleppo Syria 40 A4 36 14N 37 10E
Alexandria Egypt 52 C4 31 13N 29 55E
ALGERIA 52 A4/B4
Algiers Algeria 52 B4 36 50N 3 00E
Alicante Spain 34 B2 38 21N 0 29W
Alice Springs Australia 66 D3 23 41S 133 52E
Alloa UK 11 E2 56 07N 3 49W
Almaty Kazakhstan 41 E5 43 19N 76 55E
Alnwick UK 13 H4 55 25N 1 42W
Alps *mts.* Europe 34 C3 46 00N 7 30E
Alton UK 15 G3 51 09N 0 59W
Amazon *r.* Brazil 62 D6 2 30S 65 30W
Amble UK 13 H4 55 20N 1 34W
Ambleside UK 13 G3 54 26N 2 58W
Ambon Indonesia 45 E2 3 41S 128 10E
Amesbury UK 14 F3 51 10N 1 47W
Amlwch UK 14 C5 53 25N 4 20W
Amman Jordan 40 A4 31 04N 46 17E
Ammanford UK 14 D3 51 48N 3 58W
Amritsar India 41 E4 31 35N 74 56E
Amsterdam Netherlands 34 C4 52 22N 4 54E
Ancona Italy 36 B2 43 37N 13 31E
Andaman Islands India 41 G1 12 00N 94 00E
Andes *mts.* South America 62/63 B3/B7 10 00S 77 00W
ANDORRA 34 C3
Andover UK 15 F3 51 13N 1 28W
Anglesey *i.* UK 14 C5 53 18N 4 25W
ANGOLA 53 B2
Ankara Turkey 35 F2 39 55N 32 50E
'Annaba Algeria 52 B4 36 55N 7 47E
An Najaf Iraq 40 B4 31 59N 44 19E
Annan UK 13 F3 54 59N 3 16W
Anshan China 44 E7 41 05N 122 58E
Antananarivo Madagascar 53 D2 18 52S 47 30E
ANTIGUA AND BARBUDA 62 C8
Antofagasta Chile 63 B4 23 40S 70 23W
Antrim UK 16 E4 54 43N 6 13W
Antrim Mountains UK 16 E4/E5 55 00N 6 10W
Antwerp Belgium 34 C4 51 13N 4 25E
Appalachian Mountains USA 59 E2 37 00N 82 00W
Appennines *mts.* Italy 36 A2/C2 44 30N 10 00E
Appleby-in-Westmorland UK 13 G3 53 36N 2 29W
Aral Sea Asia 38 B5/C5 45 00N 60 00E
Aran Islands RoI 17 B3 53 10N 9 50W
Ararat, Mount Turkey 40 B4 39 44N 44 15E
Arbil Iraq 40 B4 36 12N 44 01E
Arbroath UK 11 F2 56 34N 2 35W
Arctic Ocean 72/73
Antarctica 68
Ards Peninsula UK 16 F4 54 25N 5 30W
Arequipa Peru 62 B5 16 25S 71 32W
ARGENTINA 63 C3
Århus Denmark 32 E2 56 15N 10 10E
Arica Chile 62 B5 18 30S 70 20W
Arisaig UK 11 C2 56 51N 5 51W
Arizona *state* USA 58 B2 34 00N 112 00W
Arkansas *r.* USA 59 D2 35 00N 93 00W
Arkansas *state* USA 59 D2 34 00N 93 00W
Arkhangel'sk Russia 40 H3 64 32N 40 40E
Arklow RoI 17 E2 52 48N 6 09W
Armagh UK 16 E4 54 21N 6 39W
ARMENIA 40 B4/B5
Arnold UK 15 F4 53 00N 1 09W
Arran *i.* UK 11 C1 55 35N 5 15W
Arundel UK 15 G2 50 51N 0 34W
Asansol India 42 B1 23 40N 86 59E
Ashbourne UK 14 F5 53 01N 1 43W
Ashford UK 15 H3 51 09N 0 53E
Ashgabat Turkmenistan 40 C4 37 58N 58 24E
Ashington UK 13 H4 55 11N 1 34W
Asmara Eritrea 52 C3 15 20N 38 58E
Astana Kazakhstan 39 C5 51 10N 71 28E
Asunción Paraguay 63 D4 25 15S 57 40W
Aswan Egypt 52 C4 24 05N 32 56E
Atacama Desert Chile 63 B4 22 30S 70 00W
Athens Greece 35 E2 38 00N 23 44E
Athlone RoI 17 D3 53 25N 7 56W
Atlanta USA 59 E2 33 45N 84 23W
Atlantic Ocean 72/73
Atlas Mountains Morocco 52 A4 32 00N 2 00W
At Ta'if Saudi Arabia 40 B3 21 15N 40 21E
Auchterarder UK 11 E2 56 18N 3 43W
Auchtermuchty UK 11 E2 56 17N 3 15W
Auckland New Zealand 67 H2 36 51S 174 46E
Austin USA 59 D2 30 18N 97 47W
AUSTRALIA 66/67
AUSTRIA 34 D3
Aviemore UK 11 E3 57 12N 3 50W
Avignon France 34 C3 43 56N 4 48E
Avon *r.* UK 14 F4 52 15N 1 55W
Axminster UK 14 E2 50 47N 3 00W
Ayers Rock *mt.* Australia 66 D3 25 20S 131 01E
Aylesbury UK 15 G3 51 50N 0 50W
Ayr UK 11 D1 55 28N 4 38W
AZERBAIJAN 40 B4/B5

B

Baffin Bay Canada 56 F4/G4 72 00N 64 00W
Baffin Island Canada 56 F4 70 00N 75 00W
Baghdad Iraq 40 B4 33 20N 44 26E
BAHAMAS, THE 57 F2
BAHRAIN 40 C3
Bakewell UK 14 F5 53 13N 1 40W
Baku Azerbaijan 40 B5 40 22N 49 53E
Bala UK 14 D4 52 54N 3 35W
Balearic Islands Spain 34 C2/C3 40 00N 2 00E
Bali *i.* Indonesia 45 D2 8 30S 115 00E
Balikesir Turkey 35 E2 39 37N 27 51E
Balkhash, Lake Kazakhstan 38 C5 46 00N 75 00E
Ballantrae UK 12 D4 55 06N 5 00W
Ballater UK 11 E3 57 03N 3 03W
Ballybofey RoI 16 D4 54 48N 7 47W
Ballycastle UK 16 E5 55 12N 6 15W
Ballymena UK 16 E4 54 52N 6 17W
Ballymoney UK 16 E5 55 04N 6 31W
Baltimore USA 59 F2 39 18N 76 38W
Bamako Mali 52 A3 12 40N 7 59W
Bamburgh UK 13 H4 55 36N 1 42W
Banbridge UK 16 E4 54 21N 6 16W
Banbury UK 15 F4 52 04N 1 20W
Banchory UK 11 F3 57 30N 2 30W
Banda Aceh Indonesia 45 B3 5 30N 95 20E
Bandar Seri Begawan Brunei 45 D3 4 53N 114 57E
Bandung Indonesia 45 C2 6 57S 107 34E
Bangalore India 41 E2 12 58N 77 35E
Bangkok Thailand 45 C4 13 44N 100 30E
BANGLADESH 42 B1/C2
Bangor UK 16 F4 54 40N 5 40W
Bangor UK 14 C5 53 13N 4 08W
Bangui CAR 52 B3 4 23N 18 37E
Banjarmasin Indonesia 45 D2 3 22S 114 33E
Banjul The Gambia 52 A3 13 28N 16 39W
Baotou China 44 C7 40 38N 109 59E
BARBADOS 62 D8
Barcelona Spain 34 C3 41 25N 2 10E
Bari Italy 36 C2 41 07N 16 52E
Barking UK 15 H3 51 33N 0 06E
Barmouth UK 14 C4 52 43N 4 03W
Barnard Castle UK 13 H3 54 33N 1 55W
Barnet UK 15 G3 51 39N 0 12W
Barnsley UK 13 H2 53 34N 1 28W
Barnstaple UK 14 C3 51 05N 4 04W
Barra *i.* UK 11 A2/A3 57 00N 7 25W
Barranquilla Colombia 62 B8 11 10N 74 50W
Barreiras Brazil 62 E5 12 09S 44 58W
Barrow-in-Furness UK 13 F3 54 07N 3 14W
Barry UK 14 D3 51 24N 3 18W
Barton-upon-Humber UK 13 J2 53 41N 0 27W
Basel Switzerland 34 C3 47 33N 7 36E
Basingstoke UK 15 F3 51 16N 1 05W
Basra Iraq 40 B4 30 30N 47 50E
Bath UK 14 E3 51 23N 2 22W
Bathgate UK 11 E1 55 55N 3 39W
Baton Rouge USA 59 D2 30 30N 91 10W
Baykal, Lake Russia 44 C8 54 00N 109 00E
Bearsden UK 11 D1 55 56N 4 20W
Beccles UK 15 J4 52 28N 1 34E
Bedford UK 15 G4 52 08N 0 29W
Bedworth UK 15 F4 52 29N 1 28W
Beijing China 44 D6 39 55N 116 26E
Beira Mozambique 53 C2 19 49S 34 52E
Beirut Lebanon 40 A4 33 52N 35 30E
BELARUS 33 F2/G2
Belém Brazil 62 E6 1 27S 48 29W
Belfast UK 16 F4 54 35N 5 55W
BELGIUM 34 C4
Belgrade Serbia 35 E3 44 50N 20 30E
Belize Belize 57 E1 17 29N 88 10W
BELIZE 57 E1
Belo Horizonte Brazil 63 E5 19 54S 43 54W
Benbecula *i.* UK 11 A3 57 25N 7 20W
Ben Cruachan *mt.* UK 11 C2 56 26N 5 09W
Benghazi Libya 52 C4 32 07N 20 04E
BENIN 52 B3
Ben Lawers *mt.* UK 11 D2 56 33N 4 15W
Ben Lomond *mt.* UK 11 D2 56 12N 4 38W
Ben More *mt.* UK 11 B2 56 25N 6 02W
Ben More *mt.* UK 11 D2 56 25N 6 02W
Ben Nevis *mt.* UK 11 C2 56 48N 5 00W
Ben Wyvis *mt.* UK 11 D3 57 40N 4 35W
Bérgamo Italy 36 A3 45 42N 9 40E
Bergen Norway 32 D3 60 23N 5 20E
Berlin Germany 34 D4 52 32N 13 25E
Bermuda *i.* Atlantic Ocean 57 F2 32 50N 64 20W
Bern Switzerland 34 C3 46 57N 7 26E
Berwick-upon-Tweed UK 11 H4 55 46N 2 00W
Bethesda UK 14 C5 53 11N 4 03W
Beverley UK 13 J2 53 51N 0 26W
Bexley UK 15 H3 51 27N 0 09E
BHUTAN 42 B2/C2
Bicester UK 15 F3 51 54N 1 09W
Bideford UK 14 C3 51 01N 4 13W
Bideford Bay UK 14 C3 51 05N 4 25W
Biggar UK 11 E1 55 38N 3 32W
Biggleswade UK 15 G4 52 05N 0 17W
Bilbao Spain 34 B3 43 15N 2 56W
Birkenhead UK 13 F2 53 24N 3 02W
Birmingham UK 14 F4 52 30N 1 50W
Birmingham USA 59 E2 33 30N 86 55W
Biscay, Bay of Atlantic Ocean 34 B3 45 30N 2 50W
Bishkek Kyrgyzstan 41 E5 42 53N 74 46E
Bishop Auckland UK 13 H3 54 40N 1 40W
Bishop's Stortford UK 15 H3 51 53N 0 09E
Bissau Guinea-Bissau 52 A3 11 52N 15 39W
Blackburn UK 13 G2 53 45N 2 29W
Black Mountains UK 14 D3/D4 51 55N 3 10W
Blackpool UK 13 F2 53 50N 3 03W
Black Sea Europe 35 E3/F3 43 00N 35 00E
Blaenau Ffestiniog UK 14 D4 52 59N 3 56W
Blairgowrie UK 11 E2 56 36N 3 21W
Blandford Forum UK 14 E2 50 52N 2 11W
Blantyre Malawi 53 C2 15 46S 35 00E
Blyth UK 13 H4 55 07N 1 30W
Boa Vista Brazil 62 C7 3 23S 55 30W
Bodmin UK 14 C2 50 29N 4 43W
Bognor Regis UK 15 G2 50 47N 0 41W
Bogotá Colombia 62 B7 4 38N 74 05W
Boise USA 58 B3 43 38N 116 12W
BOLIVIA 62 C5
Bologna Italy 36 B2 44 30N 11 20E
Bolton UK 13 G2 53 35N 2 26W
Bonar Bridge *tn.* UK 11 D3 57 53N 4 21W
Bonn Germany 34 C4 50 44N 7 06E
Bootle UK 13 F2 53 28N 3 00W
Bordeaux France 34 B3 44 50N 0 34W
Borneo *i.* Indonesia/Malaysia 45 D2/D3 1 00N 113 00E
Bornholm *i.* Denmark 32 E2 55 02N 15 00E
Boscastle UK 14 C2 50 41N 4 42W
BOSNIA-HERZEGOVINA 34/35 D3
Boston UK 15 G4 52 29N 0 01W
Boston USA 59 F3 42 20N 71 05W
BOTSWANA 53 C1
Bournemouth UK 14 F2 50 43N 1 54W
Bracknell UK 15 G3 51 26N 0 46W
Bradford UK 13 H2 53 48N 1 45W
Braemar UK 11 E3 57 01N 3 23W
Brahmaputra *r.* India/Bangladesh 42 C2 27 00N 94 00E
Braintree UK 15 H3 51 53N 0 32E
Brampton UK 13 G3 54 57N 2 43W
Brásília Brazil 62 E5 15 45S 47 57W
Brasov Romania 35 E3 45 39N 25 35E
Bratislava Slovakia 34 D3 48 10N 17 10E
Bray RoI 17 E3 53 12N 6 06W
BRAZIL 62 B6/F6
Brazilian Highlands Brazil 62 E5 17 00S 44 00W
Brazzaville Congo 52 B2 4 14S 15 14E
Brechin UK 11 F2 56 44N 2 40W
Brecon UK 14 D3 51 57N 3 24W
Brecon Beacons *mts.* UK 14 D3 51 53N 3 30W
Bremen Germany 34 C4 53 05N 8 48E
Brent UK 15 G3 51 34N 0 17W
Brentwood UK 15 H3 51 38N 0 18E
Bréscia Italy 36 B3 45 33N 10 13E
Bressay *i.* UK 10 G6 60 08N 1 05W
Brest France 34 B3 48 23N 4 30W
Brest Belarus 33 F2 52 08N 23 40E
Bridgend UK 14 D3 51 31N 3 35W
Bridgnorth UK 14 E4 52 33N 2 25W
Bridgwater UK 14 E3 51 08N 3 00W
Bridlington UK 13 H3 54 05N 0 12W
Bridport UK 14 E2 50 44N 2 46W
Brigg UK 13 J2 53 34N 0 30W
Brighton UK 15 G2 50 50N 0 10W
Brisbane Australia 67 F3 27 28S 153 03E
Bristol UK 14 E3 51 27N 2 35W
Bristol Channel UK 14 C3/D3 51 20N 3 50W
Brixham UK 14 D2 50 23N 3 30W
Brno Czech Republic 34 D3 49 13N 16 40E
Broadford UK 11 C3 57 14N 5 54W
Brodick UK 11 C1 55 35N 5 09W
Bromley UK 15 H3 51 31N 0 01W
Bromsgrove UK 14 E4 50 20N 2 03W
Bromyard UK 14 E4 52 11N 2 30W
Brora UK 11 E4 58 01N 3 51W
Brough UK 13 G3 54 32N 2 19W
BRUNEI 45 D3
Brussels Belgium 34 C4 50 50N 4 21E
Bucharest Romania 35 E3 44 25N 26 07E
Buckfastleigh UK 14 D2 50 29N 3 46W
Buckhaven UK 11 E2 56 11N 3 03W
Buckingham UK 15 G3 52 00N 1 00W
Budapest Hungary 35 D3 47 30N 19 03E
Bude UK 14 C2 50 50N 4 33W
Bude Bay UK 14 C2 50 50N 4 40W
Buenos Aires Argentina 63 D3 34 40S 58 30W
Buffalo USA 59 F3 42 52N 78 55W
Builth Wells UK 14 D4 52 09N 3 24W
Bujumbura Burundi 52 C2 3 22S 29 19E
Bukhara Uzbekistan 40 D4 39 47N 64 26E
Bulawayo Zimbabwe 53 C1 20 10S 28 43E
BULGARIA 35 E3
Buncrana RoI 16 D5 55 08N 7 27W
Bungay UK 15 J4 52 28N 1 26E
Burgas Bulgaria 35 E3 42 30N 27 29E
BURKINA 52 A3
Burnley UK 13 G2 53 48N 2 14W
Burry Port UK 14 C3 51 42N 4 15W
Bursa Turkey 35 E3 40 12N 29 04E
Burton upon Trent UK 14 F4 52 48N 1 36W
BURUNDI 52 C2
Bury UK 13 G2 53 36N 2 17W
Bury St. Edmunds UK 15 H4 52 15N 0 43E
Bute *i.* UK 11 C1 55 50N 5 05W
Buxton UK 14 F5 53 15N 1 55W

C

Cabinda *province* Angola 52 B2 5 00S 12 00E
Cádiz Spain 34 B2 36 32N 6 18W
Caernarfon UK 14 C5 53 08N 4 16W
Caernarfon Bay UK 14 C5 53 05N 4 30W
Caerphilly UK 14 D3 51 35N 3 14W
Cágliari Italy 36 A1 39 13N 9 08E
Caha Mountains RoI 17 B1 51 40N 9 40W
Cairn Gorm *mt.* UK 11 E3 57 07N 3 40W
Cairngorms *mts.* UK 11 E3 57 10N 3 30W
Cairns Australia 67 E4 16 54S 145 45E
Cairo Egypt 52 C4 30 03N 31 15E
Calais France 34 C4 50 57N 1 52E
Calgary Canada 58 B4 51 05N 114 05W
Cali Colombia 62 B7 3 24N 76 30W
California *state* USA 58 B2 35 00N 119 00W
Callander UK 11 D2 56 15N 4 13W
Calligarry UK 11 C3 57 02N 5 58E
Calne UK 14 E3 51 27N 2 00W
Camberley UK 15 G3 51 21N 0 45W
CAMBODIA 45 C4
Camborne UK 14 B2 50 12N 5 19W
Cambrian Mountains UK 14 D4 52 15N 3 45W
Cambridge UK 15 H4 52 12N 0 07E
CAMEROON 52 B3
Cameroun, Mount Cameroon 52 B3 4 13N 9 10E
Campbeltown UK 11 C1 55 26N 5 36W
Campos Brazil 63 E4 21 46S 41 21W
Campsie Fells *hills* UK 11 D2 56 00N 4 15W
CANADA 57 C3/G3
Canary Islands Spain 52 A4 28 30N 15 10W
Canberra Australia 67 E2 35 17S 149 09E
Cannock UK 14 E4 52 42N 2 01W
Cantabrian Mountains Spain 34 B3 43 00N 5 30W
Canterbury UK 15 J3 51 17N 1 05E
Cape Town RSA 53 B1 33 56S 18 28E
CAPE VERDE 70
Caracas Venezuela 62 C8 10 35N 66 56W
Cardiff UK 14 D3 51 30N 3 13W
Cardigan UK 14 C4 52 06N 4 40W
Caribbean Sea Central America 62 B8/C8 15 00N 75 00W
Carlisle UK 13 G3 54 54N 2 55W
Carmarthen UK 14 C3 51 51N 4 20W
Carn Eige *mt.* UK 11 C3 57 22N 5 07W
Carnforth UK 13 G3 54 08N 2 46W
Carnoustie UK 11 F2 56 30N 2 44W
Carpathians *mts.* Europe 35 E3 49 00N 22 00E
Carrauntoohill *mt.* RoI 17 B1 52 00N 9 45W
Carrickfergus UK 16 F4 54 43N 5 49W
Cartagena Colombia 62 B8 10 24N 75 33W
Cartagena Spain 34 B2 37 36N 0 59W
Casablanca Morocco 52 A4 33 39N 7 35W
Caspian Sea Asia 40 B4/C5 41 00N 50 00E
Castlebar RoI 17 B3 53 52N 9 17W
Castlebay *tn.* UK 11 A2 56 57N 7 28W
Castleblaney RoI 16 E4 54 07N 6 44W
Castle Douglas UK 12 F3 54 57N 3 56W
Castleford UK 13 H2 53 43N 1 21W
Castletown Isle of Man 12 E3 54 04N 4 38W
Catánia Italy 36 C1 37 31N 15 06E
Caucasus *mts.* Asia 40 B5 43 00N 43 00E
Cavan RoI 16 D3 53 58N 7 21W
Cayenne French Guiana 62 D7 4 55N 52 18W
CENTRAL AFRICAN REPUBLIC 52 B3/C3
Ceuta *territory* Spain 34 B2 35 53N 5 19W
CHAD 52 B3/C3
Chad, Lake West Africa 52 B3 13 50N 14 00E
Changchun China 44 E7 43 50N 125 20E
Chang Jiang *r.* China 44 C6/D6 30 00N 116 00E
Changsha China 44 D5 28 10N 113 00E
Channel Islands British Isles 32 C1 49 30N 2 30W
Charlotte USA 59 E2 35 03N 80 50W
Chatham UK 15 H3 51 23N 0 32E
Cheadle UK 13 G2 53 24N 2 13W
Chelmsford UK 15 H3 51 44N 0 28E
Cheltenham UK 14 E3 51 54N 2 04W
Chengdu China 44 C6 30 37N 104 06E
Chennai India 41 F2 13 05N 80 18E
Chepstow UK 14 E3 51 39N 2 41W
Chernivtsi Ukraine 35 E3 48 19N 25 52E
Cheshunt UK 15 G3 51 43N 0 02W
Chester UK 13 G2 53 12N 2 54W

Chesterfield UK	15	F5	53 15N	1 25W
Chester-le-Street UK	13	H3	54 52N	1 34W
Cheviot Hills UK	13	G4	55 25N	2 20W
Cheviot, The *sum.* UK	13	G4	55 29N	2 20W
Cheyenne USA	58	C3	41 08N	104 50W
Chiang Mai Thailand	44	B4	18 48N	98 59E
Chiba Japan	48	D2	35 38N	140 07E
Chicago USA	59	E3	41 50N	87 45W
Chichester UK	15	G2	50 50N	0 48W
CHILE	62	B1/C5		
Chillán Chile	63	B3	36 37S	72 10W
Chiloé Island Chile	63	B2	42 30S	74 00W
Chiltern Hills UK	15	F3/G3	51 40N	1 00W
Chimbote Peru	62	B6	9 04S	78 34W
CHINA	44			
Chippenham UK	14	E3	51 28N	2 07W
Chipping Norton UK	15	F3	51 56N	1 32W
Chipping Sodbury UK	14	E3	51 33N	2 24W
Chisinau Moldova	35	E3	47 00N	28 50E
Chittagong Bangladesh	42	C1	22 20N	91 48E
Chongqing China	44	C5	29 30N	106 35E
Chorley UK	13	G2	53 40N	2 38W
Christchurch New Zealand	67	H1	43 32S	172 38E
Christchurch UK	14	F2	50 44N	1 45W
Cincinnati USA	59	E2	39 10N	83 30W
Cirencester UK	14	F3	51 44N	1 59W
Ciudad Juárez Mexico	58	C2	31 42N	106 29W
Clachan UK	11	C1	55 45N	5 34W
Clacton-on-Sea UK	15	J3	51 48N	1 09E
Cleethorpes UK	13	J2	53 34N	0 02W
Clevedon UK	14	E3	51 27N	2 51W
Cleveland Hills UK	13	H3	54 25N	1 15W
Clitheroe UK	13	G2	53 53N	2 23W
Clones RoI	16	D4	54 11N	7 15W
Clonmel RoI	17	D2	52 21N	7 42W
Clyde *r.* UK	11	E1	55 45N	4 55W
Clydebank UK	11	D1	55 54N	4 24W
Coalisland UK	16	E4	54 32N	6 42W
Coalville UK	15	F4	52 44N	1 20W
Coatbridge UK	11	D1	55 52N	4 01W
Cockermouth UK	13	F3	54 40N	3 21W
Colchester UK	15	H3	51 54N	0 54E
Coldstream *tn.* UK	11	F1	55 39N	2 15W
Coleraine UK	16	E5	55 08N	6 40W
Coll *i.* UK	11	B2	56 40N	6 35W
Cologne Germany	34	C4	50 56N	6 57E
COLOMBIA	62	B7		
Colombo Sri Lanka	41	E1	6 55N	79 52E
Colonsay *i.* UK	11	B2	56 05N	6 15W
Colorado *r.* USA/Mexico	58	C2	38 00N	109 00W
Colorado *state* USA	58	C2	39 00N	106 00W
Columbia USA	59	E2	34 00N	81 00W
Columbia *r.* Canada/USA	58	A3/B3	50 30N	119 00W
Columbus USA	59	E2	39 59N	83 03W
Colwyn Bay *tn.* UK	14	D5	53 18N	3 43W
Como, Lake Italy	36	A3	46 00N	9 00E
COMOROS	53	D2		
Conakry Guinea	52	A3	9 30N	13 43W
Concepción Chile	63	B3	36 50S	73 03W
CONGO	52	B2/B3		
Congo *r.* Congo/Congo Dem. Rep.	52	B2/C3	3 00S	16 00E
Coniston Water *l.* UK	13	F3	54 20N	3 05W
Connecticut *state* USA	59	F3	41 00N	73 00W
Consett UK	13	H3	54 51N	1 49W
Conwy UK	14	D5	53 17N	3 50W
Cook, Mount New Zealand	67	H1	43 36S	170 09E
Cookstown UK	16	E4	54 39N	6 45W
Copenhagen Denmark	32	E2	55 43N	12 34E
Corby UK	15	G4	52 49N	0 32W
Córdoba Argentina	63	C3	31 25S	64 11W
Corfu Greece	35	D2	39 00N	19 00E
Cork RoI	17	C1	51 54N	8 28W
Corpus Christi USA	59	D1	27 47N	97 26W
Corsica *i.* France	36	A2	42 00N	9 00E
COSTA RICA	57	E1		
CÔTE D'IVOIRE	52	A3		
Cotopaxi *vol.* Ecuador	62	B6	0 40S	78 28W
Cotswold Hills UK	14	E3/F3	51 40N	2 10W
Coventry UK	15	F4	52 25N	1 30W
Cowes UK	15	F2	50 45N	1 18W
Craigavon UK	16	E4	54 28N	6 25W
Craighouse UK	11	C1	55 51N	5 57W
Craignure UK	11	C2	56 28N	5 42W
Cramlington UK	13	H4	55 05N	1 35W
Crawley UK	15	G3	51 07N	0 12W
Crediton UK	14	D2	50 47N	3 39W
Creeslough RoI	16	D5	55 07N	7 55W
Crete *i.* Greece	35	E2	35 00N	25 00E
Crewe UK	13	G2	53 05N	2 27W
Crewkerne UK	14	E2	50 53N	2 48W
Crianlarich UK	11	D2	56 23N	4 37W
Crieff UK	11	E2	56 23N	3 52W
Crimea *p.* Ukraine	35	F3	46 00N	34 00E
CROATIA	34/35	D3		
Cromarty UK	11	D3	57 40N	4 02W
Cromer UK	15	J4	52 56N	1 18E
Crossmaglen UK	16	E4	54 05N	6 37W
Croydon UK	15	G3	51 23N	0 06W
Crumlin UK	16	E4	54 37N	6 14W
CUBA	57	E2/F2		
Cuiabá Brazil	62	D5	15 32S	56 05W
Cuillin Hills UK	11	B3	57 15N	6 15W
Cullen UK	11	F3	57 41N	2 49W
Cullompton UK	14	D2	50 52N	3 24W
Cumbernauld UK	11	E1	55 57N	4 00W
Cumnock UK	11	D1	55 27N	4 16W
Cupar UK	11	E2	56 19N	3 01W
Curitiba Brazil	63	E4	25 25S	49 25W
Cuzco Peru	62	B5	13 32S	1 57W
Cwmbran UK	14	D3	51 39N	3 00W
CYPRUS	35	F2		
CZECH REPUBLIC	34/34	D3		

D

Dakar Senegal	52	A3	14 38N	17 27W
Dalbeattie UK	12	F3	54 56N	3 49W
Dalian China	44	E6	38 53N	121 37E
Dallas USA	59	D2	32 47N	96 48W
Damascus Syria	40	A4	33 30N	36 19E
Danube *r.* Europe	35	E3	44 00N	25 00E
Dar es Salaam Tanzania	53	C2	6 51S	39 18E
Darfur *mts.* Sudan	52	C3	12 40N	24 20E
Darling *r.* Australia	67	E2	31 00S	144 00E
Darlington UK	13	H3	54 31N	1 34W
Dartford UK	15	H3	51 27N	0 13E
Dartmoor UK	14	C2/D2	50 35N	3 50W
Dartmouth UK	14	D2	50 21N	3 35W
Darvel UK	11	D1	55 37N	4 18W
Darwin Australia	66	D4	12 24S	130 52E
Davao The Philippines	45	E3	7 05N	125 38E
Daventry UK	15	F4	52 16N	1 09W
Dawlish UK	14	D2	50 35N	3 28W
Deal UK	15	J3	51 14N	1 24E
Dee *r.* UK	11	F3	57 05N	2 10W
Dee *r.* UK	14	D5	53 16N	3 10W
Delaware *state* USA	59	F2	39 00N	75 00W
Delhi India	41	E3	28 40N	77 14E
Demavand, Mount Iran	40	C4	35 56N	52 08E
DEMOCRATIC REPUBLIC OF CONGO	52/53	C2/C3		
Denbigh UK	14	D5	53 11N	3 25W
DENMARK	32	D2/E2		
Denver USA	58	C2	39 45N	105 00W
Derby UK	15	F4	52 55N	1 30W
Derwent *r.* UK	13	J2	53 50N	0 55W
Derwent Water *l.* UK	13	F3	54 35N	3 09W
Des Moines USA	59	D3	41 35N	93 35W
Detroit USA	59	E3	42 23N	83 05W
Devizes UK	14	F3	51 22N	1 59W
Dewsbury UK	13	H2	53 42N	1 37W
Dhaka Bangladesh	42	C1	23 42N	90 22E
Didcot UK	15	F3	51 37N	1 15W
Dijon France	34	D3	47 20N	5 02E
Dili Indonesia	45	E2	8 33S	125 34E
Dingle Bay RoI	17	A2	52 05N	10 15W
Dingwall UK	11	D3	57 35N	4 29W
Dire Dawa Ethiopia	52	D3	9 35N	41 50E
Diss UK	15	J4	52 23N	1 06W
Diyarbakir Turkey	40	B4	37 55N	40 14E
DJIBOUTI	52	D3		
Djibouti Djibouti	52	D3	11 35N	43 11E
Dnipropetrovsk Ukraine	35	F3	48 29N	35 00E
Dodoma Tanzania	53	C2	6 10S	35 40E
Doha Qatar	40	C3	25 15N	51 36E
Dolgellau UK	14	D4	52 44N	3 53W
DOMINICA	62	C8		
DOMINICAN REPUBLIC	62	B8/C8		
Donaghadee UK	16	F4	54 39N	5 33W
Doncaster UK	13	H2	53 32N	1 07W
Donegal RoI	16	C4	54 39N	8 07W
Donegal Bay *b.* RoI	16	C4	54 30N	8 30W
Donets'k Ukraine	35	F3	48 00N	37 50E
Dorchester UK	14	E2	50 43N	2 26W
Dorking UK	15	G3	51 14N	0 20W
Douala Cameroon	52	B3	4 04N	9 43E
Douglas Isle of Man	12	E3	54 09N	4 29W
Douro *r.* Spain/Portugal	34	B3	41 30N	6 30W
Dover UK	15	J3	51 08N	1 19E
Dover, Strait of English Channel	15	J2/J3	51 00N	1 20W
Downham Market UK	15	H4	52 36N	0 23E
Downpatrick UK	16	F4	54 20N	5 43W
Dresden Germany	34	D4	51 03N	13 45E
Drogheda RoI	17	E3	53 43N	6 21W
Droitwich UK	14	E4	52 16N	2 09W
Dromore UK	16	E4	54 25N	6 09W
Drummore UK	12	E3	54 42N	4 54W
Drumnadrochit UK	11	D3	57 20N	4 30W
Dubai UAE	40	C3	25 14N	55 17E
Dublin RoI	17	E3	53 20N	6 15W
Dudley UK	14	E4	52 30N	2 05W
Dufftown UK	11	E3	57 26N	3 08W
Dumbarton UK	11	D1	55 57N	4 35W
Dumfries UK	12	F4	55 04N	3 37W
Dunbar UK	11	F2	56 00N	2 31W
Dunblane UK	11	E2	56 12N	3 59W
Duncansby Head *c.* UK	10	E4	58 39N	3 02W
Dundalk RoI	16	E4	54 01N	6 25W
Dundee UK	11	F2	56 28N	3 00W
Dunfermline UK	11	E2	56 04N	3 29W
Dungannon UK	16	E4	54 31N	6 46W
Dungiven UK	16	E4	54 55N	6 55W
Dún Laoghaire RoI	17	E3	53 17N	6 08W
Dunoon UK	11	D1	55 57N	4 56W
Duns UK	11	F1	55 47N	2 20W
Dunstable UK	15	G3	51 53N	0 32W
Dunvegan UK	11	B3	57 26N	6 35W
Durban RSA	53	C1	29 53S	31 00E
Durham UK	13	H3	54 47N	1 34W
Dursley UK	14	E3	51 42N	2 21W
Dushanbe Tajikistan	40	D4	38 38N	68 51E
Düsseldorf Germany	34	C4	51 13N	6 47E
Dyce UK	11	F3	57 12N	2 11W

E

Ealing UK	15	G3	51 31N	0 18W
Eastbourne UK	15	H2	50 46N	0 17E
East Dereham UK	15	H4	52 41N	0 56E
East Kilbride UK	11	D1	55 46N	4 10W
Eastleigh UK	15	F2	50 58N	1 22W
EAST TIMOR	45	E2		
Ebbw Vale UK	14	D3	51 47N	3 12W
Ebro *r.* Spain	34	B3	42 00N	1 15E
ECUADOR	62	B6		
Edinburgh UK	11	E1	55 57N	3 13W
Edmonton Canada	58	B4	53 34N	113 25W
EGYPT	52	C4		
Eigg *i.* UK	11	B2	56 55N	6 10W
Elgin UK	11	E3	57 39N	3 20W
El Gîza Egypt	52	C4	30 01N	31 12E
Ellesmere Port UK	13	G2	53 17N	2 54W
Ellon UK	11	F3	57 22N	2 05W
El Paso USA	58	C2	31 45N	106 30W
EL SALVADOR	57	E1		
Ely UK	15	H4	52 24N	0 16E
Enfield UK	15	G3	51 39N	0 05W
England *country* UK	14/15			
English Channel UK/France	32	C1/C2	50 00N	2 00W
Enniskillen UK	16	D4	54 21N	7 38W
Entebbe Uganda	54	A3	0 04N	32 27E
EQUATORIAL GUINEA	52	B3		
Erie, Lake Canada/USA	59	E3	42 15N	81 00W
ERITREA	52	C3/D3	14 40N	40 15E
Esfahan Iran	40	C4	32 41N	51 41E
Essen Germany	34	C4	51 27N	6 57E
ESTONIA	33	F2		
ETHIOPIA	52	C3/D3		
Etna, Mount Italy	36	B1	37 45N	15 00E
Everest, Mount China/Nepal	41	F3	27 59N	86 56E
Evesham UK	14	F4	52 06N	1 56W
Exeter UK	14	D2	50 43N	3 31W
Exmoor UK	14	D2	51 08N	3 40W
Exmouth UK	14	D2	50 37N	3 25W
Eyemouth UK	11	F1	55 25N	2 06W
Eye Peninsula UK	10	B4	58 10N	6 10W

F

Fair Isle *i.* UK	10	G5	59 32N	1 38W
Faisalabad Pakistan	41	E4	31 25N	73 09E
Fakenham UK	15	H4	52 50N	0 51E
Falkirk UK	11	E1	55 59N	3 48W
Falkland Islands South Atlantic Ocean	63	C1/D1	52 30S	60 00W
Falmouth UK	14	B2	50 08N	5 04W
Fareham UK	15	F2	50 51N	1 10W
Faringdon UK	15	F3	51 40N	1 35W
Farnborough UK	15	G3	51 17N	0 46W
Farnham UK	15	G3	51 13N	0 49W
Faroe Islands Atlantic Ocean	32	C3	62 00N	7 00W
FEDERATED STATES OF MICRONESIA	71			
Felixstowe UK	15	J3	51 58N	1 20E
Fens, The UK	15	G4/H4	52 45N	0 05E
Ferrara Italy	36	B2	44 50N	11 38E
Fès Morocco	52	A4	34 05N	5 00W
FIJI	67	H4		
FINLAND	33	F3		
Fionnphort UK	11	B2	56 19N	6 23W
Firth of Clyde *est.* UK	11	C1/D1	55 45N	5 00W
Firth of Forth *est.* UK	11	E2/F2	56 05N	3 00W
Fishguard UK	14	C3	51 59N	4 59W
Flamborough Head *c.* UK	13	H3	54 06N	0 04W
Fleetwood UK	13	F2	53 56N	3 01W
Flint UK	14	D5	53 15N	3 07W
Florence Italy	36	B2	43 47N	11 15E
Florianópolis Brazil	63	E4	27 35S	48 31W
Florida *state* USA	59	E1	28 00N	82 00W
Fóggia Italy	36	C2	41 28N	15 33E
Folkestone UK	15	J3	51 05N	1 11E
Forfar UK	11	F2	56 38N	2 54W
Formby UK	13	F2	53 34N	3 05W
Forres UK	11	E3	57 37N	3 38W
Fortaleza Brazil	62	F6	3 45S	38 35W
Fort Augustus UK	11	D3	57 09N	4 41W
Forth *r.* UK	11	D2	56 10N	4 10W
Fort William UK	11	C2	56 49N	5 07W
Fort Worth USA	59	D2	32 45N	97 20W
Foula *i.* UK	10	F6	60 08N	2 05W
Fowey UK	14	C2	50 20N	4 38W
Foyle *r.* UK/RoI	16	D4	54 58N	7 35W
FRANCE	34	B3/C3		
Frankfurt-am-Main Germany	34	C4	50 06N	8 41E
Fraserburgh UK	11	F3	57 42N	2 00W
Freetown Sierra Leone	52	A3	8 30N	13 17W
French Guiana *territory* France	62	D7	5 00N	53 00W
Frome UK	14	E3	51 14N	2 20W
Fuji-san *mt.* Japan	48	C2	35 23N	138 42E
Fukui Japan	48	C2	36 04N	136 12E
Fukuoka Japan	48	B1	33 39N	130 21E
Fukushima Japan	48	D2	37 44N	140 28E
Furnace UK	11	C2	56 09N	5 12W
Fushun China	44	E7	41 50N	123 54E

G

GABON	52	B2/B3		
Gaborone Botswana	53	C1	24 45S	25 55E
Gainsborough UK	13	J2	53 24N	0 48W
Gairloch *tn.* UK	11	C3	57 42N	5 40W
Galashiels UK	11	F1	55 37N	2 49W
Galty Mountains RoI	17	C2	52 22N	8 10W
Galway RoI	17	B3	53 16N	9 03W
Galway Bay *b.* RoI	17	B3	53 15N	9 15W
GAMBIA, THE	52	A3		
Ganges *r.* India/Bangladesh	41	E3/F3	24 00N	88 00E
Garda, Lake Italy	36	B3	45 00N	10 00E
Garelochhead UK	11	D2	56 05N	4 50W
Gatehouse of Fleet UK	12	E3	54 53N	4 11W
Gateshead UK	13	H3	54 58N	1 35W
Gdansk Poland	33	E2	54 22N	18 41E
Geneva Switzerland	34	C3	46 13N	6 09E
Genoa Italy	36	A2	44 24N	8 56E
Georgetown Guyana	62	D7	6 46N	58 10W
GEORGIA	40	B5		
Georgia *state* USA	59	E2	33 00N	83 00W
GERMANY	34	C3/D4		
GHANA	52	A3		
Gibraltar *territory* UK	34	B2	36 09N	5 21W
Gifu Japan	48	C2	35 27N	136 46E
Gillingham UK	15	H3	51 24N	0 33E
Girvan UK	12	E4	55 15N	4 51W
Glasgow UK	11	D1	55 53N	4 15W
Glastonbury UK	14	E3	51 09N	2 43W
Glenluce UK	12	E3	54 53N	4 49W
Glenrothes UK	11	E2	56 12N	3 10W
Gloucester UK	14	E3	51 53N	2 14W
Gobi Desert Mongolia	44	B7/C7	48 30N	100 00E
Good Hope, Cape of RSA	53	B1	34 30S	19 00E
Goole UK	13	J2	53 42N	0 52W
Göteborg Sweden	32	E2	57 45N	12 00E
Gotland *i.* Sweden	33	E2	57 30N	18 40E
Gower *p.* UK	14	C3	51 35N	4 10W
Grampian Mountains UK	11	D2/E2	56 45N	4 00W
Grand Rapids *tn.* USA	59	E3	42 57N	86 40W
Grangemouth UK	11	E2	56 01N	3 44W
Grantham UK	15	G4	52 55N	0 39W
Grantown-on-Spey UK	11	E3	57 20N	3 58W
Gravesend UK	15	H3	51 27N	0 24E
Graz Austria	34	D3	47 05N	15 22E
Great Dividing Range *mts.* Australia	67	E2/F3	35 00N	148 00E
Great Driffield UK	13	J3	54 01N	0 26W
Great Malvern UK	14	E4	52 07N	2 19W
Great Ouse *r.* UK	15	H4	52 40N	0 20E
Great Salt Lake USA	58	B3	41 10N	112 40W
Great Torrington UK	14	C2	51 57N	4 09W
Great Whernside *sum.* UK	13	H3	54 10N	1 59W
Great Yarmouth UK	15	J4	52 37N	1 44E
GREECE	35	E2/E3		
GREENLAND	57	G4/H4		
Greenock UK	11	D1	55 57N	4 45W
Grenada	62	C8		
Grimsby UK	13	J2	53 35N	0 05W
Groznyy Russia	40	B5	43 21N	45 42E
GUAM	71			
Guangzhou China	44	D4	23 08N	113 20E
GUATEMALA	57	E1		
Guatemala Guatemala	57	E1	14 38N	90 22W
Guayaquil Ecuador	62	B6	2 13S	79 54W
Guildford UK	15	G3	51 14N	0 35W
GUINEA	52	A3		
GUINEA-BISSAU	52	A3		
Guisborough UK	13	H3	54 32N	1 04W
Guiyang China	44	C5	26 35N	106 40E
Gulf, The Middle East	40	B3/C3	27 20N	51 00E
GUYANA	62	D7		

H

HAITI	62	B8		
Hakodate Japan	48	D3	41 46N	140 44E
Halifax UK	13	H2	53 44N	1 52W
Halkirk UK	10	E4	58 30N	3 30W
Haltwhistle UK	13	G3	54 58N	2 27W
Hamburg Germany	34	D4	53 33N	10 00E
Hamilton UK	11	D1	55 47N	4 03W
Hangzhou China	44	E6	30 18N	120 07E
Hannover Germany	34	C4	52 23N	9 44E
Hanoi Vietnam	44	C5	21 01N	105 52E
Harare Zimbabwe	53	C2	17 50S	31 03E
Harbin China	44	E7	45 45N	126 41E
Harlech UK	14	C4	52 52N	4 07W
Harlow UK	15	H3	51 47N	0 08E
Haroldswick UK	10	H6	60 47N	0 50W
Harris *i.* UK	11	A3/B3	57 50N	6 55W
Harrogate UK	13	H2	54 00N	1 33W
Harrow UK	15	G3	51 34N	0 20W
Hartland Point *c.* UK	14	C3	51 02N	4 31W
Harwich UK	15	J3	51 57N	1 17E
Haslemere UK	15	G3	51 06N	0 43W
Hastings UK	15	H2	50 51N	0 36E
Hatherleigh UK	14	C2	50 49N	4 04W
Havana Cuba	57	E2	23 07N	82 25W
Havant UK	15	G2	50 51N	0 59W
Haverhill UK	15	H4	52 05N	0 26E
Havering UK	15	H3	51 34N	0 14E
Hawaiian Islands Pacific Ocean	70		20 00N	156 00W
Hawick UK	11	F1	55 25N	2 47W
Hay-on-Wye UK	14	D4	52 04N	3 07W
Haywards Heath UK	15	G3	51 00N	0 06W
Hefei China	44	D6	31 55N	117 18E
Helensburgh UK	11	D2	56 01N	4 44W
Helmsdale UK	11	E4	58 07N	3 40W
Helsinki Finland	33	F3	60 08N	25 00E
Helston UK	14	B2	50 05N	5 16W
Helvellyn *mt.* UK	13	F3	54 32N	3 02W
Hemel Hempstead UK	15	G3	51 46N	0 28W
Hemsworth UK	13	H2	53 38N	1 21W
Henley-on-Thames UK	15	G3	51 32N	0 56W
Hereford UK	14	E4	52 04N	2 43W
Hexham UK	13	G3	54 58N	2 06W
Heysham UK	13	G3	54 02N	2 54W
High Wycombe UK	15	G3	51 38N	0 46W
Hillingdon UK	15	G3	51 32N	0 27W
Himalaya *mts.* Asia	41	E4/F3	28 00N	85 00E
Hinckley UK	15	F4	52 33N	1 21W
Hiroshima Japan	48	B1	34 23N	132 27E
Hitchin UK	15	G3	51 57N	0 17W
Hobart Australia	67	E1	42 53S	147 19E
Hô Chi Minh Vietnam	45	C4	10 46N	106 43E
Hodeida Yemen Rep.	40	B2	14 50N	42 58E
Hohhot China	44	D7	40 49N	117 37E
Hokkaido *i.* Japan	48	D3	43 30N	143 00E
Holsworthy UK	14	C2	50 49N	4 21W
Holyhead UK	14	C5	53 19N	4 38W
Holy Island UK	14	C5	53 16N	4 39W
Homyel' Belarus	33	G2	52 25N	31 00E

HONDURAS 57 E1
Hong Kong China 44 D4 23 00N 114 00E
Honiara Solomon Islands
67 F5 9 28S 159 57E
Honiton UK 14 D2 50 48N 3 13W
Honshu *i.* Japan 48 B1/D3 37 15N 139 00E
Horn, Cape Chile 63 C1 56 00S 67 15W
Hornsea UK 13 J2 53 55N 0 10W
Horsham UK 15 G3 51 04N 0 21W
Hounslow UK 15 G3 51 28N 0 21W
Houston USA 59 D1 29 45N 95 25W
Hove UK 15 G2 50 49N 0 11W
Hoy *i.* UK 10 E4 58 48N 3 20W
Huang He *r.* China 44 D6 36 00N 116 00E
Huddersfield UK 13 H2 53 39N 1 47W
Hudson Bay Canada 56 E3/E4 60 00N 89 00W
HUNGARY 34/35 D3/E3
Hunstanton UK 15 H4 52 57N 0 30E
Huntingdon UK 15 G4 52 20N 0 12W
Huntly UK 11 F3 57 27N 2 47W
Huron, Lake Canada/USA
59 E3 45 00N 83 00W
Hyderabad India 41 E2 17 22N 78 26E
Hyderabad Pakistan 40 D3 25 22N 68 22E

I
Ibadan Nigeria 52 B3 7 23N 3 56E
Ibiza *i.* Balearic Islands 34 C2 39 00N 1 20E
ICELAND 32 A3/B3
Idaho *state* USA 58 B3 44 00N 115 00W
Ilfracombe UK 14 C3 51 13N 4 08W
Ilhéus Brazil 62 F5 14 50S 39 06W
Ilkeston UK 15 F4 52 59N 1 18W
Ilkley UK 13 H2 53 55N 1 50W
Illinois *state* USA 59 E3 40 00N 89 00W
Ilminster UK 14 E2 50 56N 2 55W
Immingham UK 13 J2 53 36N 0 11W
Imphal India 41 G3 24 47N 93 55E
Inchon South Korea 44 E6 37 30N 126 38E
INDIA 41 E1/E4
Indiana *state* USA 59 E3 40 00N 86 00W
Indianapolis USA 59 E2 39 45N 86 10W
Indian Ocean 73
INDONESIA 45 B3/F2
Indore India 41 E3 22 42N 75 54E
Indus *r.* Asia 40/41 D3/E4 27 00N 68 00E
Inishowen Peninsula RoI
16 D5 55 15N 7 15W
Inner Hebrides *is.* UK 11 B2/B3 56 45N 6 45W
Innsbruck Austria 34 D3 47 17N 11 25E
Inveraray UK 11 C2 56 13N 5 05W
Inverbervie UK 11 F2 56 51N 2 17W
Invergarry UK 11 D3 57 02N 4 47W
Invergordon UK 11 D3 57 42N 4 10W
Inverkeithing UK 11 E2 56 02N 3 25W
Invermoriston UK 11 D3 57 13N 4 38W
Inverness UK 11 D3 57 27N 4 15W
Inverurie UK 11 F3 57 17N 2 23W
Iowa *state* USA 59 D3 42 00N 94 00W
Ipoh Malaysia 45 C3 4 36N 101 05E
Ipswich UK 15 J4 52 04N 1 10E
Iquique Chile 63 B4 20 15S 70 08W
Iquitos Peru 62 B6 3 51S 73 13W
Iraklíon Greece 35 E2 35 20N 25 08E
IRAN 40 B4/C4
IRAQ 40 B4
Irish Sea British Isles 12 D2/E2 53 30N 5 30W
Irkutsk Russia 44 C8 52 18N 104 15E
Irrawaddy *r.* Myanmar 44 B4/B5 26 00N 97 30E
Irvine UK 11 D1 55 37N 4 40W
Islamabad Pakistan 41 E4 33 42N 73 10E
Islay *i.* UK 11 B1 55 48N 6 12W
Isle of Man British Isles 12 E3 54 15N 4 30W
ISRAEL 40 A4
Istanbul Turkey 35 E3 41 02N 28 57E
ITALY 36
Izmir Turkey 35 E2 38 25N 27 10E

J
Jackson USA 59 D2 32 20N 90 11W
Jacksonville USA 59 E2 30 20N 81 40W
Jaipur India 41 E3 26 53N 75 50E
Jakarta Indonesia 45 C2 6 08S 106 45E
JAMAICA 62 B8
James Bay Canada 59 E4/F4 53 45N 81 00W
Jammu and Kashmir *state* Southern Asia
41 E4 29 40N 76 30E
Jamshedpur India 41 F3 22 47N 86 12E
JAPAN 48
Java *i.* Indonesia 45 C2/D2 7 00S 110 00E
Jaya Peak Indonesia 66 D5 4 05S 137 09E
Jedburgh UK 11 F1 55 29N 2 34W
Jedda Saudi Arabia 40 A3 21 30N 39 10E
Jerusalem Israel/West Bank
40 A4 31 47N 35 13E
Jilin China 44 E7 43 53N 126 35E
Jinan China 44 D6 36 41N 117 00E
Johannesburg RSA 53 C1 26 10S 28 02E
John o'Groats UK 10 E4 58 38N 3 05W
Johnstone UK 11 D1 55 50N 4 31W
Johor Bahru Malaysia 45 C3 1 27N 103 45E
Jönköping Sweden 32 E2 57 45N 14 10E
JORDAN 40 A4
Juba Sudan 52 C3 4 50N 31 35E
Jura *i.* UK 11 B1/C2 55 55N 6 00W
Jura *mts.* France/Switzerland
36 A3 46 30N 6 00E

K
Kabul Afghanistan 40 D4 34 30N 70 00E
Kalahari Desert Southern Africa
53 C1 23 30S 23 00E
Kaliningrad Russia 33 F2 54 40N 20 30E
Kampala Uganda 52 C3 0 19N 32 35E
Kandahar Afghanistan 40 D4 31 35N 65 45E
Kano Nigeria 52 B3 12 00N 8 31E
Kanpur India 41 F3 26 27N 80 14E
Kansas *state* USA 59 D2 38 00N 98 00W
Kansas City USA 59 D2 39 02N 94 33W
Karachi Pakistan 40 D3 24 52N 67 03E
Kathmandu Nepal 41 F3 27 42N 85 19E
Katowice Poland 33 E2 50 15N 18 59E
Kaunas Lithuania 33 F2 54 52N 23 55E
KAZAKHSTAN 39 B5/D5
Kazan' Russia 33 H2 55 45N 49 10E
Keady UK 16 E4 54 15N 6 42W
Keighley UK 13 H2 53 52N 1 54W
Keith UK 11 F3 57 32N 2 57W
Kells RoI 17 E3 53 44N 6 53W
Kelso UK 11 F1 55 36N 2 25W
Kendal UK 13 G3 54 20N 2 45W
Kenilworth UK 15 F4 52 21N 1 34W
Kentucky *state* USA 59 E2 37 00N 85 00W
KENYA 54
Kenya, Mount Kenya 54 B2 0 10S 37 19E
Kerman Iran 40 C4 30 18N 57 05E
Keswick UK 13 F3 54 37N 3 08W
Kettering UK 15 G4 52 24N 0 44W
Keynsham UK 14 E3 51 26N 2 30W
Kharkiv Ukraine 35 F3 50 00N 36 15E
Khartoum Sudan 52 C3 15 33N 32 35E
Khulna Bangladesh 42 B1 22 49N 89 34E
Kidderminster UK 14 E4 52 23N 2 14W
Kidsgrove UK 14 E5 53 05N 2 14W
Kidwelly UK 14 C3 51 45N 4 18W
Kiel Germany 34 D4 54 20N 10 08E
Kielder Water *res.* UK 13 G4 55 10N 2 30W
Kiev Ukraine 33 G2 50 25N 30 30E
Kigali Rwanda 52 C2 1 56S 30 04E
Kilimanjaro, Mount Tanzania
54 B2 3 04S 37 22E
Kilkeel UK 16 E4 54 04N 6 00W
Kilkenny RoI 17 D2 52 39N 7 15W
Killarney RoI 17 B2 52 03N 9 30W
Kilmacrenan RoI 16 D5 55 02N 7 47W
Kilmaluag UK 11 B3 57 41N 6 17W
Kilmarnock UK 11 D1 55 36N 4 30W
Kinabalu, Mount Malaysia
45 D3 6 03N 116 32E
Kinbrace UK 10 E4 58 15N 3 56W
Kingsbridge UK 14 D2 50 17N 3 46W
King's Lynn UK 15 H4 52 45N 0 24E
Kingston Jamaica 62 B8 17 58N 76 48W
Kingston upon Hull UK 13 J2 53 45N 0 20W
Kingston upon Thames UK
15 G3 51 25N 0 18W
Kingswood UK 14 E3 51 28N 2 30W
Kington UK 14 D4 52 12N 3 01W
Kingussie UK 11 D3 57 05N 4 03W
Kinloch UK 11 B3 57 01N 6 17W
Kinross UK 11 E2 56 13N 3 27W
Kinshasa Congo Dem. Rep.
52 B2 4 18S 15 18E
Kintyre *p.* UK 11 C1 55 30N 5 35W
KIRIBATI 70
Kirkby UK 13 G2 53 29N 2 54W
Kirkcaldy UK 11 E2 56 07N 3 10W
Kirkcudbright UK 12 E3 54 50N 4 03W
Kirkintilloch UK 11 D1 55 57N 4 10W
Kirkuk Iraq 40 B4 35 28N 44 26E
Kirkwall UK 10 F4 58 59N 2 58W
Kirov Russia 33 H2 58 00N 49 38E
Kirriemuir UK 11 E2 56 41N 3 01W
Kisangani Congo Dem. Rep.
52 C3 0 33N 25 14E
Kisumu Kenya 54 A2 0 08S 34 47E
Kita-Kyushu Japan 48 B1 33 52N 130 49E
Knaresborough UK 13 H3 54 00N 1 27W
Knighton UK 14 D4 52 21N 3 03W
Kobe Japan 48 C1 34 40N 135 12E
Kolkata India 41 F3 22 30N 88 20E
Konya Turkey 35 F2 37 51N 32 30E
Kosciuszko, Mount Australia
67 E2 36 27S 148 17E
Kota Kinabalu Malaysia 45 D3 5 59N 116 04E
Kryvyy Rih Ukraine 35 F3 47 55N 33 24E
Kuala Lumpur Malaysia 45 C3 3 09N 101 42E
Kuching Malaysia 45 D3 1 35N 110 21E
Kunming China 44 C5 25 04N 102 41E
Kursk Russia 33 G2 51 45N 36 14E
KUWAIT 40 B3
Kuwait Kuwait 40 B3 29 20N 48 00E
Kwangju South Korea 44 E6 35 07N 126 52E
Kyle of Lochalsh UK 11 C3 57 17N 5 43W
Kyoto Japan 48 C2 35 02N 135 45E
KYRGYZSTAN 41 E5
Kyushu *i.* Japan 48 B1 32 20N 131 00E

L
Laâyoune Western Sahara
52 A4 27 10N 13 11W
Ladoga, Lake Russia 33 G3 61 00N 30 00E
Lagos Nigeria 52 B3 6 27N 3 28E
Lahore Pakistan 41 E4 31 35N 74 18E
Lairg UK 11 D4 58 01N 4 25W
Lake District UK 13 F3/G3 54 30N 3 00W
Lammermuir Hills UK 11 F1 55 50N 2 45W
Lampeter UK 14 C4 52 07N 4 05W
Lanark UK 11 E1 55 41N 3 48W
Lancaster UK 13 G3 54 03N 2 48W
Land's End *c.* UK 14 B2 50 03N 5 44W
Langholm UK 13 F4 55 09N 3 00W
Lanzhou China 44 C6 36 01N 103 45E
LAOS 44/45 C4/C5
La Paz Bolivia 62 C5 16 30S 68 10W
Largs UK 11 D1 55 48N 4 52W
Larne UK 16 F4 54 51N 5 49W
Las Vegas USA 58 B2 36 10N 115 10W
LATVIA 33 F2
Launceston UK 14 C2 50 38N 4 21W
Lausanne Switzerland 36 A3 46 32N 6 39E
LEBANON 40 A4
Ledbury UK 14 E4 52 02N 2 25W
Leeds UK 13 H2 53 50N 1 35W
le Havre France 34 C3 49 30N 0 06E
Leicester UK 15 F4 52 38N 1 05W
Leighton Buzzard UK 15 G3 51 55N 0 41W
Leipzig Germany 34 D4 51 20N 12 25E
le Mans France 34 C3 48 00N 0 12E
Leominster UK 14 E4 52 14N 2 45W
Lerwick UK 10 G6 60 09N 1 09W
LESOTHO 53 C1
Letchworth UK 15 G3 51 58N 0 14W
Letterkenny RoI 16 D4 54 57N 7 44W
Lewes UK 15 H2 50 52N 0 01E
Lewis *i.* UK 10/11 B3/B4 58 15N 6 30W
Leyburn UK 13 H3 54 19N 1 49W
Leyland UK 13 G2 53 42N 2 42W
Lhasa China 44 B5 29 08N 87 43E
LIBERIA 52 A3
Libreville Gabon 52 B3 0 30N 9 25E
LIBYA 52 B4/C4
Lichfield UK 14 F4 52 42N 1 48W
LIECHTENSTEIN 34 C3
Lille France 34 C4 50 39N 3 05E
Lilongwe Malawi 53 C2 13 58S 33 49E
Lima Peru 62 B5 12 06S 8 40W
Limassol Cyprus 35 F2 34 04N 33 03E
Limavady UK 16 E5 55 03N 6 57W
Limerick RoI 17 C2 52 04N 8 38W
Lincoln UK 13 J2 53 14N 0 33W
Lincoln Wolds *hills* UK 13 J2 53 25N 0 05W
Linlithgow UK 11 E1 55 59N 3 37W
Lisbon Portugal 34 B2 38 44N 9 08W
Lisburn UK 16 E4 54 31N 6 03W
Liskeard UK 14 C2 50 28N 4 28W
LITHUANIA 33 F2
Littlehampton UK 15 G2 50 48N 0 33W
Little Rock USA 59 D2 34 42N 92 17W
Liverpool UK 13 G2 53 25N 2 55W
Livingston UK 11 E1 55 53N 3 32W
Livorno Italy 36 B2 43 33N 10 18E
Lizard UK 14 B1 49 57N 5 13W
Lizard Point UK 14 B1 49 56N 5 13W
Ljubljana Slovenia 36 B3 46 04N 14 30E
Llandeilo UK 14 D3 51 53N 3 59W
Llandovery UK 14 D3 51 59N 3 48W
Llandrindod Wells UK 14 D4 52 15N 3 23W
Llandudno UK 14 D5 53 19N 3 49W
Llanelli UK 14 C3 51 42N 4 10W
Llangollen UK 14 D4 52 58N 3 10W
Llanidloes UK 14 D4 52 27N 3 32W
Lleyn Peninsula UK 14 C4 52 53N 4 30W
Lochaline *tn.* UK 11 C2 56 32N 5 47W
Loch Fyne *b.* UK 11 C2 56 10N 5 05W
Lochgilphead *tn.* UK 11 C2 56 03N 5 26W
Loch Linnhe *b.* UK 11 C2 56 35N 5 25W
Loch Lomond *l.* UK 11 D2 56 10N 4 35W
Loch Long *l.* UK 11 D2 56 10N 4 50W
Lochmaddy *tn.* UK 11 A3 57 36N 7 08W
Lochnagar *mt.* UK 11 E2 56 57N 3 16W
Loch Ness *l.* UK 11 D3 57 02N 4 30W
Lochranza *tn.* UK 11 C1 55 42N 5 18W
Loch Tay *l.* UK 11 D2 56 31N 4 10W
Lockerbie UK 13 F4 55 07N 3 22W
Lodz Poland 33 E2 51 49N 19 28E
Loire *r.* France 34 C3 47 30N 1 00W
Lombok *i.* Indonesia 45 D2 8 30S 116 30E
Lomé Togo 52 B3 6 10N 1 21E
London UK 15 G3 51 30N 0 10W
Londonderry UK 16 D4 54 59N 7 19W
Long Eaton UK 15 F4 52 54N 1 15W
Longford RoI 17 D3 53 44N 7 47W
Looe UK 14 C2 50 21N 4 27W
Los Angeles USA 58 B2 34 00N 118 15W
Lossiemouth UK 11 E3 57 43N 3 18W
Lostwithiel UK 14 C2 50 25N 4 40W
Lough Allen *l.* RoI 16 C4 54 15N 8 00W
Loughborough UK 15 F4 52 47N 1 11W
Lough Corrib *l.* RoI 17 B3 53 10N 9 10W
Lough Derg *l.* RoI 17 C2 52 55N 8 15W
Lough Foyle *est.* UK/RoI
16 D5 55 10N 7 10W
Lough Mask *l.* RoI 17 B3 53 40N 9 30W
Lough Neagh *l.* UK 16 E4 54 35N 6 30W
Lough Ree *l.* RoI 17 D3 53 35N 8 00W
Lough Swilly *b.* RoI 16 D5 55 20N 7 35W
Louisiana *state* USA 59 D2 32 00N 92 00W
Louisville USA 59 E2 38 13N 85 48W
Louth UK 13 J2 53 22N 0 01W
Lower Lough Erne *l.* UK 16 D4 54 25N 7 45W
Lowestoft UK 15 J4 52 29N 1 45E
Luanda Angola 53 B2 8 50S 13 15E
Lubango Angola 53 B2 14 55S 13 30E
Lubumbashi Congo Dem. Rep.
53 C2 11 41S 27 29E
Lucknow India 41 F3 26 50N 80 54E
Ludhiana India 41 E4 30 56N 75 52E
Ludlow UK 14 E4 52 22N 2 43W
Luleå Sweden 33 F3 65 35N 22 10E
Lundy *i.* UK 14 C3 51 11N 4 40W
Luoyang China 44 D6 34 47N 112 26E
Lurgan UK 16 E4 54 28N 6 20W
Lusaka Zambia 53 C2 15 26S 28 20E
Luton UK 15 G3 51 53N 0 25W
LUXEMBOURG 34 C3/C4
Luxembourg Lux. 34 C3 49 37N 6 08E
Luxor Egypt 52 C4 25 41N 32 24E
Luzon *i.* The Philippines
44/45 E4 15 00N 122 00E
L'viv Ukraine 35 E3 49 50N 24 00E
Lybster UK 10 E4 58 18N 3 13W
Lyme Regis UK 14 E2 50 44N 2 57W
Lymington UK 15 F2 50 46N 1 33W
Lynton UK 14 D2 51 15N 3 50W
Lyons France 34 C3 45 46N 4 50E
Lytham St. Anne's UK 13 F2 53 45N 3 01W

M
Mablethorpe UK 13 K2 53 21N 0 15E
Macao China 44 D4 22 10N 113 40E
Macclesfield UK 13 G2 53 16N 2 07W
Macduff UK 11 F3 57 40N 2 29W
MACEDONIA, FORMER YUGOSLAV REPUBLIC OF (FYROM) 35 E3
Machynlleth UK 14 D4 52 35N 3 51W
MADAGASCAR 53 D1/D2
Madeira Islands Atlantic Ocean
52 A4 32 45N 17 00W
Madrid Spain 34 B3 40 25N 3 43W
Madurai India 41 E1 9 55N 78 07E
Maghera UK 16 E4 54 51N 6 40W
Magherafelt UK 16 E4 54 45N 6 36W
Maidenhead UK 15 G3 51 32N 0 44W
Maidstone UK 15 H3 51 17N 0 32E
Malabo Equatorial Guinea
52 B3 3 45N 8 48E
Málaga Spain 34 B2 36 43N 4 25W
MALAWI 53 C2
MALAYSIA 45 C3/D3
MALDIVES 39 C3
MALI 52 A3/B3
Malin Head *c.* RoI 16 D5 55 30N 7 20W
Mallaig UK 11 C3 57 00N 5 50W
Mallorca *i.* Balearic Islands
34 C2 39 50N 2 30E
Malmesbury UK 14 E3 51 36N 2 06W
Malmö Sweden 32 E2 55 35N 13 00E
MALTA 36 B1
Malton UK 13 J3 54 08N 0 48W
Managua Nicaragua 57 E1 12 06N 86 18W
Manaus Brazil 62 D6 3 06S 60 00W
Manchester UK 13 G2 53 30N 2 15W
Mandalay Myanmar 44 B5 21 57N 96 04E
Mangalore India 41 E2 12 54N 74 51E
Mangotsfield UK 14 E3 51 29N 2 31W
Manila The Philippines 45 E4 14 37N 120 58E
Mansfield UK 15 F5 53 09N 1 11W
Maputo Mozambique 53 C1 25 58S 32 35E
Maracaibo Venezuela 62 B8 10 44N 71 37W
Maracaibo, Lake Venezuela
62 B7 9 50N 71 30W
Mar del Plata Argentina 63 D3 38 00S 57 32W
Margate UK 15 J3 51 24N 1 24E
Mariupol Ukraine 35 F3 47 05N 37 34E
Market Drayton UK 14 E4 52 54N 2 29W
Market Harborough UK 15 G4 52 29N 0 55W
Market Rasen UK 13 J2 53 24N 0 21W
Marlborough UK 14 F3 51 26N 1 43W
Marlow UK 15 G3 51 35N 0 48W
Marseilles France 34 C3 43 18N 5 22E
MARSHALL ISLANDS 71
Maryland *state* USA 59 F2 39 00N 77 00W
Maryport UK 12 F3 54 43N 3 30W
Maseru Lesotho 53 C1 29 19S 27 29E
Mashhad Iran 40 C4 36 16N 59 34E
Massachusetts *state* USA
59 F3 42 00N 72 00W
Massif Central *mts.* France
34 C3 45 00N 3 30E
Matsue Japan 48 B2 35 29N 133 04E
Matsuyama Japan 48 B1 33 50N 132 47E
MAURITANIA 52 A3/A4
MAURITIUS 71
Maybole UK 12 E4 55 21N 4 41W
Mecca Saudi Arabia 40 A3 21 26N 39 49E
Medan Indonesia 45 B3 3 35N 98 39E
Medellín Colombia 62 B7 6 15N 75 36W
Medina Saudi Arabia 40 A3 24 30N 39 35E
Mediterranean Sea Africa/Europe
34/35
Meerut India 41 E3 29 00N 77 42E
Mekong *r.* South Asia 44 C5 15 00N 105 00E
Melbourne Australia 67 E2 37 49S 144 58E
Melrose UK 11 F1 55 36N 2 44W
Melton Mowbray UK 15 G4 52 46N 0 53W
Memphis USA 59 E2 35 10N 90 00W
Mendip Hills UK 14 E3 51 18N 2 45W
Mendoza Argentina 63 C3 32 48S 68 52W
Menorca *i.* Balearic Islands
34 C2 39 45N 4 15E
Mere UK 14 E3 51 06N 2 16W
Mersey *r.* UK 13 G2 53 20N 2 55W
Merthyr Tydfil UK 14 D3 51 46N 3 23W
Merton UK 15 G3 51 25N 0 12W
Messina Italy 36 C1 38 13N 15 33E
MEXICO 57 D2/E1
Mexico City Mexico 57 E1 19 25N 99 10W
Mexico, Gulf of Mexico 59 D1/E1 25 00N 90 00W
Miami USA 59 E1 25 45N 80 15W
Michigan *state* USA 59 E3 45 00N 85 00W
Michigan, Lake Canada/USA
59 E3 45 00N 87 00W
Middlesbrough UK 13 H3 54 35N 1 14W
Milan Italy 36 A3 45 28N 9 12E
Mildenhall UK 15 H4 52 21N 0 30E
Milford Haven UK 14 B3 51 44N 5 02W
Milton Keynes UK 15 G4 52 02N 0 42W
Milwaukee USA 59 E3 43 03N 87 56W
Minch, The *sd.* UK 11 B3/C4 58 00N 6 00W
Mindanao *i.* The Philippines
45 E3 8 00N 125 00E
Minehead UK 14 D2 51 13N 3 29W
Minneapolis USA 59 D3 45 00N 93 15W
Minnesota *state* USA 59 D3 47 00N 95 00W
Minsk Belarus 33 F2 53 51N 27 30E
Mississippi *r.* USA 59 D2 33 00N 90 30W
Mississippi *state* USA 59 D2/E2 32 00N 90 00W
Missouri *r.* USA 58 B3 48 00N 109 00W
Missouri *state* USA 59 D2 38 00N 93 00W
Mobile USA 59 E2 30 40N 88 05W
Módena Italy 36 B2 44 39N 10 55E
Moffat UK 12 F4 55 20N 3 27W
Mogadishu Somalia 52 D3 2 02N 45 21E

Mold UK 14 D5 53 10N 3 08W
MOLDOVA 35 E3
Mombasa Kenya 54 B2 4 04S 39 40E
MONACO 36 A2
Monadhliath Mountains UK 11 D3 57 10N 4 00W
Monaghan RoI 16 E4 54 15N 6 58W
MONGOLIA 44 B7/D7
Monmouth UK 14 E3 51 50N 2 43W
Monrovia Liberia 52 A3 6 20N 10 46W
Montana *state* USA 58 B3/C3 47 00N 111 00W
Mont Blanc *mt.* France/Italy 34 C3 45 50N 6 52E
MONTENEGRO 35 D3
Monterrey Mexico 58 C1 25 40N 100 20W
Montevideo Uruquay 63 D3 34 55S 56 10W
Montgomery UK 14 D4 52 34N 3 10W
Montréal Canada 59 F3 45 32N 73 36W
Montrose UK 11 F2 56 43N 2 29W
Monza Italy 36 A3 45 35N 9 16E
Moray Firth *est.* UK 11 E3 57 45N 3 45W
Morecambe UK 13 G3 54 04N 2 53W
MOROCCO 52 A4
Moroni Comoros 53 D2 11 40S 43 16E
Moscow Russia 33 G2 55 45N 37 42E
Mosul Iraq 40 B4 36 21N 43 08E
Motherwell UK 11 D1 55 48N 3 59W
MOZAMBIQUE 53 C2
Muck *i.* UK 11 B2 56 50N 6 15W
Mukalla Yemen Rep. 40 B2 14 34N 49 09E
Mull *i.* UK 11 B2/C2 56 25N 6 00W
Mullingar RoI 17 D3 53 32N 7 20W
Mull of Kintyre *c.* UK 11 C1 55 17N 5 55W
Multan Pakistan 41 E4 30 10N 71 36E
Mumbai India 41 E2 18 56N 72 51E
Munich Germany 34 D3 48 08N 11 35E
Murmansk Russia 33 G3 68 59N 33 08E
Murray *r.* Australia 67 E2 35 40S 144 00E
Muscat Oman 40 C3 23 37N 58 38E
Musselburgh UK 11 E1 55 57N 3 04W
Mwanza Tanzania 52 C2 2 31S 32 56E
MYANMAR 44/45 B4/B5

N
Naas RoI 17 E3 53 13N 6 39W
Nagasaki Japan 48 A1 32 45N 129 52E
Nagoya Japan 48 C2 35 08N 136 53E
Nagpur India 41 E3 21 10N 79 12E
Nairn UK 11 E3 57 35N 3 53W
Nairobi Kenya 54 B2 1 17S 36 50E
Namib Desert Namibia 53 B1 22 00S 14 00E
NAMIBIA 53 B1
Nanchang China 44 D5 28 33N 115 58E
Nanjing China 44 D6 32 03N 118 47E
Naples Italy 36 B2 40 50N 14 15E
Nassau The Bahamas 59 F1 25 05N 77 20W
Nasser, Lake Egypt 52 C4 22 35N 31 40E
Natal Brazil 62 F6 5 46S 35 15W
NAURU 67 G5
Ndjamena Chad 52 B3 12 10N 14 59E
Neath UK 14 D3 51 40N 3 48W
Nebraska *state* USA 58/59 C3/D3 42 00N 102 00W
Nelson UK 13 G2 53 51N 2 13W
NEPAL 41 F3
NETHERLANDS 34 C4
Nevada *state* USA 58 B2 39 00N 118 00W
Newark USA 59 F3 40 43N 74 11W
Newark-on-Trent UK 15 G5 53 05N 0 49W
Newbury UK 15 F3 51 25N 1 20W
New Caledonia *i.* Pacific Ocean 67 G3 22 00S 165 00E
Newcastle UK 16 F4 54 12N 5 54W
Newcastle Emlyn UK 14 C4 52 02N 4 28W
Newcastle-under-Lyme UK 14 E5 53 00N 2 14W
Newcastle upon Tyne UK 13 H3 54 59N 1 35W
New Cumnock UK 11 D1 55 24N 4 12W
Newfoundland *i.* Canada 56 G3 53 51N 56 56W
New Galloway UK 12 E4 55 05N 4 10W
New Hampshire *state* USA 59 F3 43 00N 72 00W
New Jersey *state* USA 59 F2 40 00N 75 00W
Newmarket UK 15 H4 52 15N 0 25E
New Mexico *state* USA 58 C2 35 00N 107 00W
New Orleans USA 59 D1 30 00N 90 03W
Newport UK 14 E4 52 47N 2 22W
Newport UK 14 D3 51 35N 3 00W
Newport UK 15 F2 50 42N 1 18W
New Quay UK 14 C4 52 13N 4 22W
Newquay UK 14 B2 50 25N 5 05W
Newry UK 16 E4 54 11N 6 20W
New South Wales *state* Australia 67 E2 32 00S 145 00E
Newton Abbot UK 14 D2 50 32N 3 36W
Newton Aycliffe UK 13 H3 54 37N 1 34W
Newtonmore UK 11 D3 57 04N 4 08W
Newton Stewart UK 12 E3 54 57N 4 29W
Newtown UK 14 D4 52 32N 3 19W
Newtownabbey UK 16 F4 54 40N 5 54W
Newtownards UK 16 F4 54 36N 5 41W
Newtownhamilton UK 16 E4 54 12N 6 35W
Newtownstewart UK 16 D4 54 43N 7 24W
New York USA 59 F3 40 40N 73 50W
New York *state* USA 59 F3 43 00N 76 00W
NEW ZEALAND 67 G1/H2
Niamey Niger 52 B3 13 32N 2 05E
NICARAGUA 57 E1
Nicaragua, Lake Nicaragua 56 E1 11 50N 86 00W
Nice France 34 C3 43 42N 7 16E
Nicobar Islands India 41 G2 8 30N 94 00E
Nicosia Cyprus 35 F2 35 11N 33 23E
NIGER 52 B3
Niger *r.* Africa 52 A3/B3 11 00N 5 00W
NIGERIA 52 B3
Nile *r.* Sudan/Egypt 52 C3/C4 28 00N 31 00E
Nizhniy Novgorod Russia 33 H2 56 20N 44 00E
Norfolk USA 59 F2 36 54N 76 18W
Northallerton UK 13 H3 54 20N 1 26W
Northampton UK 15 G4 52 14N 0 54W
North Berwick UK 11 F2 56 04N 2 44W
North Carolina *state* USA 59 F2 36 00N 80 00W
North Channel British Isles 12 D3/D4 55 20N 5 50W
North Dakota *state* USA 58/59 C3/D3 47 00N 102 00W
North Downs *hills* UK 15 G3/H3 51 15N 0 30E
Northern Ireland *country* UK 16 D4/D5
NORTHERN MARIANAS 71
Northern Territory Australia 66 D3/D4 19 00S 132 00E
NORTH KOREA 44 E6/E7
North Sea Atlantic Ocean 32 D2 57 00N 4 00E
North Uist *i.* UK 11 A3 57 04N 7 15W
Northwest Highlands UK 10/11 C3/D4 58 00N 5 00W
Northwich UK 13 G2 53 16N 2 32W
North York Moors UK 13 J3 55 22N 0 45W
NORWAY 32/33 D2/F4
Norwich UK 15 J4 52 38N 1 18E
Nottingham UK 15 F4 52 58N 1 10W
Nouakchott Mauritania 52 A3 18 09N 15 58W
Novara Italy 36 A3 45 27N 8 37E
Novgorod Russia 33 G2 58 30N 31 20E
Nullarbor Plain Australia 66 C2 30 30S 129 00E
Nuremberg Germany 34 D3 49 27N 11 05E
Nuuk Greenland 57 G4 64 10N 51 40W
Nyasa, Lake Malawi/Mozambique 53 C2 12 00S 35 00E

O
Oban UK 11 C2 56 25N 5 29W
Ochil Hills UK 11 E2 56 15N 3 30W
Odense Denmark 32 E2 55 24N 10 25E
Oder *r.* Europe 34 D4 53 00N 14 30E
Odessa Ukraine 35 F3 46 30N 30 46E
Ohio *r.* USA 59 E2 39 00N 86 00W
Ohio *state* USA 59 E2/E3 40 00N 83 00W
Okavango Swamp Botswana 53 C2 19 00S 23 00E
Okehampton UK 14 C2 50 44N 4 00W
Oklahoma *state* USA 59 D2 36 00N 98 00W
Oklahoma City USA 59 D2 35 28N 97 33W
Öland *i.* Sweden 32 E2 56 45N 51 50E
Oldham UK 13 G2 53 33N 2 07W
Old Head of Kinsale *c.* RoI 17 C1 51 40N 8 30W
Oldmeldrum UK 11 F3 57 20N 2 20W
Omagh UK 16 D4 54 36N 7 18W
Omaha USA 59 D3 41 15N 96 00W
OMAN 40 C2/C3
Oman, Gulf of Iran/Oman 40 C3/D3 24 30N 58 30E
Omdurman Sudan 52 C3 15 37N 32 29E
Onega, Lake *l.* Russia 33 G3 62 00N 40 00E
Ontario, Lake Canada/USA 59 F3 43 45N 78 00W
Oporto Portugal 34 B3 41 09N 8 37W
Oran Algeria 52 A4 35 45N 0 38W
Oregon *state* USA 58 A3/B3 44 00N 120 00W
Orinoco *r.* Venezuela/Colombia 62 C7 6 40N 64 30W
Orkney Islands UK 10 E4/E5 59 00N 3 00W
Orléans France 34 C3 47 54N 1 54E
Osaka Japan 48 C1 34 40N 135 30E
Oslo Norway 32 E2 59 56N 10 45E
Ostrava Czech Rep. 35 D3 49 50N 18 15E
Oswestry UK 14 D4 52 52N 3 03W
Ouagadougou Burkina 52 A3 12 20N 1 40W
Oundle UK 15 G4 52 29N 0 29W
Outer Hebrides *is.* UK 10/11 A2/B4 58 00N 7 00W
Oxford UK 15 F3 51 46N 1 15W

P
Pacific Ocean 72/73
Padang Indonesia 45 C2 1 00S 100 21E
Padstow UK 14 C2 50 33N 4 56W
Padua Italy 36 B3 45 24N 11 53E
Paisley UK 11 D1 55 50N 4 26W
PAKISTAN 40/41 D3/E4
PALAU 71
Palawan *i.* The Philippines 45 D3 10 00N 119 00E
Palembang Indonesia 45 C2 2 59S 104 45E
Palermo Italy 36 B1 38 08N 13 23E
Palma Balearic Islands 34 C2 39 35N 2 39E
Pamirs *mts.* Asia 41 E4 38 00N 74 00E
PANAMA 62 A7/B7
Panamá City Panama 62 B7 8 57N 19 30W
PAPUA NEW GUINEA 67 E5
PARAGUAY 63 C4/D4
Paraguay *r.* South America 63 D4 21 20S 58 20W
Paramaribo Suriname 62 D7 5 52N 55 14W
Paraná Argentina 63 C3 31 45S 60 30W
Paraná *r.* South America 63 D4 30 00S 59 50W
Paris France 34 C3 48 52N 2 20E
Parma Italy 36 B2 44 48N 10 19E
Parnaíba Brazil 62 E6 2 58S 41 46W
Patna India 41 F3 25 37N 85 12E
Patras Greece 35 E2 38 14N 21 44E
Peebles UK 11 E1 55 39N 3 12W
Pekanbaru Indonesia 45 C3 0 33N 101 30E
Pembroke UK 14 C3 51 41N 4 55W
Penicuik UK 11 E1 55 50N 3 14W
Pennines *hills* UK 13 G3 54 30N 2 10W
Pennsylvania *state* USA 59 F3 41 00N 78 00W
Penrith UK 13 G3 54 40N 2 44W
Pentland Hills UK 11 E1 55 45N 3 30W
Penzance UK 14 B2 50 07N 5 33W
Perth UK 11 E2 56 42N 3 28W
Perth Australia 66 B2 31 57S 115 52E
PERU 62 B5/B6
Perugia Italy 36 B2 43 07N 12 23E
Pescara Italy 36 B2 42 27N 14 13E
Peshawar Pakistan 41 E4 34 01N 71 33E
Peterhead UK 11 G3 57 30N 1 46W
Peterlee UK 13 H3 54 46N 1 19W
Petersfield UK 15 G3 51 00N 0 56W
Philadelphia USA 59 F2 40 00N 75 10W
PHILIPPINES, THE 44/45 E3/E4
Phnom Penh Cambodia 45 C4 11 35N 104 55E
Phoenix USA 58 B2 33 30N 112 03W
Pickering UK 13 J3 54 14N 0 46W
Piraeus Greece 35 E2 37 57N 23 42E
Pisa Italy 36 B2 43 43N 10 24E
Pitlochry UK 11 E2 56 43N 3 45W
Plovdiv Bulgaria 35 E3 42 08N 24 45E
Plymouth UK 14 C2 50 23N 4 10W
Po *r.* Italy 36 A2/B2 45 00N 12 00E
Podgorica Montenegro 35 D3 42 28N 19 17 E
Pointe Noire *tn.* Congo 52 B2 4 46S 11 53E
POLAND 32/32 E2/F2
Pontardulais UK 14 C3 51 43N 4 02W
Pontefract UK 13 H2 53 42N 1 18W
Pontypool UK 14 D3 51 43N 3 02W
Pontypridd UK 14 D3 51 37N 3 22W
Poole UK 14 F2 50 43N 1 59W
Poolewe UK 11 C3 57 45N 5 37W
Portadown UK 16 E4 54 26N 6 27W
Port Askaig UK 11 B1 55 51N 6 07W
Port-au-Prince Haiti 62 B8 18 33N 72 20W
Port Ellen UK 11 B1 55 39N 6 12W
Port Glasgow UK 11 D1 55 56N 4 41W
Port Harcourt Nigeria 52 B3 4 43N 7 05E
Porthmadog UK 14 C4 52 55N 4 08W
Portknockie UK 11 F3 57 42N 2 52W
Portland USA 58 A3 45 32N 122 40W
Portlaoise RoI 17 D3 53 02N 7 17W
Port Moresby PNG 67 E5 9 30S 147 07E
Portnahaven UK 11 B1 55 41N 6 31W
Pôrto Alegre Brazil 63 D3 30 03S 51 10W
Port of Ness *tn.* UK 10 B4 58 29N 6 13W
Port of Spain Trinidad and Tobago 62 C8 10 38N 61 31W
Porto Novo Benin 52 B3 6 30N 2 47E
Pôrto Velho Brazil 62 C6 8 45S 63 54W
Portree UK 11 B3 57 24N 6 12W
Portrush UK 16 E5 55 12N 6 40W
Portsmouth UK 15 F2 50 48N 1 05W
Portsoy UK 11 F3 57 41N 2 41W
Port Talbot UK 14 D3 51 36N 3 47W
PORTUGAL 34 B2/B3
Poznan Poland 32 E2 52 25N 16 53E
Prague Czech Rep. 34 D3 50 06N 14 26E
Prato Italy 36 B2 43 53N 11 06E
Preseli Mountains UK 14 C3 51 58N 4 45W
Preston UK 13 G2 53 46N 2 42W
Prestwick UK 11 D1 55 30N 4 37W
Pretoria RSA 53 C1 25 45S 28 12E
Providence USA 59 F3 41 50N 71 28W
Puerto Montt Chile 63 B2 41 28S 73 00W
PUERTO RICO 62 C8
Pune India 41 E2 18 34N 73 58E
Punta Arenas Chile 63 B1 53 10S 70 56W
Pusan South Korea 44 E6 35 05N 129 02E
Pwllheli UK 14 C4 52 53N 4 25W
Pyongyang North Korea 44 E6 39 00N 125 47E
Pyrénées *mts.* France/Spain 34 C3 42 50N 0 30E

Q
QATAR 40 C3
Qingdao China 44 E6 36 04N 120 22E
Qiqihar China 44 E7 47 23N 124 00E
Quantock Hills UK 14 D2 51 05N 3 15W
Québec Canada 59 F3 46 50N 71 15W
Queensland *state* Australia 67 E3 22 00S 143 00E
Quetta Pakistan 40 D4 30 12N 67 00E
Quezon City The Philippines 45 E4 14 39N 121 02E
Quito Ecuador 62 B6 0 14S 78 30W

R
Raasay *i.* UK 11 B3 57 25N 6 05W
Rabat Salé Morocco 52 A4 34 02N 6 51W
Ramsgate UK 15 J3 51 20N 1 25E
Randalstown UK 16 E4 54 45N 6 19W
Rathlin Island UK 16 E5 55 20N 6 10W
Ravenna Italy 36 B2 44 25N 12 12E
Rawalpindi Pakistan 41 E4 33 36N 73 04E
Reading UK 15 G3 51 28N 0 59W
Recife Brazil 62 F6 8 06S 34 53W
Redbridge UK 15 H3 51 34N 0 05E
Redcar UK 13 H3 54 37N 1 04W
Redditch UK 14 F4 52 19N 1 56W
Redhill *tn.* UK 15 G3 51 14N 0 11W
Redruth UK 14 B2 50 13N 5 14W
Red Sea Middle East 52 C4/D3 27 00N 35 00E
Reggio di Calabria Italy 36 C1 38 06N 15 39E
Reggio nell'Emilia Italy 36 B2 44 42N 10 37E
Reigate UK 15 G3 51 14N 0 13W
Reims France 34 C3 49 15N 4 02E
Reno USA 58 B2 39 32N 119 49W
REPUBLIC OF IRELAND 16/17
REPUBLIC OF SOUTH AFRICA 53 C1
Reykjavík Iceland 32 A3 64 09N 21 58W
Rhayader UK 14 D4 52 18N 3 30W
Rhine *r.* Europe 34 C3 50 30N 7 30E
Rhode Island *state* USA 59 F3 41 00N 71 00W
Rhodes *i.* Greece 35 E2 36 00N 28 00E
Rhondda UK 14 D3 51 40N 3 30W
Rhône *r.* Switzerland/France 34 C3 45 00N 4 50E
Rhum *i.* UK 11 B2/B3 57 00N 6 20W
Rhyl UK 14 D5 53 19N 3 29W
Ribeirão Preto Brazil 63 E4 21 09S 47 48W
Richmond UK 13 H3 54 24N 1 44W
Richmond USA 59 F2 37 34N 77 27W
Richmond upon Thames UK 15 G3 51 28N 0 19W
Riga Latvia 33 F2 56 53N 24 08E
Rimini Italy 36 B2 44 03N 12 34E
Ringwood UK 14 F2 50 51N 1 47W
Rio Branco *tn.* Brazil 62 C6 9 59S 67 49W
Rio de Janeiro *tn.* Brazil 63 E4 22 53S 43 17W
Rio Grande *r.* Mexico/USA 58 C2 29 30N 105 00W
Ripon UK 13 H3 54 08N 1 31W
Riyadh Saudi Arabia 40 B3 24 39N 46 46E
Rochdale UK 13 G2 53 38N 2 09W
Rochester USA 59 F3 43 12N 77 37W
Rocky Mountains Canada/USA 56 C3/D2 46 00N 110 00W
ROMANIA 35 E3
Rome Italy 36 B2 41 53N 12 30E
Romsey UK 15 F2 50 59N 1 30W
Rosario Argentina 63 C3 33 00S 60 40W
Rosehearty UK 11 F3 57 42N 2 07W
Rosslare RoI 17 E2 52 15N 6 22W
Ross-on-Wye UK 14 E3 51 55N 2 35W
Rostock Germany 34 D4 54 06N 12 09E
Rostov-on-Don Russia 33 G1 47 15N 39 45E
Rotherham UK 13 H2 53 26N 1 20W
Rothes UK 11 E3 57 31N 3 13W
Rothesay UK 11 C1 55 51N 5 03W
Rotterdam Netherlands 34 C4 51 54N 4 28E
Royal Leamington Spa UK 15 F4 52 18N 1 31W
Royal Tunbridge Wells UK 15 H3 51 08N 0 16E
Rugby UK 15 F4 52 23N 1 15W
Rugeley UK 14 F4 52 46N 1 55W
Runcorn UK 13 G2 53 20N 2 44W
RUSSIAN FEDERATION 39 A5/J6
RWANDA 52 C2
Ryde UK 15 F2 50 44N 1 10W
Rye UK 15 H2 50 57N 0 44E
Ryukyu Islands Japan 38 F4 27 30N 127 30E

S
Sacramento USA 58 A2 38 32N 121 30W
Saffron Walden UK 15 H4 52 01N 0 15E
Sahara Desert North Africa 52 A4/B4 22 50N 0 00
St. Agnes UK 14 B2 50 18N 5 13W
St. Albans UK 15 G3 51 46N 0 21W
St. Andrews UK 11 F2 56 20N 2 48W
St. Austell UK 14 C2 50 20N 4 48W
St-Étienne France 34 C3 45 26N 4 23E
St. George's Channel British Isles 14 A3/B4 52 00N 6 00W
St. Helens UK 13 G2 53 28N 2 44W
St. Ives UK 15 G4 52 20N 0 05W
St. Ives UK 14 B2 50 12N 5 29W
ST. KITTS AND NEVIS 62 C8
St. Lawrence *r.* Canada/USA 59 F3 47 30N 70 00W
St. Louis USA 59 D2 38 40N 90 15W
ST. LUCIA 62 C8
St. Neots UK 15 G4 52 14N 0 17W
St. Paul USA 59 D3 45 00N 93 10W
St. Petersburg Russia 33 G2 59 55N 30 25E
ST. VINCENT AND THE GRENADINES 62 C8
Sakhalin *i.* Russia 44 G7/G8 50 00N 143 00E
Salalah Oman 40 C2 17 00N 54 04E
Salcombe UK 14 D2 50 13N 3 47W
Sale UK 13 G2 53 26N 2 19W
Salerno Italy 36 B2 40 40N 14 46E
Salford UK 13 G2 53 30N 2 16W
Salisbury UK 14 F3 51 05N 1 48W
Salisbury Plain UK 14 F3 51 10N 1 55W
Salta Argentina 63 C4 24 46S 65 28W
Saltash UK 14 C2 50 24N 4 12W
Saltcoats UK 11 D1 55 38N 4 47W
Salt Lake City USA 58 B3 40 45N 111 55W
Salvador Brazil 62 F5 12 58S 38 29W
Salween *r.* Myanmar/China 44 B5 21 00N 99 00E
Salzburg Austria 34 D3 47 48N 13 03E
Samarkand Uzbekistan 40 D4 39 40N 66 57E
SAMOA 70
Samsun Turkey 35 F3 41 17N 36 22E
Sana Yemen Rep. 40 B2 15 23N 44 14E
San Cristobal Venezuela 62 B7 7 46N 72 15W
San Diego USA 58 B2 32 45N 117 10W
San Francisco USA 58 A2 37 45N 122 27W
San José Costa Rica 57 E1 9 59N 84 04W
San Juan Puerto Rico 62 C8 18 29N 66 08W
SAN MARINO 36 B2 44 00N 12 00E
Sanquhar UK 12 F4 55 22N 3 56W
San Salvador El Salvador 57 E1 13 40N 89 10W
Santa Cruz Bolivia 62 C5 17 50S 63 10W
Santander Spain 34 B3 43 28N 3 48W
Santarém Brazil 62 D6 2 26S 54 41W
Santiago Chile 63 B3 33 30S 70 40W
Santo Domingo Dominican Republic 62 C8 18 30N 69 57W
Saône *r.* France 34 C3 47 30N 5 30E
São Paulo Brazil 63 E4 23 33S 46 39W
SÃO TOMÉ AND PRINCIPE 52 B3
Sapporo Japan 48 D3 43 05N 141 21E

Place	Page	Grid	Lat	Long
Sarajevo Bosnia-Herzegovina	35	D3	43 52N	18 26E
Sardinia i. Italy	36	A1/A2	40 00N	9 00E
Sassari Italy	36	A2	40 43N	8 34E
SAUDI ARABIA	40	B3		
Savannah USA	59	E2	32 04N	81 07W
Sawel mt. UK	16	D4	54 49N	7 02W
Scafell Pike mt. UK	13	F3	54 27N	3 14W
Scalasaig UK	11	B2	56 04N	6 12W
Scalloway UK	10	G6	60 08N	1 17W
Scapa UK	10	F4	58 58N	2 59W
Scarborough UK	13	J3	54 17N	0 24W
Scilly, Isles of UK	32	C1	49 56N	6 20W
Scotland country UK	10/11			
Scunthorpe UK	13	J2	53 35N	0 39W
Seascale UK	12	F3	54 24N	3 29W
Seattle USA	58	A3	47 35N	122 20W
Seine r. France	34	C3	49 15N	1 15E
Selby UK	13	H2	53 48N	1 04W
Selkirk UK	11	F1	55 33N	2 50W
Semarang Indonesia	45	D2	6 58S	110 29E
Sendai Japan	48	D2	38 16N	140 52E
SENEGAL	52	A3		
Seoul South Korea	44	E6	37 32N	127 00E
Seram i. Indonesia	45	E2/F2	3 30S	129 30E
SERBIA	35	D3/E3		
Sevastopol Ukraine	35	F3	44 36N	33 31E
Sevenoaks UK	15	H3	51 16N	0 12E
Severn r. UK	14	E3	51 30N	2 30W
Seville Spain	34	B2	37 24N	5 59W
SEYCHELLES	71			
Sfax Tunisia	52	B4	34 45N	10 43E
Sgurr Mór mt. UK	11	C3	57 42N	5 03W
Shaftesbury UK	14	E3	51 01N	2 12W
Shanghai China	44	E6	31 06N	121 22E
Shanklin UK	15	F2	50 38N	1 10W
Shannon r. RoI	17	B2/C2	52 45N	8 57W
Sheerness UK	15	H3	51 27N	0 45E
Sheffield UK	13	H2	53 23N	1 30W
Shenyang China	44	E7	41 50N	123 26E
Shepton Mallet UK	14	E3	51 12N	2 33W
Sherborne UK	14	E2	50 57N	2 31W
Shetland Islands UK	10	G6	60 00N	1 15W
Shikoku i. Japan	48	B1	33 40N	134 00E
Shiraz Iran	40	C3	29 38N	52 34E
Shrewsbury UK	14	E4	52 43N	2 45W
Sicily i. Italy	36	B1/C1	37 00N	14 00E
Sidlaw Hills UK	11	E2	56 30N	3 10W
Sidmouth UK	14	D2	50 41N	3 15W
SIERRA LEONE	52	A3		
Sierra Nevada mts. USA	59	A2/B2	37 00N	119 00W
Simferopol Ukraine	35	F3	44 57N	34 05E
Sinai p. Egypt	52	C4	28 32N	33 59E
SINGAPORE	45	C3		
Siracusa Italy	36	C1	37 04N	15 19E
Skegness UK	13	K2	53 10N	0 21E
Skelmersdale UK	13	G2	53 55N	2 48W
Skipton UK	13	G2	53 58N	2 01W
Skopje FYROM	35	E3	42 00N	21 28E
Skye i. UK	11	B3/C3	57 20N	6 15W
Sleaford UK	15	G4	53 00N	0 24W
Slieve Donard mt. UK	16		54 11N	5 55W
Sligo RoI	16	C4	54 17N	8 28W
Slough UK	15	G3	51 31N	0 36W
SLOVAKIA	34/35	D3/E3		
SLOVENIA	36	B3/C3		
Snaefell mt. Isle of Man	12		54 16N	4 28W
Snowdon mt. UK	14	C5	53 04N	4 05W
Socotra i. Yemen Rep.	40	C2	12 05N	54 10E
Sofia Bulgaria	35	E3	42 40N	23 18E
Solapur India	41	E2	17 43N	75 56E
Solihull UK	14	F4	52 25N	1 45W
SOLOMON ISLANDS	67	F5/G5		
SOMALIA	52	D3		
Southampton UK	15	F2	50 55N	1 25W
South Australia state Australia	66	D3	27 00S	135 00E
South Carolina state USA	59	E2/F2	34 00N	81 00W
South Dakota state USA	58/59	C3/D3	45 00N	102 00W
South Downs hills UK	15	G2	50 50N	0 45W
Southend UK	11	C1	55 20N	5 38W
Southend-on-Sea UK	15	H3	51 33N	0 43E
Southern Uplands UK	12/13	E4/G4	55 30N	3 30W
SOUTH KOREA	44	E6		
South Molton UK	14	D2	51 01N	3 50W
Southport UK	13	F2	53 39N	3 01W
South Ronaldsay i. UK	10	F4	58 47N	2 56W
South Shields UK	13	H3	55 00N	1 25W
South Uist i. UK	11	A3	57 20N	7 15W
Southwold UK	15	J4	52 20N	1 40E
SPAIN	34	B2/B3		
Spalding UK	15	G2	52 47N	0 10W
Spennymoor tn. UK	13	H3	54 42N	1 35W
Spilsby UK	13	K2	53 11N	0 05E
Split Croatia	34	D3	43 31N	16 28E
Spokane USA	58	B3	47 40N	117 25W
Spurn Head UK	13	K2	53 36N	0 07E
SRI LANKA	41	F1		
Srinagar Jammu & Kashmir	41	E4	34 08N	74 50E
Stafford UK	14	E4	52 48N	2 07W
Staines UK	15	G3	51 26N	0 30W
Stamford UK	15	G2	52 39N	0 29W
Stanley Falkland Islands	63	D1	51 45S	57 56W
Start Point c. UK	14	D2	50 13N	3 38W
Stavanger Norway	32	D2	58 58N	5 45E
Stevenage UK	15	G3	51 55N	0 14W
Stirling UK	11	E2	56 07N	3 57W
Stockbridge UK	15	F3	51 07N	1 29W
Stockholm Sweden	32	E2	59 20N	18 05E
Stockport UK	13	G2	53 25N	2 10W
Stockton-on-Tees UK	13	H3	54 34N	1 19W
Stoke-on-Trent UK	14	E5	53 00N	2 10W
Stonehaven UK	11	F2	56 58N	2 13W
Stornoway UK	10	B4	58 12N	6 23W
Stourbridge UK	14	E4	52 27N	2 09W
Stourport-on-Severn UK	14	E4	52 21N	2 16W
Stowmarket UK	15	J4	52 11N	1 00E
Strabane UK	16	D4	54 49N	7 27W
Strangford Lough UK	16		54 25N	5 45W
Stranraer UK	12	D3	54 55N	5 02W
Strasbourg France	34	C3	48 35N	7 45E
Stratford-upon-Avon UK	14	F4	52 12N	1 41W
Stromness UK	10	E4	58 57N	3 18W
Stroud UK	14	E3	51 45N	2 12W
Stuttgart Germany	34	C3	48 47N	9 12E
Sucre Bolivia	63	C5	19 05S	65 15W
SUDAN	52	C3		
Sudbury UK	15	H4	52 02N	0 44E
Suez Egypt	40	A3	29 59N	32 33E
Sulawesi i. Indonesia	45	D2/E3	2 00S	120 00E
Sumatra i. Indonesia	45	B3/C2	0 00N	100 00E
Sumba i. Indonesia	45	D2/E1	10 00S	120 00E
Sumburgh Head c. UK	10	G5	59 51N	1 16W
Sunderland UK	13	H3	54 55N	1 23W
Superior, Lake Canada/USA	59	E3	48 00N	88 00W
Surabaya Indonesia	45	D2	7 14S	112 45E
Surakarta Indonesia	45	D2	7 32S	110 50E
Surat India	41	E3	21 10N	72 54E
SURINAME	62	D8		
Sutton UK	15	G3	51 22N	0 12W
Sutton Coldfield UK	14	F4	52 34N	1 48W
Sutton in Ashfield UK	15	F5	53 08N	1 15W
Swaffham UK	15	H4	52 39N	0 41E
Swanage UK	14	F2	50 37N	1 58W
Swansea UK	14	D3	51 38N	3 57W
SWAZILAND	53	C1		
SWEDEN	32/33	E2/F3		
Swindon UK	14	F3	51 34N	1 47W
SWITZERLAND	34	C3/D3		
Sydney Australia	67	F2	33 52S	151 13E
SYRIA	40	A4		
Szczecin Poland	32	E2	53 25N	14 32E
Tabriz Iran	40	B4	38 05N	46 18E
Tadcaster UK	13	H2	53 53N	1 16W
Tagus r. Spain/Portugal	34	B2	39 30N	7 00W
Tain UK	11	D3	57 48N	4 04W
Taipei Taiwan	44	E5	25 03N	121 30E
TAIWAN	44	E5		
Taiyuan China	44	D6	37 50N	112 30E
TAJIKISTAN	40/41	E4		
Takamatsu Japan	48	B1	34 20N	134 01E
Tamanrasset Algeria	52	B4	22 50N	5 28E
Tamar r. UK	14	C2	50 35N	4 15W
Tampa USA	59	E1	27 58N	82 38W
Tampere Finland	33	F3	61 32N	23 45E
Tamworth UK	14	F4	52 39N	1 40W
Tanganyika, Lake East Africa	53	C2	7 00S	30 00E
Tangshan China	44	D6	39 37N	118 05E
TANZANIA	52/53	C2		
Táranto Italy	36	C2	40 28N	17 15E
Tarbert UK	11	B3	57 54N	6 49W
Tarbert UK	11	C1	55 52N	5 26W
Tashkent Uzbekistan	40	D5	41 16N	69 13E
Tasmania state Australia	67	E1	42 00S	143 00E
Taunton UK	14	D2	51 01N	3 06W
Tavistock UK	14	C2	50 33N	4 08W
T'bilisi Georgia	40	B5	41 43N	44 48E
Tees r. UK	13	H3	54 30N	1 25W
Tegucigalpa Honduras	57	E1	14 05N	87 14W
Tehran Iran	40	C4	35 40N	51 26E
Teifi r. UK	14	C4	52 03N	4 30W
Teignmouth UK	14	D2	50 33N	3 30W
Tel Aviv-Yafo Israel	40	A4	32 05N	34 46E
Telford UK	14	E4	52 42N	2 28W
Tenby UK	14	C3	51 41N	4 43W
Tennessee state USA	59	E2	35 00N	87 00W
Terni Italy	36	B2	42 34N	12 39E
Tewkesbury UK	14	E3	51 59N	2 09W
Texas state USA	58/59	C2/D2	31 00N	100 00W
THAILAND	44/45	C2/C4		
Thames r. UK	15	G3	51 45N	1 00W
The Hague Netherlands	34	C4	52 05N	4 16E
Thessalonica Greece	35	E3	40 38N	22 58E
Thetford UK	15	H4	52 25N	0 45E
Thimphu Bhutan	42	B2	27 32N	89 43E
Thirsk UK	13	H3	54 14N	1 20W
Thornaby-on-Tees UK	13	H3	54 34N	1 18W
Thornhill UK	12	F4	55 15N	3 46W
Thurrock UK	15	H3	51 28N	0 20E
Thurso UK	10	E4	58 35N	3 32W
Tianjin China	44	D6	39 08N	117 12E
Tibet, Plateau of China	41	F4	33 00N	85 00E
Tien Shan mts. China	41	E5/F5	41 00N	76 00E
Tierra del Fuego i. Chile/Argentina	63	C1	54 00S	67 30W
Tigris r. Turkey/Iraq	40	B4	34 00N	43 00E
Tijuana Mexico	58	B2	32 29N	117 10W
Timbuktu Mali	52	A3	16 49N	2 59W
Timisoara Romania	35	E3	45 45N	21 15E
Timor i. Indonesia	45	E1/E2	9 00S	125 00E
Tiranë Albania	35	D3	41 20N	19 49E
Tiree i. UK	11	B2	56 30N	6 55W
Titicaca, Lake Peru/Bolivia	62	C5	16 00S	69 30W
Tiverton UK	14	D2	50 55N	3 29W
Tobermory UK	11	B2	56 37N	6 05W
TOGO	52	B3		
Tokyo Japan	48	C2	35 40N	139 45E
Toledo USA	59	E3	41 40N	83 35W
Tonbridge UK	15	H3	51 12N	0 16E
TONGA	70			
Torbay UK	14	D2	50 27N	3 30W
Toronto Canada	59	F3	43 42N	79 46W
Totnes UK	14	D2	50 25N	3 41W
Tottori Japan	48	B1	35 32N	134 12E
Touggourt Algeria	52	B4	33 08N	6 04E
Toulouse France	34	C3	43 33N	1 24E
Towcester UK	15	G4	52 08N	1 00W
Tralee RoI	17	B2	52 16N	9 42W
Trent r. UK	13	J2	53 10N	0 50W
Trento Italy	36	B3	46 04N	11 08E
Trieste Italy	36	B3	45 39N	13 47E
TRINIDAD AND TOBAGO	62	C8		
Tripoli Libya	52	B4	32 54N	13 11E
Trivandrum India	41	E1	8 30N	76 57E
Tromso Norway	33	E3	69 42N	19 00E
Trondheim Norway	32	E3	63 36N	10 23E
Trowbridge UK	14	E3	51 20N	2 13W
Truro UK	14	B2	50 16N	5 03W
Tucson USA	58	B2	32 15N	110 57W
Tullamore RoI	17	D3	53 16N	7 30W
Tulsa USA	59	D2	36 07N	95 58W
Tunis Tunisia	52	B4	36 50N	10 13E
TUNISIA	52	B4		
Turin Italy	34	A3	45 04N	7 40E
Turkana, Lake Ethiopia/Kenya	54	B3	4 00N	36 00E
TURKEY	35	E2/F3		
TURKMENISTAN	40	C4/D4		
Turku Finland	33	F3	60 27N	22 15E
Turriff UK	11	F3	57 32N	2 28W
TUVALU	71			
Tver' Russia	33	G2	56 49N	35 57E
Tyndrum UK	11	D2	57 27N	4 44W
Tyne r. UK	13	H3	54 58N	2 00W
Tynemouth UK	15	H4	55 01N	1 24W
Tywi r. UK	14	D3	51 45N	3 20W
Udine Italy	36	B3	46 04N	13 14E
UGANDA	52	C2/C3		
Ujung Pandang Indonesia	45	D2	5 09S	119 28E
UKRAINE	35	E4/F3		
Ulan Bator Mongolia	44	C7	47 54N	106 52E
Ulan-Ude Russia	44	C8	51 55N	107 40E
Ullapool UK	11	C3	57 54N	5 10W
Ullswater l. UK	13	G3	54 35N	2 55W
Umeå Sweden	33	F3	63 50N	20 15E
UNITED ARAB EMIRATES	40	C3		
UNITED KINGDOM	32	C2		
UNITED STATES OF AMERICA	58/59			
Unst i. UK	10	H6	60 45N	0 55W
Upper Lough Erne l. UK	16	D4	54 15N	7 30W
Uppsala Sweden	32	E2	59 55N	17 38E
Ural Mountains Russia	38	B5/B6	57 00N	60 00E
URUGUAY	63	D3		
Ürümqi China	41	F5	43 43N	87 38E
Usk r. UK	14	D3	51 59N	3 35W
Utah state USA	58	B2	39 00N	112 00W
Uttoxeter UK	14	F4	52 54N	1 52W
UZBEKISTAN	40	C5/D4		
Vadodara India	41	E3	22 19N	73 14E
Valencia Spain	34	B2	39 29N	0 24W
Valencia Venezuela	62	C8	10 14N	67 59W
Valletta Malta	36	B1	35 54N	14 32E
Valparaíso Chile	63	B3	33 05S	71 40W
Vancouver Canada	58	A3	49 13N	123 06W
Vänern, Lake Sweden	32	E2	59 00N	13 30E
Van, Lake Turkey	40	B4	38 33N	42 46E
VANUATU	67	G4		
Varanasi India	41	F3	25 20N	83 00E
VENEZUELA	62	C7		
Venice Italy	36	B3	45 26N	12 20E
Vermont state USA	59	F3	44 00N	73 00W
Verona Italy	36	B3	45 26N	11 00E
Vesuvius vol. Italy	36	B2	40 49N	14 26E
Vicenza Italy	36	B3	45 33N	11 32E
Victoria state Australia	67	E2	47 00S	143 00E
Victoria Canada	58	A3	48 26N	123 20W
Victoria, Lake East Africa	52	C2	2 00S	33 00E
Vienna Austria	34	D3	48 13N	16 22E
Vientiane Laos	44	C4	17 59N	102 38E
VIETNAM	44/45	C3/C5		
Vilnius Lithuania	33	F2	54 40N	25 19E
Virginia state USA	59	F2	38 00N	77 00W
Visakhapatnam India	41	F2	17 42N	83 24E
Vitória Brazil	63	E4	20 20S	40 18W
Vitsyebsk Belarus	33	G2	55 10N	30 14E
Vladivostok Russia	44	F7	43 09N	131 53E
Volga r. Russia	33	H2	51 30N	48 00E
Vologda Russia	33	G2	59 10N	39 55E
Volta, Lake Ghana	52	A3/B3	7 30N	0 30W
Wadebridge UK	14	C2	50 32N	4 50W
Wakayama Japan	48	C1	34 12N	135 10E
Wakefield UK	13	H2	53 42N	1 29W
Wales country UK	14	D4	52 40N	3 30W
Wallasey UK	13	F2	53 26N	3 03W
Walls UK	10	G6	60 14N	1 34W
Walsall UK	14	F4	52 35N	1 58W
Waltham Forest UK	15	H3	51 36N	0 00
Walton-on-the-Naze UK	15	J3	51 51N	1 16E
Walvis Bay tn. Namibia	53	B1	22 59S	14 31E
Wantage UK	15	F3	51 36N	1 25W
Wareham UK	14	E2	50 41N	2 07W
Warley UK	14	F4	52 30N	1 59W
Warminster UK	14	E3	51 13N	2 12W
Warrenpoint tn. UK	16		54 06N	6 15W
Warrington UK	13	G2	53 24N	2 37W
Warsaw Poland	33	F2	52 15N	21 00E
Warwick UK	15	F4	52 17N	1 34W
Washington UK	13	H3	54 54N	1 31W
Washington state USA	58	A3/B3	47 00N	120 00W
Washington D.C. USA	59	F3	38 55N	77 00W
Wash, The b. UK	15	H4	52 55N	0 10E
Waterford RoI	17	D2	52 15N	7 06W
Waterlooville UK	15	F2	50 53N	1 02W
Watford UK	15	G3	51 39N	0 24W
Wear r. UK	13	G3	54 40N	2 05W
Wellingborough UK	15	G4	52 19N	0 42W
Wellington UK	14	D2	50 59N	3 15W
Wellington New Zealand	67	H1	41 17S	174 46E
Wells-next-the-Sea UK	15	H4	52 58N	0 51E
Welshpool UK	14	D4	52 40N	3 09W
Welwyn Garden City UK	15	G3	51 48N	0 13W
West Bromwich UK	14	F4	52 31N	1 59W
Westbury UK	14	E3	51 16N	2 11W
Western Australia state Australia	66	C3	25 00S	123 00E
WESTERN SAHARA	52	A4		
Weston-super-Mare UK	14	E3	51 21N	2 59W
Westport RoI	17	B3	53 48N	9 32W
West Virginia state USA	59	F2	39 00N	81 00W
Wetherby UK	13	H2	53 56N	1 23W
Wexford RoI	17	E2	52 20N	6 27W
Weymouth UK	14	E2	50 37N	2 25W
Whitby UK	13	J3	54 29N	0 37W
Whitchurch UK	14	E4	52 58N	2 41W
Whitehaven UK	12	F3	54 33N	3 35W
White Nile r. Sudan	52	C3	11 00N	32 00E
Whithorn UK	12	E3	54 44N	4 25W
Whitley Bay tn. UK	13	H4	55 03N	1 25W
Whitney, Mount USA	58	B2	36 35N	118 17W
Wichita USA	59	D2	37 43N	97 20W
Wick UK	10	E4	58 26N	3 06W
Wicklow RoI	17	E2	52 59N	6 03W
Wicklow Mountains RoI	17	E2/E3	53 00N	6 20W
Widnes UK	13	G2	53 22N	2 44W
Wigan UK	13	G2	53 33N	2 38W
Wigston UK	15	F4	52 36N	1 05W
Wigton UK	13	G3	54 49N	3 09W
Wigtown UK	12	E3	54 52N	4 26W
Wimborne Minster UK	14	F2	50 48N	1 59W
Wincanton UK	14	E3	51 04N	2 25W
Winchester UK	15	F3	51 04N	1 19W
Windermere UK	13	G3	54 23N	2 54W
Windermere l. UK	13	G3	54 20N	2 57W
Windhoek Namibia	53	B1	22 34S	17 06E
Windsor UK	15	G3	51 29N	0 38W
Winnipeg Canada	59	D3	49 53N	97 10W
Winsford UK	13	G2	53 11N	2 31W
Wisbech UK	15	H4	52 40N	0 10E
Wisconsin state USA	59	D3/E3	45 00N	90 00W
Wishaw UK	11	E3	55 47N	3 56W
Witham UK	15	H3	51 48N	0 38E
Witney UK	15	F3	51 48N	1 29W
Woking UK	15	G3	51 20N	0 34W
Wokingham UK	15	G3	51 25N	0 51W
Wolverhampton UK	14	E4	52 36N	2 08W
Woodbridge UK	15	J4	52 06N	1 19E
Wooler UK	13	G5	55 33N	2 01W
Worcester UK	14	E4	52 11N	2 13W
Workington UK	12	F3	54 39N	3 33W
Worksop UK	15	F5	53 18N	1 07W
Worthing UK	15	G2	50 48N	0 23W
Wrath, Cape UK	11	C4	58 37N	5 01W
Wrexham UK	14	D5	53 03N	3 00W
Wroclaw Poland	32	E2	51 05N	17 00E
Wuhan China	44	D6	30 35N	114 19E
Wye r. UK	14	E3	51 40N	2 40W
Wymondham UK	15	J4	52 34N	1 07E
Wyoming state USA	58	C3	43 00N	108 00W
Xi'an China	44	C6	34 16N	108 54E
Xining China	44	C6	36 35N	101 55E
Xuzhou China	44	D6	34 17N	117 18E
Yamoussoukro Côte d'Ivoire	52	A3	6 50N	5 20W
Yangon Myanmar	44	B4	16 47N	96 10E
Yaoundé Cameroon	52	B3	3 51N	11 31E
Yell i. Shetland Islands UK	10	G6	60 35N	1 10W
YEMEN REPUBLIC	40	B2/C2		
Yeovil UK	14	E2	50 57N	2 39W
Yerevan Armenia	40	B5	40 10N	44 31E
Yogyakarta Indonesia	45	D2	7 48S	110 24E
Yokohama Japan	48	C2	35 27N	139 38E
York UK	13	H2	53 58N	1 05W
Yorkshire Wolds hills UK	13	J3	54 00N	0 45W
York, Vale of UK	13	H3	54 00N	1 20W
Youghal RoI	17	D1	51 51N	7 50W
Yucatan Peninsula Mexico	56	E1/E2	19 00N	89 00W
Zagreb Croatia	34	D3	45 48N	15 58E
Zagros Mountains Iran	40	B4/C4	32 45N	48 50E
Zambezi r. Southern Africa	53	C2	17 00S	34 00E
ZAMBIA	53	C2		
Zanzibar Tanzania	53	C2	6 10S	39 12E
Zaragoza Spain	34	B3	41 39N	0 54W
Zhengzhou China	44	D6	34 45N	113 38E
Zibo China	44	D6	36 51N	118 01E
ZIMBABWE	53	C2		
Zürich Switzerland	34	C3	47 23N	8 33E